BOOKKEEPING MADE EASY

the text of this book is printed
on 100% recycled paper

BOOKKEEPING

MADE EASY

WITH A SECTION ON BUSINESS MATHEMATICS

by Alexander L. Sheff

DIRECTOR, SCHOOL OF SPEEDWRITING

BARNES & NOBLE BOOKS

A DIVISION OF HARPER & ROW, PUBLISHERS

New York, Hagerstown, San Francisco, London

FOREWORD

Bookkeeping records the world's business transactions, without which business could not carry on. Bookkeeping is an essential, dignified and worth-while vocation, a stepping stone to high executive positions and outstanding business success. This book provides a simple and practical course in bookkeeping for ambitious men and women who wish to enter this profession as well as for progressive business men and others who find the need of bookkeeping knowledge indispensable.

There is no mystery to bookkeeping. It is based upon a few logical rules which one can very easily learn and by applying them to everyday business transactions can become so well acquainted with the subject that it becomes second-nature to him.

The author of this course has had the direction of bookkeeping instruction to thousands of young men and women during the two and a half decades he has been the head of the Eastern Business and Secretarial School, New York City. Only those methods have been used which his long and varied experience have definitely proved workable. Underlying the entire course, the principle "Learn to do by doing" is strictly adhered to. Each problem is the usual business problem and is presented so directly and illustrated so clearly that it is almost impossible for anyone possessed of normal intelligence not to be able to understand it. His experience with his students has proven that beyond any doubt.

In addition to bookkeeping, the subject of accountancy is set forth with the same clarity and simplicity. The fundamental principles of accountancy and the method by which the executive is able to compile financial data on all divisions of his business is presented in such simple terms and such clear illustrations that learning bookkeeping becomes a most absorbing experience.

"How Business is Operated" is another important feature of this book. The types and functions of nine broad divisions of business are outlined. Thus the student will gain an excellent idea of the separate functions, their interrelation, and their relations with the bookkeeping and accounting departments.

Business Mathematics is constantly used in bookkeeping of all kinds. Mathematics is here presented with special reference to problems of the retailer and manufacturer, of commission and brokerage, real estate taxes, banking and loans, insurance and investments. It also makes clear the figuring of percentage, and shows many short-cuts in calculating results. The answers to the exercises and problems are given in the back of the book.

The last chapter of the book is one to which the student will have many occasions to refer, for it contains tables of weights and measures, of simple and compound interest, and other time-saving references. It rounds out a book of incalculable value, either to those who wish to prepare to get a job or to a business man who wishes to learn how to keep his own books.

LEWIS COPELAND.

HOW TO STUDY BOOKKEEPING

At least 95% of a bookkeeper's work consists of routine tasks. Checking bills, entering them into the proper books, posting these entries, etc.—these tasks should not require any conscious effort whatsoever. They should all be done through habit.

Before forming a habit, it is necessary for us to *understand* the principle involved. The first task is, therefore, to read the problem thoroughly, understand its solution step by step, and constantly be alert to the understanding of the principle involved.

There are very few rules involved in Bookkeeping and all of these rules are based upon a fundamental rule of simple logic.

Every principle is explained by illustration. Study the illustration carefully so that you understand it without any doubt. Do each exercise without once looking at the accompanying solution. Do not hesitate to work out each problem in the manner in which you *understand* it without any reference to the solution. After your solution has been completed, compare it with the solution in the text. If there are any differences, it is essential for you to know *why* you made the mistake. Merely making the correction is not enough. Refer to that part of the text illustrating the principle which your solution showed you did not understand properly. Review this principle in the text. After having satisfied yourself that you thoroughly understand the reason for your error, do the entire problem all over again without recourse either to your former solution or the solution in the text. Compare with the text solution.

Do not feel discouraged because of the errors you have made. We learn most by making mistakes. Do not repeat the mistake, however.

Review constantly. Do not skip any lesson because each new lesson is based upon principles covered in the preceding lessons. Be very careful to prove each addition, subtraction, multiplication, or division before recording the results. The most careful bookkeeper will make clerical errors of this type. Rechecking is essential.

After the first three lessons, which cover the fundamentals, the work will become clearer with each lesson.

You will be rewarded within a brief period of time if you will adhere strictly to the foregoing suggestions.

It is a distinct advantage to allot a certain length of time each day for studying, and to adhere as closely as possible to the schedule you make for yourself. Whether you give yourself a long or a short time, be sure that you observe it regularly for the best results.

How To Study the Other Subjects

The study of Business Mathematics is simply a matter of following closely all of the author's instructions and working out each problem as it is given. Be sure that you have a full understanding of each definition, statement and diagram before you go on to the next. When you have worked out the exercises and problems—but not before—refer to the answer to each at the back of the book. If you have made an error, attack the problem again. It is better to be slow and sure than to cover the ground at the expense of accuracy.

The division on Business Organization and Practice may be studied as a change from Bookkeeping and Mathematics, but it should be given the close attention it deserves, for on it depends your understanding of the broader aspects of business.

CONTENTS

I. BOOKKEEPING

II. BUSINESS ORGANIZATION AND PRACTICE

III. BUSINESS MATHEMATICS

IV. USEFUL FACTS AND FIGURES

I

BOOKKEEPING

INTRODUCTION

BOOKKEEPING is the art of recording business transactions systematically. It is very simple and does not involve any complicated process whatsoever. It is the art of reducing each transaction to its simplest terms. It is as easy as learning a simple game of cards. You will learn bookkeeping by watching how it is done, and you will be surprised at its simplicity.

The following is a general picture of the entire bookkeeping process which will be presented in detail later, as each subject is fully explained and clearly illustrated:

A simple set of books consists of four journals and one ledger.

The Sales Journal is used to record sales of merchandise.

The Purchase Journal is used to record purchases of merchandise.

In the Cash Journal, cash receipts and cash payments are recorded.

The fourth journal is known as the General Journal. All entries which cannot be recorded into any of the aforementioned journals are entered in this journal.

In the Ledger there is one page for each record we wish to keep. There is thus one page or *account* for each of the following: Cash, Merchandise Inventory, Merchandise Sales, Merchandise Purchases, Expenses, Proprietor's Investment, Furniture, Notes Receivable, Notes Payable, etc. There will also be one page for each customer and one for each creditor.

The bookkeeper's work consists of recording transactions *as they occur* into the *journal* in which it belongs, and then "posting" (copying) these entries to their respective accounts (pages) in the ledger.

1

At the end of each month the balance of each account in the ledger is obtained and listed on a sheet of paper. This record is called a Trial Balance.

At the end of the year a statement is prepared from the Trial Balance showing all the things the business owns such as Cash, Merchandise Inventory, Customers' Balances, Notes Receivable, etc. These are called *assets*. Alongside of this list of assets a list of the business debts is listed such as Notes Payable, Creditors' balances, etc. These are called *liabilities*. The difference between the ASSETS and LIABILITIES represents the NET WORTH of the business. By comparing this net worth with the net worth appearing in a similar statement the year before, we obtain the *net increase* in the net worth for the year, called the PROFIT, or the *net decrease* in the net worth for the year, which we call the LOSS.

Here we have a simple picture of the entire process of record-keeping called Bookkeeping.

By showing this process in actual operation, the simplicity of bookkeeping will be even more apparent, especially after the student will have completed the first three lessons which deal primarily with fundamentals.

Lesson I

ACCOUNTS

As we have said before, in the ledger a page is kept for each record we have to keep. These records are called ACCOUNTS such as Cash Account, Customer's Account, Merchandise Sales Account, etc. *The ledger is therefore a book of accounts.* These accounts are eithers Assets or Liabilities. We also keep an account with the proprietor showing his investment and another account showing his drawings. These last two are called PROPRIETORSHIP ACCOUNTS.

In order to keep a record of every detail of our business, we must also keep accounts to show the costs of doing business, e.g., Expense account, Rent account, Merchandise Purchase account, Interest Cost account, etc.

Similarly we must keep a record of the income or earning accounts such as Merchandise Sales account, Interest Earned account, etc.

The ledger therefore contains asset accounts, liability accounts, proprietorship accounts, expense accounts, and earning accounts.

JOURNAL AND LEDGER PAPER

Bookkeeping records are kept on specially ruled paper. These are known as:

Journal ruling.

Ledger ruling.

The following is called *journal* ruling:

The following is called *ledger* ruling:

Observe the following:

1. The journal has two money columns: one next to the other at the extreme right of the sheet.

2. The ledger has two money columns: one in the *center* of the sheet, the other at the extreme right of the sheet.

3. The journal has *one* date column at the extreme left-hand side.

4. The ledger has *two* date columns: one at the extreme left-hand side, the other directly to the right of the double vertical lines representing the end of the first money column.

5. The journal has *one* folio column.

6. The ledger has *two* folio columns.

The student should supply himself with sufficient paper of the above rulings. They can be obtained at nearly any stationery store, as they are commonly used.

Hereafter use journal paper whenever doing any work in the journal, and use ledger paper for any ledger work.

Since Bookkeeping is the art of keeping records, it is necessary for us to acquaint ourselves with the most typical records used in business.

The following records or accounts are most frequently used: Cash, Sales, Purchases, and Expenses.

Let us consider the Cash Account.

We receive cash, and pay cash. Consequently we must separate these two; Cash receipts on one side, cash payments on the other. Hence an account must have two sides, one side representing an *increase,* the other side a *decrease.* A Cash Account will look like this:

		Cash							
Mo.	Day	Explan.	L.F.	Amount	Mo.	Day	Explan.	L.F.	Amount

Since we must first receive cash before we can pay any out, and since it is customary to begin writing from the *left* side of a page, cash receipts are recorded on the left side, cash payments on the right.

DEBIT AND CREDIT

In Bookkeeping we use technical words to describe these sides. The left side is called the DEBIT side. The right side is called the CREDIT side.

Debit and Credit mean nothing more than just that—the left side and the right side of an account respectively. The student is advised to divest himself entirely of every preconceived notion pertaining to Debit and Credit he has had until now. It will eliminate the confusion ordinarily connected with this concept.

Thus we

> *Debit* Cash when we *receive* Cash and,
>
> *Credit* Cash when we *pay* Cash; or,

Debit an account to show *anything* coming into the business;

> Credit an account to show *anything* going out of the business.

The underlying principle of double-entry bookkeeping is based on Sir Isaac Newton's third law of motion: For every action, there must be an *equal* and *contrary* reaction.

This merely signifies that for every debit there must be a credit *of the same amount*.

What does this mean?

We engage in business to make a profit. This means we must trade with each other. Jones buys $100 worth of merchandise for cash from Smith in order to sell it to Brown for $125.

Thus Jones exchanges values with Smith. Then Jones exchanges values with Brown. These exchanges of values we term *transactions*. When Jones engages in the transaction with Smith, he pays $100 in cash and receives $100 worth of merchandise. When Jones sells the merchandise to Brown, he receives $125 in cash and records a sale to Brown amounting to $125.

Thus $100 cash buys $100 worth of merchandise.

$125 cash is received for a sale amounting to $125.

Rule: In every transaction, whatever goes out pays for something coming in *valued at the same amount*.

MERCHANDISE ACCOUNTS

Any goods we buy to sell, because we are in business to sell it, is called Merchandise. We buy Merchandise, and sell Merchandise.

We have an account called Purchases, in which all merchandise bought is recorded, and another account called Sales, in which all sales of this merchandise are recorded.

We do not keep one account for merchandise; we keep two separate accounts—one for merchandise sold and one for merchandise purchased.

Sales will be recorded in the Sales account; purchases, in the Purchase account; cash, in the cash account; expense, in the Expense account, etc. Since there are *two* sides to each account, we must first ascertain on *which side* of each account we will record any of the above.

Let us consider the following transaction:

1. *We sell for cash*

When we sell for cash, two accounts are affected—Cash *comes into* the business, Merchandise Sales *goes out* of the business. Hence

Cash (coming in), is debited.

Sales (going out), is credited.

Because for every debit there must be a credit.

Since Sales always denote merchandise going out, *Sales are always Credited*. Whenever we think of Sales, remember we have in mind a *credit* to the Sales account.

Thus Sales is always a credit.

Transaction:

Jan. 4. Sold for cash merchandise $400.

7. Sold for cash merchandise $150.

Entry:

	Cash				Sales		
DR.		CR.		DR.		CR.	
Jan. 4	400					Jan. 4	400
7	150					7	150

(Dr. means Debit; Cr. means Credit)

2. *We buy merchandise for cash*

Merchandise Purchases and Cash are affected. Merchandise Purchases *come* into the business and Cash *goes out* of the business. Hence,

Purchases is debited and

Cash is credited.

Thus Purchases is always a Debit account.

Transaction:

Feb. 2. Bought for cash merchandise $160.

12. Bought for cash merchandise $250.

Entry:

	Cash				Purchases		
DR.		CR.		DR.		CR.	
		Feb. 2	160	Feb. 2	160		
		12	250	12	250		

3. We pay rent (Expense Account)

Rent is an expense.

Expense and Cash accounts are affected. Since cash goes out, **Cash is** credited and Expense is therefore debited. Hence,

Rent is debited.

Cash is credited.

Rent—the use of the premises comes in; Cash goes out. Expenses *cause* cash to go out.

Thus Expense is always a debit.

Transaction:

Jan. 10. Paid $100.00 for rent for the month.

15. Paid $5.00 for stationery and supplies for the office.

17. Paid $1.00 for stamps.

Entry:

Rent				Postage		
DR.		CR.		DR.		CR.
Jan. 10	100			Jan. 17	1	

Office Supplies				Cash		
DR.		CR.		DR.		CR.
Jan. 15	5				Jan. 10	100
					15	5
					17	1

4. We receive interest (Income Account)

We derive income or profits from sale of merchandise. Sometimes however, we receive income from sources other than merchandise sales.

Transaction:

Received $5.00 Interest for a loan of money.

Cash receipt of $5.00 and Interest Earned of $5.00 must be recorded.

Cash is debited $5.00.

Interest Earned is credited $5.00.

. Hence Earnings are Credits.

SUMMARY OF DEBITS AND CREDITS

Memorize these rules:

Cash is a debit or a credit account.
Purchases is a debit account.
Expense is a debit account.
Sales is a credit account.
Earnings is a credit account.

Also commit this to memory:

Assets are debits, e.g., Cash, Customers' balances, etc.
Liabilities are credits, e.g., Creditors' balances, Notes Payable.
Since assets are debits, liabilities (its opposite) are credits.
Expenses are debits, e.g., Rent, Wages, Interest Cost, etc.
Earnings are credits, e.g., Interest Earned, etc.

To aid us in remembering the above rules, we suggest that henceforth we say *Sales Credit* whenever we wish to say Sales account. Similarly say *Purchases Debit, Expense Debit,* and *Cash Debit* or *Cash Credit.* In this manner we will become accustomed to knowing the correct side without any hesitation.

The following chart illustrates the above:

DEBIT AND CREDIT CHART

Debit	*Credit*
Cash receipts	Cash payments
Purchases	Sales
Expense	Earnings

or

Debit	*Credit*
Increases to Assets	Decreases to Assets
Decreases to Liabilities	Increases to Liabilities
Increases to Expense	Decreases to Expense
Decreases to Earnings	Increases to Earnings

Lesson II

ACCOUNTS INVOLVED IN SALES TRANSACTIONS

To aid the student, we list a few simple transactions and show how they are resolved into their respective accounts:

(1) When we sell for cash, we
    Debit Cash, and
        Credit Sales
Cash comes in and Merchandise Sales goes out.

(2) When we sell on account, we
    Debit the customer, and
        Credit Sales
The customer's debt comes in and merchandise (Sales) goes out.

(3) When we receive cash on account, we
    Debit Cash, and
        Credit the customer
Cash comes in and the customer's debt goes out.

Transaction:
    Jan. 5. Sold to John Jones on account merchandise $280.

Entry:

Jones			Sales		
DR.		CR.	DR.		CR.
Jan. 5	280			Jan. 5	280

Transaction:
    Jan. 5. Sold to J. Jones merchandise on account $280.
         10. Received from J. Jones cash on account $100.
         15. Received from J. Jones cash in full of account $180.

Entry:

J. Jones			Cash		
DR.		CR.	DR.		CR.
Jan. 5	280	Jan. 10 100	Jan. 10	100	
		15 180	15	180	

Sales		
DR.	CR.	
	Jan. 5	280

Exercise I:

Enter the following transactions into their respective ledger accounts (Draw T accounts as above and make entries as illustrated):

Feb. 1. Sold to Wm. Jones merchandise on account $200.

   4. Sold to John Adams merchandise on account $300.

   8. Received from Wm. Jones cash on account $100.

   12. Sold for cash merchandise $200.

   15. Sold for cash merchandise $300.

   17. Received cash on account from John Adams $150.

   19. Received cash in full of bill of the 4th from Wm. Jones $100.

   20. Sold for cash merchandise $275.

   25. Received from J. Adams on account $100.

Solution:

Cash				Sales		
Feb. 8	100				Feb. 1	200
12	200				4	300
15	300				12	200
17	150				15	300
19	100				20	275
20	275					
25	100					

Wm. Jones					John Adams			
Feb. 1	200	Feb. 8	100		Feb. 4	300	Feb. 17	150
		19	100				25	100

Exercise 2:

Record the following transactions to the respective ledger accounts:

Feb. 1. Sold for cash merchandise $175.

   2. Sold for cash merchandise $200.

   3. Sold R. Allen on account merchandise $250.

   4. Sold J. Brown on account merchandise $175.

   5. Sold for cash merchandise $5.

   5. Received from R. Allen on account $100.

   6. Sold for cash merchandise $150.

   6. Received from J. Brown $175.

   7. Sold J. Brown on account merchandise $200.

Solution:

Sales

							Feb						
							'19 1					175	00
							2					200	00
							3					250	00
							4					175	00
							5					5	00
							6					150	00
							7					200	00

Cash

Feb '19	1			175	00		
	2			200	00		
	5			5	00		
	5			100	00		
	6			150	00		
	6			175	00		

Allen

Feb '19	3			250	00	Feb '19	5			100	00

Brown

Feb '19	4			175	00	Feb '19	6			175	00
	7			200	00						

ACCOUNTS WITH CUSTOMERS

A customer is one to whom we sell merchandise. We keep an account with those customers to whom we sell on account.

Transaction:

Jan. 2. We sell to J. Smith for cash $100.

We do not open an account with J. Smith because at the termination of this transaction J. Smith owes us nothing. We therefore do not have to keep an account with him.

Entry:

Debit Cash $100,
    Credit Sales $100.

Cash	Sales
Jan. 2 100.00	Jan. 2 100.00

Transaction:

Jan. 10. Sold to J. Jones on account merchandise $100.
    15. Received from J. Jones on account $75.

Entry:

Jan. 10. Debit J. Jones $100.
            Credit Sales $100.
Jan. 15. Debit Cash $75.
            Credit J. Jones $75.

LEDGER

J. Jones

Jan. 10 Sale $100	Jan. 15 Cash $75

Cash	Sales
Jan. 15 $75	Jan. 10 $100

J. Jones' account now shows a debit balance of $25 because the amount on the debit side is greater than the amount on the credit side. A customer's account will therefore show the *sale* on the debit side, and the *cash received* from him on the credit side.

Thus:

Customer's Account

DR.	CR.
Amount of Sales	Cash received

A customer's account will show a *debit* balance.

Lesson III

ACCOUNTS INVOLVED IN PURCHASE TRANSACTIONS

(1) When we buy merchandise for cash, we
> *Debit Purchases, and*
>> *Credit Cash*

Merchandise Purchases comes in and Cash goes out.

(2) When we buy merchandise on account, we
> *Debit Purchases, and*
>> *Credit the Creditor*

Merchandise Purchases comes in, our debt to the creditor goes out.

(3) When we pay cash on account, we
> *Debit the Creditor, and*
>> *Credit Cash*

Our debt comes back and cash goes out.

Exercise 3:

Jan. 2. We bought merchandise for cash $150.
3. We bought merchandise for cash $10.
3. We bought merchandise from R. Jones on account $350.
4. We bought merchandise from W. Aldrich on account $250.
6. We pay R. Jones on account $100.
8. We pay W. Aldrich on account $200.
10. We bought for cash merchandise $155.
12. We pay R. Jones in full of account $250.

Solution:

	Cash	
	Jan. 2	150
	3	10
	6	100
	8	200
	10	155
	12	250

	Purchases	
	Jan. 2	150
	3	10
	3	350
	4	250
	10	155

R. Jones			
Jan. 6	100	Jan. 3	350
12	250		

W. Aldrich			
Jan. 8	200	Jan. 4	250

ACCOUNTS WITH CREDITORS

A Creditor is one from whom we buy merchandise.

Transaction:

Jan. 5. Bought from R. Allen for cash merchandise $150.
We do not open an account for R. Allen.

Entry:

Debit Purchases.
Credit Cash.

Purchases		
Jan. 5	150	

Cash		
	Jan. 5	150

Transaction:

Jan. 7. Bought from A. Sweeney on account merchandise $300.
17. Paid A. Sweeney on account $100.

Entry:

Jan. 7. Debit Purchases $300.
Credit A. Sweeney $300.
17. Debit A. Sweeney $100.
Credit Cash $100.

LEDGER

A. Sweeney

| Jan. 17 Cash $100 | Jan. 7 Pur. $300 |

| Cash | | Purchases | |
| | Jan. 17 $100 | Jan. 7 $300 | |

A. Sweeney's account now shows a credit balance of $200. A creditor's account will always show the purchases on the credit side, and the money paid on the debit side. Thus:

Creditor's Account

DR.	CR.
Cash Paid	Amount of Purchase

A creditor's account will show a *credit* balance.

EXPENSE ACCOUNTS

A purchase of something which we are not in business to sell and which will be consumed in a short period of time is called an *Expense.*

We are in the printing business. We buy oil for running our machines. Oil is an expense called Manufacturing Expense.

When we pay cash for an expense, we
  Debit Expense and
    Credit Cash.
The expense comes in for our use, and cash goes out.

Exercise 4:
  Mar. 2. Paid $5.00 for stamps for office use.
       5. Paid factory wages $200.
       6. Paid rent for the month $150.
       7. We paid a premium of $125 for a $10,000 fire insurance policy.
       9. We paid the bookkeeper's salary $25.
      11. We bought a new cash book $2.50.
      12. We bought ink and blotters for 75¢.
      13. We paid the New York Telephone Co. $24.75.

Solution:

Cash		
	Mar. 2	5.00
	5	200.00
	6	150.00
	7	125.00
	9	25.00
	11	2.50
	12	.75
	13	24.75

Postage	
Mar. 2	5.00

Factory Wages	
Mar. 5	200.00

Rent	
Mar. 6	150.00

Insurance	
Mar. 7	125.00

Office Supplies	
Mar. 11	2.50
12	.75

Telephone	
Mar. 13	24.75

Office Salaries	
Mar. 9	25.00

It is necessary to keep a separate account for each kind of expense in order to show the cost of same.

SUMMARY

Transaction involving sales:

   (1) When we sell for cash, we
      Debit Cash, and
         Credit Sales.

   (2) When we sell on account, we
      Debit the customer, and
         Credit Sales.

   (3) When we receive cash from a customer, we
      Debit Cash, and
         Credit the customer.

Transactions involving purchases:

   (1) When we buy for cash, we
      Debit Purchases, and
         Credit Cash.

(2) When we buy on account, we
 Debit Purchases, and
  Credit the Creditor.
(3) When we pay cash on account, we
 Debit the Creditor, and
  Credit Cash.

Transaction involving expense:

 When we pay for an expense, we
  Debit Expense, and
   Credit Cash.

We have now completed the most difficult part of the course—the theory.

From now on the work becomes easier because we begin to apply these principles to actual business practice.

Examination:

 Jan. 2. Bought of J. Edwards merchandise on account $300.
   4. Sold for cash merchandise $250.
   4. Sold to T. Hudson merchandise on account $230.
   5. Bought for cash merchandise $375.
   7. We paid rent $20.
   8. Paid J. Edwards on account $100.
   10. Bought bottle of ink for the office, paid $2.
   12. Received from T. Hudson $130.
   14. Sold for cash merchandise $200.
   15. Paid stenographer's salary $25.

Record these entries to the proper ledger accounts. Check with solutions at the end of this lesson. Deduct 10% for each error. 70% Passes. If you have failed the test, correct errors, and take this examination a day later and check with solutions as before.

Solution:

Purchases

19—					
Jan. 2			300 00		
5			375 00		

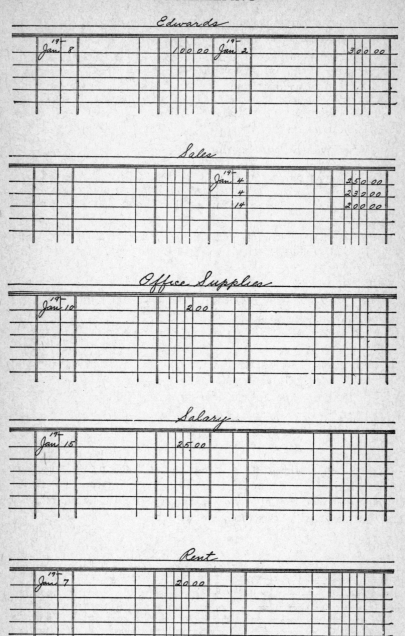

Edwards

19—			100 00	19—			300 00
Jan. 8				Jan. 2			

Sales

				19—			250 00
				Jan. 4			230 00
				4			200 00
				14			

Office Supplies

19—			2 00				
Jan. 10							

Salary

19—			25 00				
Jan. 15							

Rent

19—			20 00				
Jan. 7							

Cash

Jan⁻¹⁹ 4			250 00	Jan⁻¹⁹ 5			375 00	
12			130 00	7			20 00	
14			200 00	8			100 00	
				10			2 00	
				15			25 00	

J. Hudson

Jan⁻¹⁹ 4			230 00	Jan⁻¹⁹ 12			130 00	

Lesson IV
JOURNALS

The entries we have made until now have been made *directly* to the accounts in the ledger. A more practical method is to record each entry *first* in its entirety *as it occurs* into a *special* book called the Journal and then to post it from the Journal to the Ledger. In the average small business there are four journals—

1. The cash Journal.
    This book is used to record all cash received and all cash paid.

2. The Sales Journal.
    This book is used to record all sales on account.

3. The Purchase Journal.
    This book is used to record all merchandise purchased on account.

4. The General Journal.
    Whenever a transaction cannot be entered into any of the other three journals because no cash, sales, or purchases are involved it will be entered into the General Journal.

CASH JOURNAL VS. ACCOUNT CASH

To avoid confusion we now call attention to the fact that there is a Cash Journal, and an account in the ledger called Cash. The two are identical except for the fact that the Cash Journal contains a record of EVERY cash transactions, whereas the Cash account in the ledger merely contains ONE entry at the END of each month for the TOTAL cash received, and another entry at the END of each month for the TOTAL cash paid out.

SALES JOURNAL VS. SALES ACCOUNT

Similarly we have the Sales Journal and an account in the ledger called Sales. The TOTAL of the Sales Journal is posted at the end of each month to the Sales account.

PURCHASE JOURNAL VS. PURCHASE ACCOUNT

Likewise we have a Purchase Journal and an account in the ledger called Purchases. The TOTAL of the Purchase Journal is posted at the end of each month to the Purchase account.

THE CASH JOURNAL

This journal is used to record all cash received and paid.

Exercise 5:

Mar.　3. Received $200 for merchandise sold for cash.
　　　　3. Bought for cash merchandise $100.
　　　　4. Received from John Smith $175 on account.
　　　　6. Received from Walter Carr $250 on account.
　　　　7. Paid Harold Dawn $107 on account.
　　　10. Paid $2 for stamps.
　　　12. Sold for cash merchandise $250.
　　　15. Paid bookkeeper's salary $25.

Required:

Journalize these transactions.

Solution for Exercise 5:

C 2

Cash (Dr.) Receipts Journal

Date	Account, Cr.	Explanation	L.F.	Amount	Total
19— Mar 3	Sales		2	200 00	
4	John Smith	a/c	5	175 00	
6	Walter Carr	a/c	6	250 00	
12	Sales		2	250 00	
31	Cash, Dr.		1	875 00	875 00

C 3

Cash (Cr.) Payment Journal

Date	Account, Dr.	Explanation	L.F.	Amount	Total
19— Mar 3	Purchases		3	100 00	
7	Harold Dawn	a/c	7	107 00	
10	Postage	stamps	8	2 00	
15	Office Salaries	Bookkeeper	9	25 00	
31	Cash, Cr.		1	234 00	234 00

Cash (1)

19— Mar 31	875— 234— 641—	C2	875 00	19— Mar 31			C3	234 00	

Sales (2)

				19— Mar 3			C2	200 00	
				12	450—	C2		250 00	

Purchases (3)

19— Mar 3	100—	C3	100 00		

Solution for Exercise 5 continued:

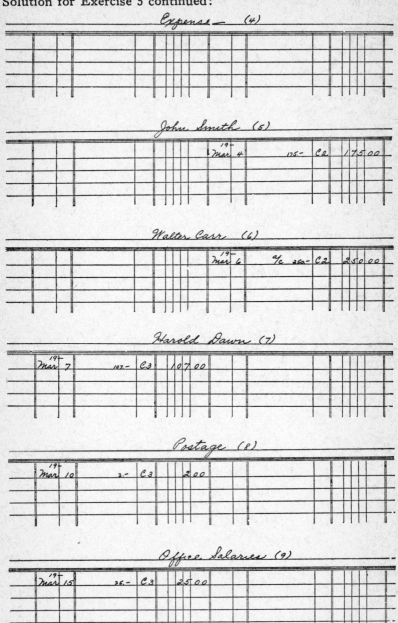

Expense — (4)

John Smith (5)

19— Mar 4		175.— C2	175 00

Walter Carr (6)

19— Mar 6	a/c 250.—	C2	250 00

Harold Dawn (7)

19— Mar 7	107.—	C3	107 00

Postage (8)

19— Mar 10	2.—	C3	2 00

Office Salaries (9)

19— Mar 15	25.—	C3	25 00

You notice that in the Cash (Dr.) Receipts Journal we have no record of the cash debit for each transaction; only the account to be *credited* is recorded. This is so because we know that every entry in the Cash (Dr.) Receipts Journal is a *debit* to Cash. There is no need to record this; it is therefore omitted. Only the *credit* is recorded. The same omission of one of the two items (debit or credit) is followed in the Sales and Purchases Journals. Hence instead of recording the debit and the credit for each transaction we record *only one*—the debit or the credit.

Thus in the Cash (Dr.) Receipt Journal we record the credits. Cash debit is understood.

Thus in the Cash (Cr.) Payment Journal we record the debits. Cash credit is understood.

Thus in the Sales (Cr.) Journal we record the debits. Sales credit is understood.

Thus in the Purchases (Dr.) Journal we record the credits. Purchase debit is understood.

The Total of each of these books will be the TOTAL of the account understood and omitted.

Thus the total of the Cash (Dr.) Receipts Journal will be Cash Debit.

Thus the total of the Cash (Cr.) Payments Journal will be Cash Credit.

Thus the total of the Sales (Cr.) Journal will be Sales Credit.

Thus the total of the Purchases (Dr.) Journal will be Purchases Debit.

Thus Special Journals eliminate one-half of the recording. In the Cash (Dr.) Receipts Journal *at the end* of the month the TOTAL of the amount column is posted to the debit side of the Cash account. However EACH credit item is posted to the credit side of the respective account *daily*.

Similarly in the Cash (Cr.) Payment Journal only the *debit* accounts are recorded because the corresponding credit for each of these debits is Cash, which is similarly not recorded, but is understood. However the *total* of the amount column is posted to the *credit* side of the Cash account *at the end* of each month. The individual debit items are posted to the debit side of their respective accounts in the ledger, *daily*.

LEDGER FOLIOS

In order to provide a ready reference, each page in each journal is numbered; each page in the ledger is also numbered. Thus C2 means Cash Book page 2, L1 means Ledger page 1, etc. In the journals we will record the pages of the ledger to which each item was posted; in the Ledger the folio letters represent the journals; viz. C2, (Cash Book page 2) C3, (Cash Book page 3) S1 (Sales Book page 1) P1 (Purchase Book page 1).

Record the ledger folios as you post, thus if interrupted in your work you will be able to tell which posting to resume with by the fact that it will *not* have a ledger folio since it has *not yet* been posted.

In checking your work later on, this system of cross-reference will be found indispensable.

SALES JOURNAL

This journal is used to record all sales of merchandise made on account—not for cash. As we have seen in the solution of Exercise 5, cash sales were recorded in the Cash Journal.

Whenever we sell merchandise, and do not receive the *full amount* of the sales in *cash,* we are said to have sold *on account*—on credit

All such transactions are entered into the Sales Journal.

Exercise 6:

April 3. Sold to William Kahn, terms 30 days, merchandise $200.00.

7. Sold to Arnold Smith on account, merchandise $300.00.

10. Sold to James Laster, terms n/30, merchandise $250.00.

n/30 means payment is to be made in 30 days.

Solution:

S1

Sales No.	Date	Account Dr.	Terms	L.F.	Amount	Total
		Sales (Cr.) Journal				
1	Apr 3	William Kahn	30 days	2	200 00	
2	7	Arnold Smith	%	3	300 00	
3	10	James Laster	n/30	4	250 00	
	30	Sales, Cr.		1		750 00

Solution for Exercise 6 continued:

Sales (1)

				19— Apr. 30		S1	750 00

William Kahn (2)

19— Apr. 3		S1	20 00				

Arnold Smith (3)

19— Apr. 7		S1	300 00				

James Laster (4)

19— Apr. 10		S1	250 00				

Notice how the *total* of the Sales Journal is posted to the credit side of the account as of the *last* day of the month; whereas the debit accounts are posted *individually* as of the date of sale.

The individual accounts are the debit accounts; the credit account-Sales is understood, and is not recorded except as a *total* at the *end* of the month. The ledger folio S1 means Sales Journal page 1.

Purchase Journal

The Purchase Journal is used to record all purchases of merchandise made on account. Cash purchases are not recorded here—they are recorded in the cash (Cr.) Payment Journal.

Exercise 7:

 May 1. Bought from Jack Stone, terms 30 days, merchandise $250.00.

    2. Bought from A. Dix Co. on account, merchandise $275.00.

   15. Bought from A. R. Jones Co., terms n/30, merchandise $150.00.

Solution:

P₁

Purchase (Dr) Journal

Purchase no.	Date	Account-Cr.	Terms	L.F.	Amount	Total
1	May 1	Jack Stone	30 days	2	250 00	
2	2	A. Dix Co.	%e	3	275 00	
3	15	A. R. Jones Co.	n/30	4	150 00	
	31	Purchases, Dr		1	675 00	675 00

Purchases (1)

May 31		P₁	675 00			

Jack Stone (2)

		May 1		P₁	250 00	

A. Dix Co. (3)

		May 2		P₁	275 00	

A. R. Jones Co. (4)

		May 15		P₁	150 00	

In the Purchase (Dr.) Journal you will observe from the above transactions the accounts to be *credited* are recorded, whereas the *total* purchases is posted as a *debit* to the Purchase account at the *end* of the month.

P1 *means* Purchase Journal, page 1.

Summary:

In the Cash (Dr.) Receipts Journal all cash receipts are entered; since all debits entered into this journal are debits to Cash, we do not record the Cash debits. Only the credits are recorded in this journal. The total for the month becomes the Cash Debit and is posted to the debit side of the Cash account.

For the same reason all the debits having Cash, as their credit, are recorded into the Cash (Cr.) Payment Journal.

Similarly all the debits to the customers' accounts having Sales as their credit, are recorded in the Sales (Cr.) Journal.

Likewise all the credits to the creditors, having Purchases as their debit, are recorded in the Purchase (Dr.) Journal.

The totals of each of these journals are posted once on the last day of the month to their respective accounts in the ledger bearing the name of the special journal. Thus the total of the Sales (Cr.) Journal is posted as a credit to the Sales account on the last day of each month.

DOUBLE ENTRY BOOKKEEPING VS. SINGLE ENTRY BOOKKEEPING

You have noticed how we have posted a debit for each credit from the journals into the ledger. If we were to add up all the debit postings in the ledger, and if we were to add up all the credit postings in the ledger, the sum of each side would be the same amount. This is obviously so because for every debit a credit of the same amount was posted. This method is called *Double Entry Bookkeeping*.

In *Single Entry Bookkeeping*, we keep only customers, creditors, and cash accounts in the ledger. Accounts with Sales, Purchases, and Expenses, would not be kept. Therefore in posting from the Sales (Cr.) Journal, only the debits to customers' accounts would be posted, the credit to Sales would *not be* posted because no Sales account is kept. Hence only *one* item is posted, not *two* as in the Double Entry method.

In view of the fact that in Double Entry Bookkeeping, the debit total must equal the credit total, we have an opportunity of checking the correctness of our postings. This affords us a *method* of checking the correctness of most of the clerical details, such as posting and footing (adding, subtracting, forwarding items, etc.).

Lesson V

SPECIAL ACCOUNTS

The proprietor must keep a record of his investment. He may have to invest more money in the future, or he may withdraw a sum of money to decrease his investment. Obviously we must keep a record of these facts. Hence an account with the proprietor must be kept. Notice how we label this account "Andrew Adams, Capital," in the solution of Exercise 8, below. If we did not add "Capital" to the name of the account, we would not recognize this account as the proprietor's account so readily.

A proprietor's capital account is a credit account.

Exercise 8:

June 1. Andrew Adams began business investing cash $1000.
      2. Bought of L. Stillman merchandise on account $200.
      3. Paid rent for the month $100.
      5. Sold for cash merchandise $75.
      6. Bought for cash merchandise $150.
      8. Paid Stillman on account $50.
     10. Sold to R. Anderson on account merchandise $125.
     15. Paid for stamps $3.00.

Journalize and post to ledger.

Solution:

c 2

Cash (Dr.) Receipts Journal

Date	Account, Cr.	Explanation	L F	Amount		Total	
19—							
June 1	Andrew Adams, Cap	Investment	4	1000 00			
5	Sales		2	75 00			
30	Cash, Dr.		1	1075 00		1075 00	

Solution for Exercise 8 continued:

C 3

Cash (Cr.) Payment Journal

Date		Account, Dr.	Explanation	L.F.	Amount		Total	
19—								
June	3	Rent	For June	8	100	00		
	7	Purchases		3	150	00		
	8	L. Stillman	⅗c	7	50	00		
	15	Postage		5	3	00		
	30	Cash, Cr.		1	303 00		303	00

81

Sales (Cr.) Journal

Date		Account, Dr.	Terms	L.F.	Amount		Total	
19—								
June	10	R. Anderson	⅗c	6	125	00		
	30	Sales, Cr.		2			125	00

P 1

Purchases (Dr.) Journal

Date		Account, Cr.	Terms	L.F.	Amount		Total	
19—								
June	2	L. Stillman	⅗c	7	200	00		
	30	Purchases, Dr.		3			200	00

Cash (1)

19—		1075					19—				
June	30	303	C2	1075	00		June	30	C3	303	00
		772.—									

Sales (2)

					19—					
					June	1	C2	75	00	
						30	200.— 81	125	00	
								200	00	

Solution for Exercise 8 continued:

Purchases (3)

19—					
June	7		C3	150 00	
	30	350—	P1	200 00
				550 00

Andrew Adams, Capital (4)

				19—					
				June	1	1000—	C2	1000 00

Postage (5)

19—					
June	15	3—	C3	3 00

R. Anderson (6)

19—					
June	10	125—	S1	125 00

L. Stillman (7)

19—					19—					
June	8		C3	50 00	June	2	200— 50— 150—	P1	200 00

Rent (8)

19—					
June	3	100—	C3	100 00

TRIAL BALANCE

At the end of each month, it is customary for us to find the balance of each account.

As we have learned, each account has one side which increases the account, and the other side which decreases the account. By subtracting the smaller amount from the larger, we obtain a balance; hence in Exercise 8, the credit side of the Cash account is smaller than the amount on the debit side, hence we obtain a *debit balance* of $772.

The Sales account has no debit postings, hence by merely totaling the credit side, we obtain a credit balance of $200.

Similarly, we proceed to obtain a balance for each account in the ledger. We then take a sheet of journal paper, head it Trial Balance, and list each account and its balance in the following manner.

The Trial Balance for Exercise 8 will look like this:

	Andrew Andrews			
	Trial Balance June 30, 19—			
	Cash		772 00	
	Sales			200 00
	Purchases		350 00	
	A. Andrews, Capital			1000 00
	Postage		3 00	
	L. Anderson		125 00	
	L. Stillman			150 00
	Rent		100 00	
			1350 00	1350 00

A Trial Balance is therefore an abstract—a list of the balances of all the accounts in the ledger which have a balance. If an account is "in balance," viz. the debit and credit amounts are the same in amount, do not list this account in the Trial Balance.

PROPRIETOR'S PERSONAL ACCOUNT

When a proprietor draws any money for his personal use, he does so because of the management services he is rendering to the business. He is entitled to compensation for his services. He may draw any amount he sees fit. He is the sole judge of that. But in drawing that amount, he does not consider his investment decreased. In establishing the selling price of his goods he has included a fee for his services. This drawing is in reality against this fee and not against his investment.

Thus a proprietor's drawing must be debited to his drawing account. This is so because Cash, being withdrawn, is credited, hence the personal account will be debited.

A proprietor's drawing account is ordinarily a debit account.

Note: Open a new account entitled "R. Walden, Drawing." The Trial Balance will thus have R. Walden, Capital and R. Walden, Drawing accounts.

Exercise 9:

July
1. R. Walden began business investing cash $5000.
2. Bought from A. Smith merchandise on account $250.
3. Sold for cash merchandise $175.
5. Paid rent $75.
7. Sold to Andrew King merchandise on account $150.
10. R. Walden drew for his personal use cash $50.
12. Paid A. Smith $100.
15. Sold A. London merchandise on account $250.

Required:

Journalize.

Solution:

Cash (Dr.) Receipts Journal

Date		Accounts, Cr.	Explanation	L.F.	Amount	Total
19—						
July	1	R. Walden, Cap.			5000 00	
	3	Sales			175 00	
	31	Cash, Dr.			5175 00	5175 00

Cash (Cr.) Payment Journal

Date		Accounts, Dr.	Explanation	L.F.	Amount	Total
19—						
July	5	Rent			75 00	
	10	R. Walden, Pers.			50 00	
	12	A. Smith			100 00	
	31	Cash, Cr.			225 00	225 00

Solution for Exercise 9 continued:

Sales (Cr.) Journal

Date	Accounts, Dr.	Terms	L.F.	Amount	Total
19— July 7	Andrew King	a/c		150 00	
15	A. London	a/c		250 00	
31	Sales, Cr.				400 00

Purchases (Dr.) Journal

Date	Accounts, Cr.	Terms	L.F.	Amount	Total
19— July 2	A. Smith	a/c		250 00	
31	Purchases, Dr.				250 00

FIXED ASSET ACCOUNTS

Things bought can be divided into three parts:

(1) Things bought to be sold, debit Purchases.

(2) Things bought to be consumed in a short time, debit Expense—such as Supplies, Stationery, Postage, etc.

(3) Things bought to be used for more than one year are called Fixed Assets, and are debited to an account describing the asset—such as Machinery, Delivery Equipment, Typewriters, etc.

Referring to the purchase of an auto-truck on August 10th, in Exercise 10, when we buy merchandise we buy it to sell. The Purchase account is debited; when we buy an auto truck, are we buying it to sell? No, we intend using it in our business to deliver merchandise. We must therefore open a special account called "Delivery Equipment." Hence we debit this account thus:

CASH PAYMENT (CR.) JOURNAL

Aug. 10. Delivery Equipment—auto-truck $350.

Exercise 10:

Aug. 1. R. Randall began business investing $4000.
2. Bought for cash merchandise $1250.
3. Sold for cash merchandise $375.
4. Drew for his personal use $25.
6. Paid bookkeeper's salary $22.
8. Sold on account to A. Kelly merchandise $350.
9. Bought from Martin Smith merchandise $300.
10. Bought for cash auto-truck for delivery service $875.
10. Bought for cash gasoline for truck $2.
10. Paid for stamps $5.
12. Paid Martin Smith in full of account $300.
13. Received from A. Kelly $150 on account.

Required:

Journalize, post, and take a Trial Balance.

Solution:

C2

Cash (Dr.) Receipts

Date	Accounts Cr.	Explanation	L.F	Amount	Total
Aug 1	R. Randall, Cap.	Investment	1	4000 00	
3	Sales	Sold for cash	2	375 00	
13	A. Kelly	Apply on acct.	3	150 00	
31	Cash, Dr.		4	4525 00	4525 00

C3

Cash (Cr.) Payment Journal

Date	Accounts Dr.	Explanation	LF	Amount	Total
Aug 2	Purchases	Bought for cash	5	1250 00	
4	R. Randall, Pers.	Withdrew	6	25 00	
6	Salaries	Paid Bookkeeper	7	22 00	
10	Delivery Equipment	Bought Truck	8	875 00	
10	Selling Expense	Bought Gasoline	9	2 00	
10	Office Supplies	Bought stamps	10	5 00	
12	Martin Smith	Paid in full	11	300 00	
31	Cash, Cr.		4	2479 00	2479 00

Solution for Exercise 10 continued:

8,

Sales (Cr.) Journal

Date		Account, Dr.	Terms	L.F	Amount		Total	
19— Aug	8	A. Kelly	a/c	3	3,50	00		
	31	Sales, Cr.		2			3,50	00

P,

Purchase (Dr.) Journal

Date		Account, Cr.	Terms	L.F	Amount		Total	
19— Aug	9	Martin Smith	a/c	11	300	00		
	31	Purchases, Dr		5			300	00

R. Randall, Capital (1)

				19— Aug	1		4000.– C2	4000	00

Sales (2)

				19— Aug	3			C2	375	00
					31		725.–	S1	350	00
									725	00

A. Kelly (3)

19— Aug	8	350.– 150.– 500.–	S1	350	00	19— Aug	13		C2	150	00

Cash (4)

19— Aug	31	4525 2479 2046	C2	4525	00	19— Aug	31		C3	2479	00

Solution for Exercise 10 continued:

Purchases (5)

19—						
Aug 2		C3	1250 00			
31	1550.-	P1	300 00			
			1550 00			

R. Randall, Personal (6)

19—				
Aug 4	25.-	C3	25 00	

Salaries (7)

19—				
Aug 6	22.-	C3	22 00	

Delivery Equipment (8)

19—				
Aug 10	875.-	C3	875 00	

Selling Expense (9)

19—				
Aug 10	2.-	C3	2 00	

Office Supplies (10)

19—				
Aug 10	5.-	C3	5 00	

Solution for Exercise 10 continued:

Martin Smith (11)

	19—				19—			
	Aug 12		C.3	300 00	Aug 9		P1	300 00

R. Randall
Trial Balance Aug. 31, 19—

R. Randall, Capital				4000 00
Sales				725 00
O. Kelly			200 00	
Cash			2046 00	
Purchases			1550 00	
R. Randall, Personal			25 00	
Salaries			22 00	
Delivery Equipment			875 00	
Selling Expense			2 00	
Office Supplies			5 00	
			4725 00	4725 00

Exercise 11:

Sept.   1. P. Church began business investing $5000.

2. Bought on account merchandise $275 from F. Derby.

3. Sold for cash merchandise $150.

4. P. Church paid the premium on his personal life insurance policy $110.
   (*Is this insurance premium a cost of operating our
   business? No. Debit P. Church, Drawing.*)

5. Bought on account from J. Keenan merchandise $250.

6. Sold R. Long on account merchandise $450.

6. P. Church invests an additional $1000.

7. Bought for cash 1 safe for the office $250.
   (*Are we buying the safe to sell? No. Debit furniture and fixtures, or Office Equipment.*)

8. Paid fire insurance premium on merchandise $150.
   (*Is this insurance premium a cost of operating our
   business? Yes. Debit Insurance.*)

9. Paid F. Derby $150 on account.

Sept. 10. Paid $2000 for a plot adjoining our building for our
future use.
(*Debit Real Estate.*)
12. Received from R. Long on account $450.
15. P. Church drew for his personal use $75.
25. P. Church withdrew from his investment $1000.
(*Debit P. Church, Capital because he withdraws this
sum from his investment, and does not expect his
business to compensate him for this sum.*)

Required:

Journalize, post, and take a Trial Balance.

Solution:

C 2

Cash (Dr.) Receipts Journal

Date	Accounts, Cr.	Explanation	L.F.	Amount	Total
Sept. 1	P. Church, Cap.	Investment	1	5000 00	
3	Sales	Sold for cash	2	150 00	
6	P. Church, Cap.	Additional Invest	1	1000 00	
12	R. Long	Apply on acc't	4	450 00	
30	Cash, Dr.		5		6600 00

C 3

Cash (Cr.) Payment Journal

Date	Account, Dr.	Explanation	L.F.	Amount	Total
Sept. 4	P. Church, Pers.	Withdrew	3	110 00	
7	Office Equipment	Bought safe	6	250 00	
8	Insurance	Paid premium	7	150 00	
9	J. Derby	Apply on acc't	8	150 00	
10	Real Estate	Bought property	9	2000 00	
15	P. Church, Pers.	Withdrew	3	75 00	
25	P. Church, Cap.	Withdrew capital	1	1000 00	
30	Cash, Cr.		5		3735 00

Solution for Exercise 11 continued:

S1

Sales (Cr.) Journal

Date	Account, Dr.	Terms	L.F.	Amount	Total
19— Sept 6	R. Long	On account	4	450 00	
30	Sales, Cr.		2		450 00

P1

Purchases (Dr.) Journal

Date	Account, Cr.	Terms	L.F.	Amount	Total
19— Sept 2	F. Derby	On account	8	275 00	
5	J. Keelan	On account	10	250 00	
30	Purchases, Dr.		11		525 00

P. Church, Capital (1)

Date			L.F.	Amount		Date				L.F.	Amount	
19— Sept 25			C3	1000 00		19— Sept 1				C2	5000 00	
						6	6000 1200 3000			C2	1000 00	
											6000 00	

Sales (2)

Date			L.F.	Amount		Date			L.F.	Amount	
						19— Sept 3			C2	150 00	
						30	600.—		S1	450 00	
										600 00	

P. Church, Personal (3)

Date			L.F.	Amount			
19— Sept 4			C3	110 00			
15	185.—		C3	75 00			

Solution for Exercise 11 continued:

R. Long (4)

Sept 6			S1	450 00	Sept 12		C2	450 00

Cash (5)

Sept 30		6600. 3735. 2865.—	C2	6600 00	Sept 30		C3	3735 00

Office Equipment (6)

Sept 7		250.—	C3	250 00	

Insurance (7)

Sept 8		150.—	C3	150 00	

F. Derby (8)

Sept 9			C3	150 00	Sept 2	375 950 125.—	P1	275 00

Real Estate (9)

Sept 10		2000.—	C3	2000 00	

Solution for Exercise 11 continued:

J. Keenan (10)

| | | | Sept 5 | 250- P₁ | 250 00 |

Purchases (11)

| Sept 30 | 525- P₁ | 525 00 | | |

P. Church
Trial Balance, Sept. 30, 19—

		Dr.	Cr.
P. Church, Capital			5000 00
Sales			600 00
P. Church, Personal		185 00	
Cash		2865 00	
Office Equipment		250 00	
Insurance		150 00	
I. Derby			125 00
Real Estate		2000 00	
J. Keenan			250 00
Purchases		525 00	
		5975 00	5975 00
		5975 00	5975 00

Lesson VI

GENERAL JOURNAL

Until now every transaction contained either cash, a sale, or a purchase. We entered these into their respective journals.

Suppose on January 5 we sold John Smith merchandise on account for $50.00. On January 15 we received cash from him for $49.00. He still owes us $1.00; we call his attention to his balance whereupon on January 18 we receive from him postage stamps amounting to $1.00 to balance his account.

How do we record the receipt of these stamps?

Are stamps cash? No, therefore we cannot use the Cash Journal.

Have we made a sale on January 18? No, therefore we cannot use the Sales Journal.

Are we purchasing any merchandise on January 18? No, therefore we cannot use the Purchase Journal.

If we cannot use *any* of these special journals, we must use another book to record miscellaneous transactions. This journal we call the *General Journal*.

This Transaction will be entered thus:

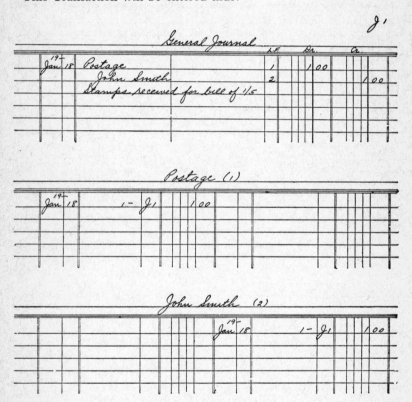

Note how the debit account is extended to the left, and its amount is written in the first column which is the debit column.

The credit account is indented, and its amount is written into the next column, the credit column, on the same line with the credit account.

Every journal entry must have a complete explanation.

We debit Postage because stamps come in to be used as an expense. (Expenses are debited for increases.)

We credit John Smith because his account is decreased. (Assets are credited for decreases.)

The form illustrated in the General Journal, is standard.

Exercise 12:

Jan.   2. The owner, S. Adams, took six 5-cent stamps for personal use.

          4. A stationer took a $3.00 book from his stock to be used by his bookkeeper.

          5. Pay our bill to Jackson in stamps, 80 cents.

          6. A furniture dealer took a $40.00 desk from his stock into his office for the bookkeeper's use.

          6. The owner, S. Adams, paid the rent of the business, $125.00, with his own money.

        12. R. Raub paid his bill of January 3 with stamps, $2.20.

        12. Paid our bill to J. Thompson, with 90 cents worth of stamps.

        14. Bought a typewriter from Milton & Co. on account $125.00 for use in office.

        14. S. Adams added to his investment by giving the business a $1500.00 automobile.

        28. Mr. S. Adams, a furniture dealer, took for himself two tables for his home, at cost $17.00.

Journalize and post.

(Solution for Exercise 12 begins on Page 44)

Exercise 13:

Oct.   1. R. Horton began business investing cash $7000.

          2. Paid rent $100.

          3. Bought on account merchandise from A. Allen $300.

          4. Sold on account to B. Burns merchandise $250.

          5. Bought stamps $10.00.

          5. R. Horton drew for his personal use $25.00.

          6. Paid A. Allen on account $100.

          7. Received from B. Burns $150.

(Exercise 13 continued on Page 47)

Solution for Exercise 12:

General Journal

			L.F.	Dr.	Cr.
Jan. 2	S. Adams, Personal		1	30	
	Postage		2		30
	Took six 5¢ stamps				
4	Office Supplies		3	3 00	
	Purchases		4		3 00
	Took supplies from stock for personal use				
5	Jackson		8	80	
	Postage		2		80
	Paid bill in stamps				
6	Furniture & Fixtures		6	40 00	
	Purchases		4		40 00
	Took desk from stock for use				
6	Rent		7	125 00	
	S. Adams, Personal		1		125 00
	Paid rent with personal funds.				
12	Postage		2	2 20	
	R. Raub		5		2 20
	Stamps received for bill of Jan. 3				
12	J. Thompson		9	90	
	Postage		2		90
	Paid bill with stamps				
14	Office Equipment		10	125 00	
	Milton & Co.		11		125 00
	Bought typewriter for use on acct.				
14	Automobile		12	1500 00	
	S. Adams, Capital		13		1500 00
	Auto contributed by Adams.				
28	S. Adams, Personal		1	17 00	
	Purchases		4		17 00
	Took mdse. for personal use.				

S. Adams, Personal (1)

Jan. 2		J1		30	Jan. 6	125.00 / 17.30 / 107.70	J1	125 00
28		J1	17 00					
			17 30					

Solution for Exercise 12 continued:

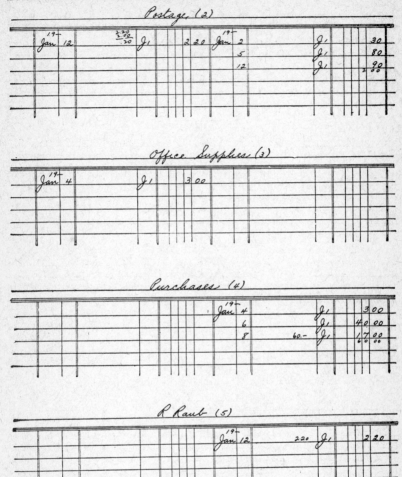

Postage (2)

Office Supplies (3)

Purchases (4)

R Raub (5)

Furniture & Fixtures (6)

Solution for Exercise 12 continued:

Rent (7)

19— Jan. 6	135.—	J1	125	00

Jackson (8)

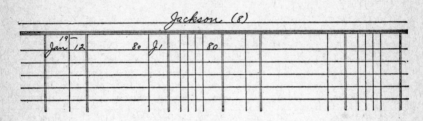

19— Jan. 12	80	J1	80

J. Thompson (9)

19— Jan. 12	90	J1	90

Office Equipment (10)

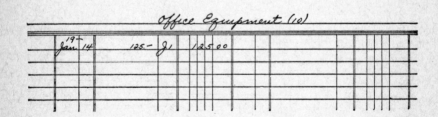

19— Jan. 14	125.—	J1	125	00

Milton & Co. (11)

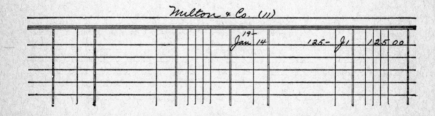

19— Jan. 14	125.—	J1	125	00

Solution for Exercise 12 continued:

Automobile (12)

Jan. 14	1500.-	J1	1500 00						

S. Adams, Capital (13)

				Jan. 14	1500.-	J1	1500 00		

S. Adams
Trial Balance. Jan. 30, 19—

S. Adams, Personal			107 70
Postage		20	
Office Supplies		3 00	
Purchases			60 00
R. Raub			2 20
Furniture & Fixtures	40 00		
Rent	125 00		
Jackson		80	
J. Thompson		90	
Office Equipment	125 00		
Milton & Co.			125 00
Automobile	1500 00		
S. Adams, Capital			1500 00
	1794 90		1794 90

(Exercise 13 continued from Page 43)

Oct. 8. R. Horton invests $2000.

10. Received from B. Burns on account $97.00.

12. Received from B. Burns stamps $3.00.

13. Bought machinery for the factory for cash **$1000**.

14. Bought oil for the machines $5.00.

   (*Debit Factory Expense.*)

15. Paid A. Allen $198.

Oct. 18. Sent A. Allen $2.00 in stamps.

> (Debit A. Allen $2.00, Credit Expense $2.00. This is so because A. Allen's account, a liability account, is decreased, therefore debited; and the Expense account is credited because when we withdraw $2.00 worth of stamps from our supply of stamps we have $2.00 worth stamps which cannot be used for expense purposes, hence the stamps account-Expense-is decreased, and must accordingly be credited. Consult the Debit and Credit Chart pertaining to decreases of Expenses and decreases of liabilities.)

Journalize, post, get Trial Balance.

Solution for Exercise 13:

C2.

Cash (Dr.) Receipts Journal

Date		Accounts, Cr.	Explanation	L.F.	Amount	Total
Oct	1	R Horton, Capital	Investment	2	7000 00	
	7	B Burns	Apply on acct.	3	150 00	
	8	R Horton, Capital	Investment	2	2000 00	
	10	B Burns	Apply on acct	3	97 00	
	31	Cash, Dr.		1	9247 00	9247 00

C3.

Cash (Cr.) Payment Journal

Date		Account, Dr.	Explanation	L.F.	Amount	Total
Oct	2	Rent	Paid Oct. rent	4	100 00	
	5	Postage	Bought stamps	5	10 00	
	5	R Horton, Pers	Withdrawal	6	25 00	
	6	A. Allen	Apply on acct	7	100 00	
	13	Machinery	Bought for cash	8	1000 00	
	14	Factory Expense	Oil for machines	9	5 00	
	15	A. Allen	Apply on acct	7	198 00	
	31	Cash, Cr.		1	1438 00	1438 00

Solution for Exercise 13 continued:

S1

Sales (Cr.) Journal

Date	Account, Dr.	Terms	L.F.	Amount	Total
19—					
Oct 4	B. Burns	On account	3	250 00	
31	Sales, Cr.		10		250 00

P1

Purchase (Dr.) Journal

Date	Account, Cr.	Terms	L.F.	Amount	Total
19—					
Oct 3	A. Allen	on account	7	300 00	
31			11		300 00

J1

General Journal

19—							
Oct 12	Postage		5	3 00			
	B. Burns		3		3 00		
	Rec'd stamps to cancel Burns' acc't						
18	A. Allen		7	2 00			
	Postage		5		2 00		
	Gave Allen stamps to settle acc't						

Cash (1)

19—						19—			
Oct 31	9247— 438— 7809—	C2	9247 00		Oct 31		C3	1438 00

R. Horton, Capital (2)

				19—			
				Oct 1		C2	7000 00
				8	9000—	C2	2000 00
							9000 00

Solution for Exercise 13 continued:

B Burns (3)

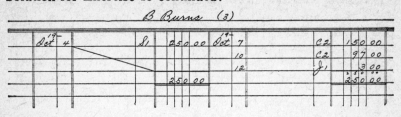

Oct 4		S1	250 00	Oct 7		C2	150 00	
				10		C2	97 00	
				12		J1	3 00	
							250 00	
			250 00				250 00	

Rent (4)

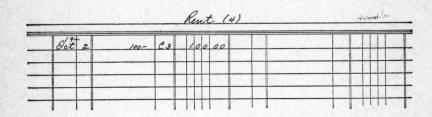

Oct 2	100.-	C3	100 00	

Postage (5)

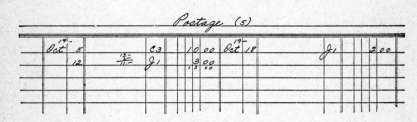

Oct 5		C3	10 00	Oct 18		J1	2 00
12		J1	3 00				
			13 00				

R Horton, Personal (6)

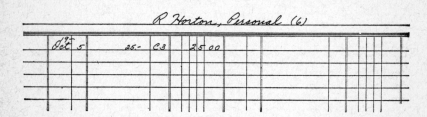

Oct 5	25.-	C3	25 00	

A. Allen (7)

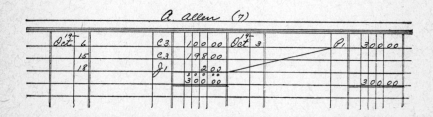

Oct 6		C3	100 00	Oct 3		P1	300 00
15		C3	198 00				
18		J1	2 00				
			300 00				300 00

Solution for Exercise 13 continued:

Machinery (8)

Oct 13		1000.-	C3	1000	00				

Factory Expense (9)

Oct 14	oil	5.-	C3	5	00				

Sales (10)

				Oct 31	250.-	S1	250	00	

Purchases (11)

Oct 31		300.-	P1	300	00				

R. Horton
Trial Balance, Oct. 31, 19—

			Dr.		Cr.	
Cash			7809	00		
R. Horton, Capital					9000	00
Rent			100	00		
Postage			1	00		
R. Horton, Personal			25	00		
Machinery			1000	00		
Factory Expense			5	00		
Sales					250	00
Purchases			300	00		
			9250	00		9250	00
			9250	00		9250	00

BALANCING AN ACCOUNT

Let us look at the ledger accounts in the Solution of Exercise 12. Observe the small-sized additions. They are called *footings* and are always in pencil. Notice the subtraction of the footings. This subtraction is always made on the side having the *larger* total, in the space reserved for the description, on the same line with the last posting on that side.

Avoid doing any work on scraps of paper. If the Trial Balance does not balance, it will be much easier to find an error in footings, if the footings are made on the ledger account.

In listing the accounts in the Trial Balance, we merely place the balance of the footings on the same side of the Trial Balance as it appears in the ledger.

Never erase a footing. *Next month's postings will be added to these footings.*

HOW TO FIND THE ERRORS

IF THE TRIAL BALANCE DOES NOT BALANCE

If the Trial Balance does not balance, we have made an error. How can we find the error? First find the difference between the two totals of the Trial Balance. Now let us look for the mistakes amounting to this figure. We have made errors either in:

1. Footings.
2. Postings, or both.

Errors in footings take less time to find, therefore start looking for this type of error first.

Errors in footings may be the following:

1. Incorrect addition in one of the journals. *To correct*—check all the additions in all the journals.

2. Incorrect addition in the ledger accounts. *To correct*—Check the additions in each ledger account.

3. Incorrect forwarding of the amounts to be subtracted e.g.—236 may have been forwarded 263. *To correct*—Check each amount forwarded.

4. Incorrect subtraction of the footings in ledger accounts. *To correct*—Prove the subtraction by adding the amount subtracted to the remainder. It must equal the amount being decreased.

Thus:

$$\begin{array}{r} 364 \\ -218 \\ \hline 146 \end{array}$$

$146 + 218 = 364$ proof

5. Incorrect amount forwarded to the Trial Balance. *To correct—* Check the amounts forwarded.

6. Forwarding the balances to the wrong side of the Trial Balance. *To correct—*Check each balance listed in the Trial Balance and see that it is placed on the same side of the Trial Balance as the balance appears in the ledger.

7. Incorrect addition in the Trial Balance. *To correct—*Check the addition of the two columns.

   Warning: In doing the additions, always add *down* the column first, then add *up* the column to check. In carrying forward an amount from one column of figures to the next, always pencil-foot the amount forwarded. Thus:

$$\begin{array}{r} 465 \\ 573 \\ 899 \\ 650 \\ \hline 2587 \end{array}$$

If you have not found the error, we must now check the postings.

How to check the Postings

1. *Checking*: Place a check ($\sqrt{}$) mark alongside of each item checked in the journals and also alongside of each item checked in the ledger. There will thus be *two* check marks for each posting checked.

2. *Check from the journals to the ledger.* Some bookkeepers check from the ledger to the journals. It is more practical to do the former.

3. *Check all debit postings first, then all credit postings.* In this manner the eye will become accustomed to looking for the posting on one side only. Often errors are overlooked because the eye is not sufficiently alert to discover the fact that the posting has been made on the wrong side.

4. *After all checking has been completed, look at each posting in the ledger to see that it has a check mark.* If the check mark is missing, the posting does not belong there. Examine to see if this posting is in error. It may be a duplicated posting, or a posting to the incorrect account.

As we check each posting be alert to observe that we did not do the following:

1. Posted incorrect amount from the journal to the ledger. *To correct*—As we check the postings carefully look for this error.
2. Posted to the wrong side. *To correct*—When checking postings, check all debit postings from all books first, then all credit postings.
3. Omitted a posting. *To correct*—When checking back the postings an unposted item will readily be found.
4. Posting to the wrong account. *To correct*—Although this type of error will not cause the Trial Balance to be out of balance, in checking the postings this error will be easily discovered.

Follow all the foregoing instructions *step by step* if your Trial Balance does not balance.

If the error is still not found, it is possible that we have overlooked it. Recheck in following way:

1. Make "T" accounts on a separate sheet of paper for each account in the ledger. e.g.

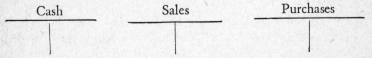

2. Copy the debit and credit footings of each account as of *last month* into the respective "T" account.
3. To prove the accuracy of each footing copied from last month's ledger footings, total all debit footings, then total all credit footings in the "T" accounts. These totals must equal the same amount if they were copied correctly because last month's Trial Balance balanced.
4. Post from all journals for the current month to the "T" accounts.

5. Take a Trial Balance of the "T" Accounts.
6. Compare this Trial Balance of the "T" accounts with the Trial Balance of the ledger accounts—account for account.
7. If the compared accounts do not agree in amount, compare each item in these acounts—the error will unquestionably be discovered.

Lesson VII

RETURNS

Sales Returns

Very frequently the goods we have sold is returned. This transaction is called a Sales Return.

There are two kinds of Sales Returns:

1. If the goods were sold for cash, we make the following entry: Debit Sales Returns, and credit Cash. Sales is a credit, its opposite—Sales Returns—is a debit account. Thus we have an count called Sales and another account called Sales Returns.

Transaction:

Paid $10 for merchandise sold on Jan. 5th returned today.

Entry:

C 3

Date	Accounts, Dr.	Cash (Cr.) Payment Journal Explanation	L. F	Amount	Total
Jan 19— 7	Sales Returns	Cash, sales ret.		10 00	

2. If the goods were sold on account we debit Sales Returns, and credit the Customer. This transaction cannot be entered into any of the special journals, because it is not a Sale on account, a Purchase on account, or Cash received or paid. It must therefore be entered into the General Journal.

Transaction:

Oct. 10. A. Smith returns merchandise in amount $25 sold on account Oct. 2.

Entry:

J1

General Journal	L.F.	Dr.	Cr.
19— Oct. 10 Sales Returns		25 00	
A. Smith			25 00
Goods sold Oct. 2, returned for			
credit.			

Exercise 14:

The following returns were made by customers:

Jan. 4. L. Carr & Son $50 sold for cash Jan. 2.

      7. D. Jones Co. $10 sold on account Jan. 3.

   15. N. Nicholas $20 sold on account Jan. 5.

   20. J. Arnold $25 sold for cash Jan. 10.

Journalize.

Solution:

C3

Cash (Cr.) Payment Journal

Date	Account, Dr.	Explanation	L.F.	Amount	Total
19— Jan. 4	Sales Returns	L. Carr & Son, sold 1/2		50 00	
20	Sales Returns	J. Arnold, sold 1/10		25 00	

J1

General Journal	L.F.	Dr.	Cr.
19— Jan. 7 Sales Returns		10 00	
D. Jones Co			10 00
Return from bill of 1/3			
15 Sales Returns		20 00	
N. Nicholas			20 00
Return from bill of 1/5			

Exercise 15:

Jan. 2. Nathan Storm began business investing $10,000.

    2. Bought on account from A. Jenkins merchandise $1500.

    3. Sold for cash merchandise $250.

    5. Paid rent $250.

    5. Sold Coleman & Jones on account merchandise $750.

    6. Sold Stewart & Co. on account merchandise $1200.

    7. Bought a safe for the office $275.

    10. Paid A. Jenkins on account $1000.

    12. Coleman & Jones return $200 merchandise sold on account on January 5.

    15. Nathan Storm drew $100 for himself.

    17. Stewart & Co. return $175 merchandise sold on the 6th.

    18. Stewart & Co. return $200 merchandise sold on the 6th.

    20. Paid $1 for replacing a broken pane of glass.

    22. Received from Stewart & Co. balance due us.

    24. Paid A. Jenkins $200.

Required:

Journalize, post, Trial Balance.

Solution:

C2

Cash (Dr.) Receipts Journal

Date	Accounts, Cr.	Explanation	L.F.	Amount	Total
19— Jan. 2	Nathan Storm, Cap.	Investment	1	10000 00	
3	Sales	Sold for cash	2	250 00	
22	Stewart & Co.	Paid in full	4	825 00	
31	Cash, Dr.		5	11075 00	11075 00

C3

Cash (Cr.) Payment Journal

Date	Accounts, Dr.	Explanation	L.F.	Amount	Total
19— Jan. 5	Rent	Paid January rent	6	250 00	
7	Office Equipment	Office safe	7	275 00	
10	A. Jenkins	Apply on account	8	1000 00	
15	Nathan Storm, Pers.	Withdrawal	9	100 00	
20	General Expense	Replace glass	10	1 00	
24	A. Jenkins	Apply on account	8	200 00	
31	Cash, Cr.		5	1826 00	1826 00

Solution for Exercise 15 continued:

S1

Sales (Cr.) Journal

Date		Accounts, Dr.	Terms	L.F.	Amount	Total
19— Jan.	5	Coleman & Jones	On account	11	750 00	
	6	Stewart & Co.	On account	4	1200 00	
	31	Sales, Cr.		2	1950 00	1950 00

P1

Purchases (Dr.) Journal

Date		Accounts, Cr.	Terms	L.F.	Amount	Total
19— Jan.	2	A. Jenkins	On account	8	1500 00	
	31	Purchases, Dr.		12		1500 00

J1

General Journal.

Date					Dr.	Cr.
19— Jan.	12	Sales Returns		3	200 00	
		Coleman & Jones		11		200 00
		Return from bill of Jan. 5.				
	17	Sales Returns		3	175 00	
		Stewart & Co		4		175 00
		Return from bill of Jan. 6.				
	18	Sales Returns		3	200 00	
		Stewart & Co		4		200 00
		Return from bill of Jan. 6.				

Nathan Storm, Capital (1)

				Date		Dr.		Cr.
				19— Jan. 2	10,000—		C2	10000 00

Sales (2)

				Date		Dr.		Cr.
				19— Jan. 3			C2	250 00
				31	2200—		S1	1950 00

Solution for Exercise 15 continued:

Sales Returns (3)

19–									
Jan. 12			J1	200 00					
17			J1	175 00					
18	575.–		J1	200 00					
				575 00					

Stewart & Co. (4)

19–					19–				
Jan. 6			S1	1200 00	Jan. 22			C2	825 00
					17			J1	175 00
					18			J1	200 00
				1200 00					1200 00

Cash (5)

19–					19–				
Jan. 31	11075– 1826– 9249–		C2	11075 00	Jan. 31			C3	1826 00

Rent (6)

19–									
Jan. 5	250.–		C3	250 00					

Office Equipment (7)

19–									
Jan. 7	275.–		C3	275 00					

A. Jenkins (8)

19–					19–				
Jan. 10			C3	1000 00	Jan. 2	1500– 1200– 300.–		P1	1500 00
24			C3	200 00					
				1200 00					

Solution for Exercise 15 continued:

Nathan Storm, Personal (9)

19—				
Jan. 15	100—	C.3	100 00	

General Expense (10)

19—				
Jan. 20	1—	C.3	1 00	

Coleman + Jones (11)

19—					19—			
Jan. 5	250— 200— 550—	S.1	750 00		Jan. 12		J.1	200 00

Purchases (12)

19—				
Jan. 31	1500—	P.1	1500 00	

Nathan Storm
Trial Balance, January 31, 19—

	Dr.	Cr.
Nathan Storm, Capital		10 000 00
Sales		2 200 00
Sales Returns	575 00	
Cash	9 249 00	
Rent	250 00	
Office Equipment	275 00	
A Jenkins		300 00
Nathan Storm, Personal	100 00	
General Expense	1 00	
Coleman + Jones	550 00	
Purchases	1 500 00	
	12 500 00	12 500 00

Purchase Returns

Very frequently we return merchandise which we have purchased. This transaction is called Purchase Returns. The very same procedure is followed as in the Sales Returns.

If the purchase was made for cash, the return is recorded in the Cash (Dr.) Receipts Journal because Purchases are decreased, and cash is increased, thus:

Transactions:

  Jan. 10. Received $25 for merchandise bought Jan. 8 and returned today.

Entry:

C 2

Date	Accounts, Cr.	Explanation	L.F.	Amount	Total
Jan. 10	Purchase Returns	bought for cash 1/8		25 00	

Cash (Dr.) Receipts Journal

If the purchase was made on account, we enter it into the General Journal.

Transaction:

  Mar. 12. Returned to Jones & Co. merchandise in amount $50— bought on account Mar. 5.

Entry:

J 1

Date			L.F.	Dr.	Cr.
Mar. 12	Jones & Co.			50 00	
	Purchase Returns				50 00
	Returned mdse. bought 3/5				

General Journal

Transaction:

  Enter the following merchandise returns made to creditors:
  April 5. M. Fenton $250 bought for cash April 2.
       6. James Preston $175 bought on account April 4.
       8. Williams & Co. $50 bought on account April 5.

Entries:

C2

Cash (Dr.) Receipts Journal

Date	Accounts Cr.	Explanation	L.F.	Amount		Total	
Apr. 5	Purchase Returns	M. Fenton bought 4/2		250	00		

J.

General Journal

			L.F.	Dr.		Cr.	
Apr. 6	James Preston			175	00		
	Purchase Returns					175	00
	Returned mdse. bought 4/4						
8	Williams & Co			50	00		
	Purchase Returns					50	00
	Returned mdse. bought 4/5						

Add the following to our Debit and Credit Chart:

Sales Returns are debits.

Purchase Returns are credits.

It may help you to remember by bearing in mind that returns are the opposite of the original action, viz. Sales is a credit, Sales Returns is a debit; Purchases is a debit, Purchase Returns is a credit.

RULE:

Purchase Returns on account are entered into the General Journal.

Sales Returns on account are entered into the General Journal.

Use the Cash (Dr.) Receipts Journal to record returns of Purchases made for cash.

Use the Cash (Cr.) Payment Journal to record returns of Sales made for cash.

Lesson VIII

NOTES

NOTES RECEIVABLE

In order to be certain that debts are paid we frequently request customers to give us promissory notes in order to have tangible evidence of debt.

Transaction:

> March 3. Sold D. Dodd merchandise on account $100.
>
>   25. Received from D. Dodd $60 cash and a 10 day note for $40.
>
> April 4. Received from D. Dodd $40 in payment for his note due today.

Entries:

C 2

Cash (Dr) Receipts Journal

Date	Accounts, Cr	Explanation	L.F.	Amount	Total
19— Mar 25	D. Dodd	a/c	1	60 00	
Apr 4	Notes Receivable		2	40 00	

S 1

Sales (Cr) Journal

Date	Accounts Dr	Terms	L.F.	Amount	Total
19— Mar 3	D. Dodd	a/c	1	100 00	

J 1

General Journal

Date			L.F.	Dr	Cr
19— Mar 25	Notes Receivable		2	40 00	
	D. Dodd		1		40 00
	Received 10 day note due April 4				

D Dodd (1)

Date		L.F.		Date		L.F.	
19— Mar 3		S 1	100 00	19— Mar 25		C 2	60 00
				25	By note	J 1	40 00
			100 00				100 00

Notes Receivable (2)

	Mar ¹⁹25	10 day, due 4/4	J1		40	00	Apr 4		C2	40	00

Dodd's note would look like this:

$40 ²⁰⁄ₓₓ   *March 25, 19 —*

Ten days after date I promise to pay to the order of R. Smith Co.

Forty and ⁿᵒ⁄₁₀₀ —————————— Dollars

at City Bank

Value received

No.———— Due April 4, 19 —   D. Dodd.

D. Dodd is called the maker of the note, R. Smith Co., the payee.
We call this note a Note Receivable because we expect to *receive cash* for it on the due date.

Observe the following:

(1) A person may owe us money:
        (a) on account.
        (b) on a note.

If he owes us money on account, *his account* will show the debt.

If he owes us money on a note, the *Notes Receivable account* will show the debt.

Thus when we receive a note from a customer, we debit *Notes Receivable,* and credit the *customer*.

(2) The receipt of the note is recorded in the General Journal.

Transaction:

    July 5. Received a 10 day note dated today from John Brown, our customer for $150.

Entry:

J^{1}

General Journal

		L.F	Dr.	Cr.
July 5	Notes Receivable		150 00	
	John Brown			150 00
	Ten day note due July 15			

(3) When we receive cash for a note, we credit *Notes Receivable* in the Cash (Dr.) Receipts Journal, *do not credit the customer.* This is due to the fact that the payment of the note decreases the Notes Receivable account, not the customer's account.

(4) The Notes Receivable account records a note on each line, and shows the due date of each note.

Memorize:

When we receive a note, we
  Debit Notes Receivable, and
    Credit the Customer, through the General Journal.
When we receive cash for a note, we
  Debit Cash, and
    Credit Notes Receivable, through the Cash
      Receipts Journal.

Exercise 16:

July   1. L. Lazarus invests $3000 cash, and $500 merchandise into the business.

Enter the cash investment into the Cash (Dr.) Receipts Journal. Then enter the merchandise investment into the General Journal thus:

J^{1}

General Journal

		L.F	Dr.	Cr.
July 1	Merchandise Inventory		500 00	
	L. Lazarus, Capital			500 00
	To record investment of mdse.			

This entry is made in the General Journal because merchandise inventory is neither cash, a sale, nor a purchase, hence cannot be recorded into any special journal. Treat this transaction as two transactions. Record the cash in the usual manner. Then record the merchandise.

July 2. Sold to H. Brown on account merchandise $275.

5. Received from H. Brown a 10 day note for $100.

7. Bought for cash merchandise $250.

8. Paid $20 for printing stationery.

10. Sold D. Davison merchandise on account $200.

12. Sold for cash merchandise $150.

15. Received from D. Davison a 10 day note for $150 and $50 in cash.

(*Make two transactions of this: first, to record the note; second, to record the cash.*)

15. Received from H. Brown payment for his note due today.

25. Received from D. Davison payment for his note due today.

Required:

Journalize, post, Trial Balance.

Solution:

C2

Cash (Dr.) Receipts Journal

Date	Account, Cr.	Explanation	LF	Amount	Total
'9— July 1	L. Lazarus, Cap.	Investment	1	3000 00	
12	Sales	Sold for cash	2	150 00	
15	D. Davison	Apply on a/c	3	50 00	
15	Notes Receivable	Brown's note due	4	100 00	
25	Notes Receivable	Davison's note due	4	150 00	
31	Cash, Dr.		5	3450 00	3450 00

C3

Cash (Cr.) Payment Journal

Date	Accounts, Dr.	Explanation	LF	Amount	Total
'9— July 7	Purchases	Bought for cash	6	250 00	
8	General Expense	Printing	7	20 00	
31	Cash, Cr.		5	270 00	270 00

Solution for Exercise 16 continued:

General Journal

J_1

			L.F.	Dr.	Cr.
19— July	1	Merchandise Inventory	9	500 00	
		L. Lazarus, Capital	1		500 00
		Merchandise invested			
	5	Notes Receivable	4	100 00	
		H. Brown	8		100 00
		Ten day note, due July 15			
	15	Notes Receivable	4	150 00	
		D. Davison	3		150 00
		Ten day note, due July 25			

Sales (Cr.) Journal

S_1

Date		Accounts, Dr.	Terms	L.F.	Amount	Total
19— July	2	H. Brown	On %c	8	275 00	
	10	D. Davison	On %c	3	200 00	
					475 00	
	31	Sales, Cr.		2		475 00

L. Lazarus, Capital (1)

19— July	1	Mdse	J_1	500 00	
	1	Cash 3500—	C2	3000 00	
				3500 00	

Sales (2)

19— July	12		C2	150 00	
	31	625—	S_1	475 00	
				625 00	

Solution for Exercise 16 continued:

D Davison (3)

July 10		S1	200 00	July 15	10 day note	Jv	150 00	
				15		C2	50 00	
			200 00				200 00	

Notes Receivable (4)

July 5	Brown	J1	100 00	July 15	Brown	C2	100 00	
15	Davison	J1	150 00	25	Davison	C2	150 00	
			250 00				250 00	

Cash (5)

July 31	3450- 270- 3180-	C2	3450 00	July 31		C3	270 00

Purchases (6)

July 7	250-	C3	250 00	

General Expense (7)

July 8	20-	C3	20 00	

Solution for Exercise 16 continued:

H. Brown (8)

19—						19—					
July 2	$\frac{225-}{100-}$ $\frac{175-}{}$	S1	275	00		July 5	10 day note	J1	100	00

Merchandise Inventory (9)

19—					
July 1		500-	J1	500	00

L. Lazarus
Trial Balance - July 31, 19—

L. Lazarus, Capital					3500	00
Sales					625	00
Cash		3180	00			
Purchases		250	00			
General Expense		20	00			
H. Brown		175	00			
Merchandise Inventory		500	00		4125	00
		4125	00		4125	00

NOTES PAYABLE

Notes Payable follow the same rules as Notes Receivable, and are similar in every detail, except that Notes Payable are liabilities because they represent debts of the business, hence Notes Payable is a *credit* account.

Memorize these rules:

(1) When we give a note to a creditor, we
    Debit the Creditor, and
        Credit Notes Payable in the General Journal.

(2) When we pay cash for a note, we
    Debit Notes Payable, and
        Credit Cash, in the Cash (Cr.) Payment Journal.

Transactions:

> Aug. 1. We bought on account from J. Jones merchandise $400.00.
>   3. We bought on account from R. Rose merchandise $275.00.
>   5. We gave J. Jones a 20 day note in full of the 1st.
>   13. Gave R. Rose $175.00 cash and 30 day note for balance.
>   25. Paid J. Jones note due today.

Entries:

P1

Purchases (Dr) Journal

Date	Accounts, Cr.	Terms	L.F.	Amount	Total
Aug 1	J. Jones	a/c	1	400 00	
3	R. Rose	a/c		275 00	
31	Purchases, Dr			675 00	675 00

J1

General Journal

Date		L.F.	Dr.	Cr.
Aug 5	J. Jones		400 00	
	Notes Payable			400 00
	Gave 20 day note due 8/25 on a/c			
13	R Rose		100 00	
	Notes Payable			100 00
	Gave 30 day note due 9/12 on a/c			

C3

Cash (Cr) Payment Journal

Date	Accounts, Dr	Explanation	L.F.	Amount	Total
Aug 13	R Rose	on account		175 00	
25	Notes Payable	J Jones note		400 00	
31	Cash, Cr			575 00	575 00

Gave 30 day note due September 12 in full of account. To figure due date of above note: This note will run 18 days in August, hence it will fall due on the 12th day $(18 + ? = 30)$ of September.

Lesson IX

REVIEW

Exercise 17A:

Exercises A and B cover two months' transactions. Have separate pages for each journal, open three accounts on each page of the ledger:

Oct. 1. T. Andrews began business investing $5000 cash and $2000 merchandise.

2. Paid rent $150.

2. Bought on account merchandise:

R. Adams	$250
J. Smith	$375
J. Ackerman	$575

3. Sold for cash to A. Anderson merchandise $320.

3. Bought for cash from Williams & Co merchandise $473.

4. Paid $1000 for a Ford delivery truck.

4. Paid $100 premium on $5000 liability insurance on the truck.

4. Paid $15.75 for auto license for the year.

6. The following merchandise was returned for credit:

R. Adams	$100
J. Smith	$150

8. Sold to K. Dale, terms 10 day note, merchandise $270.

8. Sold to J. Wilder, terms ½ cash, balance 15 day note, merchandise $300 (two transactions).

10. Sold on account merchandise:

W. Swing	$175
L. Copeland	$190

12. Paid J. Smith $100 on account.

12. L. Copeland returns merchandise $90.

15. Our delivery truck was in a smash-up, repairs amount to $150.

> (*Debit selling expense since delivery cost is added to selling price.*)

15. W. Swing sends his 10 day note for $75 and cash for the balance.

15. Paid office salaries $150, T. Andrews drew $100, paid wages $350.

18. K. Dale sends us check for note due today.
18. Sent J. Smith a 30 day note for the balance of his account.
23. Received cash for J. Wilder's note due today.
25. Received check from W. Swing for note due today.
31. Paid office salaries $150, T. Andrews drew $120, paid wages $475.

Journalize, post, Trial Balance.

Do not erase footings because the next exercise is a continuation of this exercise. Consult instructions at the end of this exercise before continuing with this work.

Exercise 17B:

Nov. 1. Paid rent $150.
5. Bought for cash merchandise $375.
7. Returned $150 merchandise bought for cash Nov. 5, received check for same (one transaction).
7. Paid J. Smith for our note due today.
8. Sent R. Adams our check for $75 and a 10 day note for the balance.
10. Sold Charles Fenton Co. merchandise $600 terms ⅓ cash, ⅓ 15 day note, balance n/30 (on account). (Enter the *entire* sale first, then receipt of cash, then receipt of note; do nothing to show balance on account, because balance is already on our books.)
12. Sold D. King merchandise $250, received his 15 day note (two transactions).
RULE: If the sale or purchase is not *all for cash,* it is to be considered *all on account.*
13. Bought merchandise on account from:
R. Adams, Chicago, Ill., $230 terms F.O.B. Chicago.
(Buyer pays freight from Chicago to place of destination.)
J. Ackerman $385.
15. We return to J. Ackerman $115 merchandise and give him a 10 day note for $170 and a 15 day note for $100 (three transactions).
15. Paid office salaries $150, T. Andrews drew $100, paid wages $400.

17. Paid $12 to American Express Co. for delivery of merchandise bought from R. Adams on Nov. 13. (Debit Freight-Inward account.)

18. Sent R. Adams check for note due today.

20. Sent letters to our customers advertising a special sale $40 (Debit Selling Expense).

21. Bought from J. Ackerman merchandise $645; paid $200 cash and a 60 day note for the balance.

22. Sold K. Dale merchandise $750; terms ½ cash, balance 45 day note.

25. Received check from Charles Fenton for note due today.

25. Sent check to J. Ackerman for note due today.

27. Received cash from D. King for note due today.

30. Paid J. Ackerman by check for note due today.

30. Paid office salaries $150, T. Andrews drew $250, paid wages $375.

Required:

1. Post to the ledger accounts opened last month, add any new accounts necessary. Make sure you do not open another account for any account already on the books.

   Do not skip any line. Post to the very next line underneath the last posting of last month. The pencil footing will be in the *same space* as the first posting for this month. Pencil footings never occupy the space of one line. In balancing the accounts for the month of November, add the footings of October to the postings of November. Subtract on the larger side, in the space of the last posting on that side.

2. Obtain a Trial Balance.

   This Trial Balance will contain the *balance* of each ledger account up to date including all postings for October. In business a Trial Balance is a *cumulative* summary of balances. January will contain only the January items. February will contain the balances of all accounts covering *all* transaction for the months of January and February. The March Trial Balance will contain the balances of all accounts for all postings covering January, February and March. This cumulative process continues up to the Trial Balance of December 31. We will learn later how we "close our books" on December 31.

NOTE:

Our special Journals are closed and ruled at the *end of each month*.
Our ledger is closed *at the end of the year*.

Solution for Exercises

C 2

Cash (Dr.) Receipts Journal

Date		Accounts Cr.	Explanation	L.F.	Amount	Total
Oct	1	T. Andrews, Capital	Investment	1	5000 00	
	3	Sales	Sold for cash	1	320 00	
	8	J. Wilder	Apply on acc't	1	150 00	
	15	W. Swing	Apply on acc't	2	100 00	
	18	Notes Receivable	K. Dale's note	2	270 00	
	23	Notes Receivable	J. Wilder's note	2	150 00	
	25	Notes Receivable	Swing's note	2	75 00	
	31	Cash, Dr.		2	6065 00	6065 00
						6065 00
Nov	1	Balance		✓		2731 25
	7	Purchases	Ret. mdse for cash	3	150 00	
	10	Charles Fenton & Co.	Apply on account	8	200 00	
	22	K. Dale	Apply on account	6	375 00	
	25	Notes Receivable	Charles Fenton Co's	2	200 00	
	27	Notes Receivable	D. King's note	2	250 00	
	31	Cash, Dr.		2	1175 00	1175 00
						3906 25
Dec	1	Balance				1159 25

17A and 17B:

C3

Cash (Cr.) Payment Journal

Date	Accounts, Dr.	Explanation	LF	Amount	Total
Oct '19 2	Rent	Paid Oct rent	3	150 00	
3	Purchases	Bought for cash	3	473 00	
4	Delivery Truck	Bought Ford truck	3	1000 00	
4	Insurance	Premium on truck	4	100 00	
4	Selling Expense	Auto license	4	15 75	
12	J. Smith	Apply on acct.	4	100 00	
15	Selling Expense	Paid for repairs	5	150 00	
15	Salaries	Pd salaries to date	5	150 00	
15	I Andrews, Per.	Withdrew	5	100 00	
15	Wages	Pd wages to date	6	350 00	
31	Salaries	Pd salaries to date	5	150 00	
31	I Andrews, Pers.	Withdrew	5	120 00	
31	Wages	Pd wages to date	6	475 00	
31	Cash, Cr.		2	3333 75	3333 75
31	Balance				2731 25
					6065 00
Nov '19 1	Rent	Paid Nov. rent	3	150 00	
5	Purchases	Bought for cash	3	375 00	
7	Notes Payable	Smith's note	8	125 00	
8	R Adams	Apply on acct	7	75 00	
15	Salaries	Pd salaries to date	5	150 00	
15	I Andrews, Pers.	Withdrew	5	100 00	
15	Wages	Pd wages to date	6	400 00	
17	Freight Inward	Pd frt., A. C. Co.	8	12 00	
18	Notes Payable	R. Adams note	8	75 00	
20	Selling Expense	Advertising	5	40 00	
21	J. Ackerman	Apply on acct	7	200 00	
25	Notes Payable	Ackerman's note	8	170 00	
30	Notes Payable	Ackerman's note	8	100 00	
30	Salaries	Pd. salaries to date	5	150 00	
30	Wages	Pd wages to date	6	375 00	
30	I Andrews, Pers.	Withdrew	5	250 00	
30	Cash, Cr.		2	2747 00	2747 00
30	Balance		✓		1159 25
					3906 25

Solution for Exercise 17A and 17B continued:

81

Sales (Cr.) Journal

Date		Accounts, Dr.	Terms	L.F	Amount	Total
Oct	8	K. Dale	10-day note	6	270 00	
	8	J. Wilder	½ cash, bal 15da note	1	300 00	
	10	W. Swing	on account	2	175 00	
	10	L. Copeland	on account	6	190 00	
	31	Sales, Cr.		1	935 00	935 00
Nov	10	Charles Denton & Co.	⅓ cash, ⅓ note, ⅓ n/30	8	600 00	
	12	D. King	15 day note	9	250 00	
	22	K. Dale	½ cash, bal 45da note	6	750 00	
	30	Sales, Cr.		1	1600 00	1600 00

J.1

General Journal

Date			L.F	Dr.	Cr.
Oct	1	Merchandise Inventory	7	2000 00	
		D. Andrews, Capital	1		2000 00
		To record investment of inventory			
	6	R. Adams	7	100 00	
		Purchases	3		100 00
		Returned merchandise for credit			
	6	J. Smith	4	150 00	
		Purchases	3		150 00
		Returned merchandise for credit			
	8	Notes Receivable	2	270 00	
		K. Dale	6		270 00
		Ten day note, due Oct. 18			
	8	Notes Receivable	2	150 00	
		J. Wilder	1		150 00
		15 day note, due Oct. 23			
	12	Sales	1	90 00	
		L. Copeland	6		90 00
		Gave credit for mdse. returned			
	15	Notes Receivable	2	75 00	
		W. Swing	2		75 00
		10 days, due Oct. 25			
	18	J. Smith	4	125 00	
		Notes Payable	8		125 00
		30 days, due November 7			

Solution for Exercise 17A and 17B continued:

P₁

Purchase (Dr) Journal

Date	Accounts, Dr.	Terms	LF	Amount	Total
19—					
Oct 2	R Adams	on account	7	250 00	
2	J. Smith	on account	4	375 00	
2	J. Ackerman	on account	7	575 00	
31	Purchases, Dr.		3	1200 00	1200 00
Nov 13	R Adams	on account	7	230 00	
13	J. Ackerman	on account	7	385 00	
21	J. Ackerman	$200 cash, bal. 60 da. note	7	645 00	
30	Purchases, Dr.		3	1260 00	1260 00

J2

General Journal

Date	Account	LF	Dr	Cr
19—				
Nov 8	R Adams	7	75 00	
	Notes Payable	8		75 00
	10 days, due Nov 18			
10	Notes Receivable	2	200 00	
	Charles Fenton Co	8		200 00
	15 days, due Nov 25			
12	Notes Receivable	2	250 00	
	A King	9		250 00
	15 days, Due Nov 27			
15	J. Ackerman	7	115 00	
	Purchases	3		115 00
	Returned mdse for credit			
15	J. Ackerman	7	170 00	
	Notes Payable	8		170 00
	10 days, due Nov 25			
15	J. Ackerman	7	100 00	
	Notes Payable	8		100 00
	15 days, due Nov 30			
21	J. Ackerman	7	445 00	
	Notes Payable	8		445 00
	60 days – due January 20			
22	Notes Receivable	2	375 00	
	K Dale	6		375 00
	45 days, due January 6.			

Solution for Exercise 17A and 17B continued:

J Andrews, Capital (1)

					Oct	1	Cash	C2	5000	00
					Nov	30	Mdse 7000-	J1	2000	00
									7000	00

Sales (1)

Oct	12	mdse ret'd	J1	90 00	Oct	3		C2	320	00
						31	1255- 720- 7165-	S1	935	00
					Nov	30	2855- 2365-	S1	1600	00
									2855	00

J Wilder (1)

Oct	8		S1	300 00	Oct	8		C2	150	00
						8	Notes Rec.	J1	150	00
				300 00					300	00

Cash (2)

Oct	31	6065.25 555.25 273.25	C2	6065 00	Oct	31		C3	3333	75
Nov	30	7240.- 6080.75 1159.25	C2	1175 00	Nov	30		C3	2747	00
				7240 00					6080	75

Notes Receivable (2)

Oct	8	K.Dale 10/18	J1	270 00	Oct	18		C2	270	00
	8	Wilder 10/23	J1	150 00		23		C2	150	00
	15	Ewing 10/25	J1	75 00		25		C2	75	00
Nov	10	Denton 11/25	J2	200 00	Nov	25		C2	200	00
	12	King 11/27	J2	250 00		27		C2	250	00
	22	Dale 1/6	J2	375 00					945	00
		1320.- 745.- 575.-		1320 00						

Solution for Exercise 17A and 17B continued:

W. Swing (2)

	19—					19—				
	Oct	10		S1	175 00	Oct	15		C2	100 00
							15	Notes Rec.	J1	75 00
					175 00					1 75 00

Rent (3)

	19—				
	Oct	2	.150.—	C3	150 00
	Nov	1	300.—	C3	150 00
					300 00

Purchases (3)

	19—					19—				
	Oct	3		C3	473 00	Oct	6		J1	100 00
		31	1673.— 1933.—	P1	1200 00		6		J1	150 00
	Nov	5		C3	375 00	Nov.	7		C2	150 00
		30	3305.— 2743.—	P1	1260 00		15		J2	115 00
					3308 00					515 00

Delivery Truck (3)

	19—				
	Oct	4	1000.—	C3	1000 00

Insurance (4)

	19—				
	Oct	4	100.—	C3	100 00

Solution for Exercise 17A and 17B continued:

General Expense (4)

Oct 4		15.75	C3	15 75	

J. Smith (4)

Oct 6			J1	150 00	Oct 2		P1	375 00
12			C3	100 00				
18			J1	125 00				
				375 00				375 00

J Andrews, Personal (5)

Oct 15			C3	100 00	
31	220.-		C3	120 00	
Nov 15			C3	100 00	
30	570.-		C3	250 00	

Salaries (5)

Oct 15			C3	150 00	
31	300.-		C3	150 00	
Nov 15			C3	150 00	
30	600.-		C3	150 00	

Selling Expense (5)

Oct 15	150.-		C3	150 00	
Nov 20	190.-		C3	40 00	

Solution for Exercise 17A and 17B continued:

F. Dale (6)

Oct 19 8		S1	270 00	Oct 19 8	Note	J1	270 00
Nov 22		S1	750 00	Nov 22		C2	375 00
				22	Note	J2	375 00
			750 00				750 00
							750 00

L. Copeland (6)

Oct 19 10	190- 90- 100-	S1	190 00	Oct 19 12	mdse ret'd	J1	90 00

Wages (6)

Oct 19 15		C3	350 00		
31	825-	C3	475 00	825 00
Nov 15		C3	400 00	
30	1600-	C3	375 00	1600 00

Merchandise Inventory (7)

Oct 19 1	2000-	J1	2000 00

R. Adams (7)

Oct 19 6	mdse ret'd	J1	100 00	Oct 19 2	250- 100- 150-	P1	250 00
Nov 8		C3	75 00	Nov 13	480- 250- 230-	P1	230 00
8	note	J2	75 00	250 00				480 00

Solution for Exercise 17A and 17B continued:

J. Ackerman (7)

19—					19—					
Nov	15		J2	115 00	Oct	2	525.–	P1	575 00
	15		J2	170 00	Nov	13		P1	385 00
	15		J2	100 00		21	1605.– / 1030.– / 535.–	P1	645 00
	21		J2	445 00					1 605 00
	21		C3	200 00					
				1 030 00					

Notes Payable (8)

19—					19—					
Nov	7		C3	125 00	Oct	18		J1	125 00
	18		C3	75 00	Nov	8		J2	75 00
	25		C3	170 00		15		J2	170 00
	30		C3	100 00		15		J2	100 00
				470 00		21	915.– / 470.– / 445.–	J2	445 00
									915 00

Freight – In (8)

19—					
Nov	7	12.–	C3	12 00

Charles Fenton Co. (8)

19—						19—					
Nov	10	600.– / 400.– / 200.–	S1	600 00	Nov	10		C2	200 00
						10	Note	J2	200 00
									400 00

D. King (9)

19—						19—					
Nov	12		S1	250 00	Nov	12	Note	J2	250 00

Solution for Exercise 17A and 17B continued:

T. Andrews
Trial Balance, October 31, 19—

		Dr.	Cr.
T. Andrews, Capital			7000 00
Sales			1165 00
Cash		2731 25	
Rent		150 00	
Purchases		1423 00	
Delivery Truck		1000 00	
Insurance		100 00	
General Expense		15 75	
Selling Expense		150 00	
Salaries		300 00	
T. Andrews, Personal		220 00	
Wages		825 00	
L. Copeland		100 00	
R. Adams			150 00
J. Ackerman			575 00
Merchandise Inventory		2000 00	
Notes Payable			125 00
		9015 00	9015 00

T. Andrews
Trial Balance, Nov. 30, 19—

		Dr.	Cr.
T. Andrews, Capital			7000 00
Sales			2765 00
Notes Receivable		375 00	
Cash		1159 25	
Rent		300 00	
Purchases		2793 00	
Delivery Truck		1000 00	
Insurance		100 00	
General Expense		15 75	
Selling Expense		190 00	
Salaries		600 00	
T. Andrews, Personal		570 00	
Wages		1600 00	
L. Copeland		100 00	
R. Adams			230 00
J. Ackerman			575 00
Mdse. Inventory		2000 00	
Notes Payable			445 00
Charles Fenton Co.		200 00	
Freight-In		12 00	
		11015 00	11015 00

Lesson X

BANK STATEMENT

On the first day of each month, it is customary for us to receive a statement from our bank. This statement lists all transactions with our bank during the *preceding* month.

A bank statement will look like this:

XYZ BANK AND TRUST COMPANY

Account Number
00-00-000

STATEMENT OF ACCOUNT	
Balance Forward	
12/7	306 14

John Doe & Company
000 Main Street
Sample City, N.Y.

**(Please advise in writing
of change of address)**

Date	Checks		Date	Checks	Date	Deposits
12 8	SC	50	12 8	100 00	12 9	610 00
12 16		80 00	12 20	40 15	12 15	169 10
12 28		150 00	12 30	200 00		
1 5	NB	2 50				

CODE
C—certified check, OD—overdraft,
NB—new bank book, SC—service
charge (for previous month's activity)

Balance at end of Period	
1/6	512 09

**Please examine statement carefully; if no errors are reported within
10 days, your account will be considered correct.**

Note the fact that all checks paid by the bank are listed on the left hand side; all deposits on the right hand side; the initial balance and every deposit is listed on the extreme right hand side. The final balance is the last balance on the latter side. All checks paid by the bank are returned with this statement.

It is necessary for us to prove the accuracy of this bank statement by comparing our cash balance with the bank's balance. This proof is called "Bank Reconcilation Statement."

Since we deposit all money received, and pay all money by checks, our balance ought to equal the bank's balance.

The following form is most frequently used:

BANK RECONCILIATION STATEMENT

March 31, 19—

Bank balance $1250.00

Less Outstanding Checks:

Check #262	$ 50.00	
Check #266	110.00	
Check #267	130.00	290.00

Our balance .... $ 960.00

An outstanding check is one which has been issued but has not been presented for payment at the bank.

To make a Bank Reconciliation Statement:

1. Arrange all checks enclosed in the bank statement in the order in which they were issued (since each check has a number, all checks will be arranged numerically).

2. Check these returned checks against the corresponding stubs in the check book—make a check mark ($\sqrt{}$) on each stub.

   (a) Be careful to see that the amount on the stub is exactly the same as the amount on the check.

   (b) When you begin to check the return vouchers (checks) against the stubs, if any of these return vouchers were listed as outstanding last month, make a check mark ($\sqrt{}$) against that item only *in last month's* Bank Reconciliation Statement.

   This is done because the Bank Reconciliation Statement of the previous month contains a list of all the checks which were outstanding up to that day, hence it is not necessary to place a check mark (√) on the corresponding stub in the check book because that check is listed in last month's Bank Reconciliation Statement. Therefore, make a check mark alongside of the check listed as outstanding in last month's Bank Reconciliation Statement.

3. When the checking has been completed, list up in this month's statement all checks which have not been checked, beginning with last month's Bank Reconciliation Statement.

These items are not checked because they are outstanding; they have not arrived at the bank as yet, and therefore have not been paid. They are called the "Outstanding Checks."

TROUBLESOME FACTORS

Very frequently unusual occurrences will cause the Bank Reconciliation Statement not to balance. Adjustments—corrections—must accordingly be made.

We list herewith some of the most frequent adjustments:

1. *Bank Charges—*

Very frequently banks make special charges for collecting out-of-town checks or for any other special services rendered by the bank. We are informed of these charges when we receive our bank statement. Since our Cash Book will not show this, it will be necessary to correct our Cash Book accordingly. Record this expense in this month's Cash Book because the Cash Book for last month has already been closed.

2. *Checks issued but not recorded in Check Book—*

Frequently checks are issued and the recording of same is carelessly omitted. Record in the Cash Book for the current month.

3. *Deposits made without any record in the Cash Book—*

Occasionally, through inadvertence, deposits are made by the employer and the bookkeeper is not informed. Enter this also in the Cash Book for the current month.

4. *Check entered on check stub for larger or smaller amount than the check—*

When checking the returned checks against the check stubs, if the amount on the check differs from the amount on the stub, the correction must be made in the current Cash Book.

5. *Receipts not deposited—*

Our receipts may not agree with the deposits. Frequently the last deposit does not appear on the bank statement for the current month. It is listed as the first deposit the following month. To reconcile deduct this deposit from our balance.

The following model may be used to reconcile the bank statement in the event any of the aforementioned corrections are to be made.

BANK RECONCILIATION STATEMENT

June 30, 19—

Our Balance				5437.50
Add—				
(case 4) Check #42 entered for 65-				
issued for	50-	15-		
(case 3) Deposit June 26 not entered	145-			160.00
				5597.50
Less				
(case 1) Bank Charge	2.10			
(case 2) Check not entered	35.00			
(case 4) Check #46 for 162-				
entered for 152-	10.00			
(case 5) Deposit not recorded by				
bank	165.25		212.35	
Outstanding Checks			5809.85	
#47 25-				
#49 15-	40.00		40.00	
Bank Balance			5849.85	

Lesson XI

INTEREST BEARING NOTES

NOTES RECEIVABLE BEARING INTEREST

Transaction:

July 10. Received the following note:

$1000 ⁰⁰/₁₀₀   New York, N.Y. July 10, 19—
            Ten days   after date I promise to pay to
the order of Jones & Co
One Thousand and ⁿ°/₁₀₀   Dollars
at Sterling National Bank, New York, N.Y.
Value received with interest at 6%
No.____ Due July 20, 19-   A. Ronald
AD 41

When we, Jones & Co., receive the note we will credit A. Ronald for
$1000; since no interest has as yet been earned, we record no interest.
The entry is:

J. 1

		General Journal	L.F.	Dr.	Cr.
July 10	Notes Receivable			1000 00	
	A. Ronald				1000 00
	Received 10 day 6% interest bearing note				
	due 7/20				

This entry is the same as if it were a non-interest bearing note, except
for the explanation.

When the note falls due the following entry is made:

C 2

Cash (Dr) Receipts Journal

Date	Accounts Cr	Explanation	L.F.	Amount	Total
July 20	Notes Receivable	A. Ronald	1	1000 00	
20	Interest Earned	on above	2	1 67	

Notes Receivable (1)

July 10	Ronald 6% due 7/20	J1	1000 00	July 20		C 2	1000 00

Interest Earned (2)

					19— July 20		C2		1 67

Observe the fact that two different accounts are affected, 2 lines are used; Interest and Notes Receivable are not the same account, hence Interest Earned will always be recorded on the *next line* underneath the Notes Receivable entry in the Cash (Dr.) Receipts Journal.

NOTES PAYABLE BEARING INTEREST

Transaction:

Gave Lewis Copeland the following note:

$250 $\frac{00}{xx}$　　　　New York, N.Y. July 10, 19 —
　　　Thirty days after date I promise to pay to
the order of　　*Lewis Copeland*
Two hundred and fifty and $\frac{no}{100}$ ———— Dollars
at 122 East 42 Street, New York, N.Y. Room 306
Value received
No. 6　Due August 9, 19-　　*Jones & Co.*

When we give the note, we make this entry:

General Journal

			LF	Dr.		Cr.	
19— July 10	Lewis Copeland			250	00		
	Notes Payable					250	00
	For 30 day note - 6% - due Aug 9.						

Note—The rate of interest is recorded in the explanation in order to indicate the fact that it is an interest bearing note.

When the note falls due, the following entry is made:

C 3

Cash (Cr.) Payment Journal

Date	accounts, Dr.	Explanation	L.F.	Amount		Total	
Aug 9	Notes Payable	Lewis Copeland	1	250	00		
9	Interest Cost	on above	2	1	25		

Notes Payable (1)

Aug 9		C 3	250	00	July 10	L Copeland c/o J1	250	00

Interest Cost (2)

Aug 9		C 3		1	25		

Memorize and add this to our Debit and Credit Chart:

Interest Earned is a Credit Account.

Interest Cost is a Debit Account.

NOTE—Interest is recorded only when it is *paid* and requires a *separate* line in the Cash Book.

Exercise 18:

June 2. Received a 10 day note from L. Richards for $150 on account.

> If no interest is stated, it is a non-interest bearing note.

     4. Sent a 20 day 6% interest bearing note to A. Walters for $200.

     5. Paid L. Jackson's note due today amount $150, time 30 days.

     6. Sent check to R. Dix for our $175 thirty day note, bearing 6% interest.

     8. Received a check from T. Atlee for his $300, 60 day, 6% interest bearing note.

June 10. Received a check from Smith Co. for their $275, 30 day note.

12. Received a check from L. Richards for his note due today.

17. Received 30 day note for $250 from M. Anderson.

24. We sent A. Walters our check for our note due today.

Required: Make original entries only.

J¹

General Journal

Date			L.F	Dr	Cr
June 2	Notes Receivable			150 00	
		L. Richards			150 00
		10 days due 6/12			
4	A. Walters			200 00	
		Notes Payable			200 00
		20 days @ 6% - due 6/24			
17	Notes Receivable			250 00	
		M. Anderson			250 00
		30 days - due 7/17			

C2

Cash (Dr) Receipts Journal

Date	Accounts, Cr.	Explanation	L.F	Dr	Cr
June 8	Notes Receivable	J. Atlee		300 00	
8	Interest Earned	on above		3 00	
10	Notes Receivable	Smith Co.		275 00	
12	Notes Receivable	L. Richards		150 00	
	Cash, Dr.			728 00	728 00

C3

Cash (Cr.) Payment Journal

Date	Account, Dr	Explanation	L.F	Dr	Cr
June 5	Notes Payable	L. Jackson		150 00	
6	Notes Payable	L. Dix		175 00	
6	Interest Cost	On above		88	
24	Notes Payable	A. Walters		200 00	
24	Interest Cost	On above		67	
	Cash, Cr.			526 55	526 55

Lesson XII

COLUMNAR CASH BOOK

It is customary to use the term "Cash Book" instead of Cash Journal. Observe how the following transactions are entered in the accompanying solution.

Exercise 19:

Sept. 1. A. Glover invested $3000 in his business.
2. Sold for cash merchandise $250.
3. Received from A. Smith on account $300.
3. Sold for cash to W. Jones $50.
4. Sold for cash to A. Johnson $150.
5. Received $100 for A. Reynolds' note due today and $2 interest on same.
6. Sold for cash to B. Altman $275.
8. Received $25 refund on goods returned to L. Arnold Co. from bill of Aug. 10.
10. Sold for cash $100 to Andrew Geller.
12. Sold for cash to J. B. Preston $175.

Required: Make original entries only.

(Solution for Exercise 19 appears on Page 93)

There are five cash sale transactions in this exercise. If we were to use a one-column Cash Book, as we have until now, we would have had to post *five times* to the Sales Account from this book. By having a special column for Cash Sales we make only *one* posting—the TOTAL Cash Sales at the *end* of the month. Do you realize how many postings are saved this way?

The items which are not to be posted, because they will be posted in total, are checked ($\sqrt{}$).

There is no account for "Sundries" in the ledger, hence do not post this total.

Exercise 20:

The Cash (Cr.) Payment Journal will have the following columns:

(Exercise 20 continued on Page 94)

C 2

Cash (Dr.) Receipts Journal

Date	Accounts, Cr.	Explanation	L.F.	Dr. Cash	Cr. Sales	Cr. Sundries
Sept 1	A. Glover, Capital	Investment	12	3000 00		3000 00
2	Sales	misc.	✓	250 00	250 00	
3	A. Smith	On account	5	300 00		300 00
3	Sales	H. Jones	✓	50 00	50 00	
4	Sales	A. Johnson	✓	150 00	150 00	
5	Notes Receivable	A. Reynolds	6	100 00		100 00
5	Interest earned	On above	7	2 00		2 00
6	Sales	B. Altman	✓	275 00	275 00	
8	Purchase Ret.	L. Arnold Co.	8	25 00		25 00
10	Sales	A. Seller	✓	100 00	100 00	
12	Sales	J. B. Preston	✓	175 00	175 00	
				4427 00	1000 00	3427 00
				4427 00	1000 00	3427 00
	Cash, Dr.		1	4427 00		
	Sales, Cr.		2		1000 00	
	Sundries, Cr.		✓		3427 00	
				4427 00	4427 00	

(Exercise 20 continued from Page 92)

Net Cash Cr.; Purchase Dr.; M. Morrow, Personal Dr.; General Expense Dr.; Sundries Dr.

Oct. 1. Paid rent $100.
  2. Bought for cash from D. Whitman $250.
  3. Bought for cash from C. Hayes $100.
  4. M. Morrow, Prop., withdrew for his personal use $25.
  5. M. Morrow, Prop., withdrew for his personal use $75.
  6. Paid to replace broken window pane $2.
  7. Paid American Towel Service $3 for towel service.
  8. Bought for cash from A. Towner $175.
  10. Paid M. Johnson's note for $250, and interest $3, due today.
  12. Paid refund on cash sale $10 to R. Smith on bill of 6th.
  13. Paid petty cash $15.
  15. Bought for cash merchandise $25.
  15. Proprietor drew $65.
Required: Make original entries only.

(Solution for Exercise 20 appears on Page 95)

Exercise 21:

Record the following transactions into a Cash (Dr.) Receipt Book and Cash (Cr.) Payment Book having the same columnar headings as in the last exercise.

Nov. 1. J. Whitman began business investing $10,000 in cash.
  2. Bought for cash from J. Davis & Co. merchandise $1200.
  3. Sold for cash to R. Albert merchandise $400.
  3. Sold Norton & Hayes for cash $375.
  4. Paid rent $200.
  5. Bought from Singer Sewing Machine Co. 3 machines for our factory for cash $400.
  6. Paid $32 freight on goods bought from J. Davis & Co.
  6. Received a check of $854.25 for a 30 day, 6% interest bearing note due today.
  8. J. Whitman drew $125.
  9. Paid $5 for petty cash.
  10. Received check for $52 for a cash sale.
  10. Received $100 on account from R. Smith Co.
  12. Paid Office Salaries $150, factory wages $375.

(Exercise 21 continued on Page 96)

C 3

Cash (C) Payment Journal

Date	Accounts, Dr.	Explanation	L.F.	Net Cash Cr.	Purchases Dr.	M. Morrow Personal Dr.	General Expense Dr.	Sundries Dr.
1917 Oct. 1	Rent	Dr. Oct.	12	100 00				100 00
2	Purchases		1	250 00	250 00			
3	Purchases	D. Whitman	1	100 00	100 00			
4	M. Morrow, Personal	C. Hayes	1	25 00		25 00		
5	M. Morrow, Personal		1	75 00		75 00		
6	General Expense	Window pane	1	2 00			2 00	
7	General Expense	Amer. Towel Co.	1	3 00			3 00	
8	Purchases	A. Turner	1	175 00	175 00			
10	Notes Payable	A. Johnson	13	250 00				250 00
10	Interest Cost	Dr. above	14	3 00				3 00
12	Sales Return	R. Smith bill 1/6	9	10 00				10 00
13	General Expense	Petty cash	1	15 00			15 00	
15	Purchases	Misc.	1	25 00	25 00			
15	M. Morrow, Personal		1	65 00		65 00		
				1098 00	550 00	165 00	20 00	363 00
				1098 00	550 00	165 00	20 00	363 00
	Purchases, Dr.		3	550 00				
	M. Morrow, Pers. Dr.		19	165 00				
	General Expense Dr.		16	20 00				
	Sundries Dr.		1	363 00				
	Cash, Cr.		1	1098 00	1098 00			
				1098 00	1098 00			

(*Exercise 21 continued from Page 94*)

Nov. 12. Paid 60 day note, 6% interest, due today, face of note $350.

    15. Sold for cash merchandise $350.

    15. Bought for cash merchandise $175.

    15. J. Whitman drew $275.

Required: Make original entries.

(*Solution for Exercise 21 appears on Pages 97 and 98*)

Lesson XIII

TRADE DISCOUNT

SALES DISCOUNT

Terms:

When a sale is made, the seller and buyer agree when payment is to be made. The terms of the sale must be determined when each sale is made.

If the terms are net 10 days, the payment must be made in 10 days from the date of the bill. Thus if the bill is $100, date of the bill Jan. 10, terms net 10 days, the buyer must pay $100 on Jan. 20.

However, in order to induce the buyer to pay within a certain period of time a small amount is permitted to be deducted by him if payment is made within the time agreed upon.

Thus if we sold to J. Jones on Jan. 10 merchandise for $100 terms 2% 10 days—net 30 days, the buyer has the privilege of deducting 2% discount—$2 from his bill, if he pays on Jan. 20. And if he does not do so, he must pay in full $100 on Feb. 9.

If he pays on Jan. 20, he will pay $98.

If he pays on Feb. 9, he will pay $100.

NOTE—2% discount is not 2% interest.

Interest denotes a per cent *per annum* whereas discount is the per cent on the entire bill *irrespective of time*.

$$\text{Prin.} \times \text{Rate} = \text{Discount.}$$

Hence $100 \times \dfrac{2}{100} = \$2$ discount.

If it were 2% interest it would be figured:

$$\text{Prin.} \times \text{Rate} \times \text{Time} = \text{Interest}$$

$$100 \times \frac{2}{100} \times \frac{10}{360} = 6 \text{ cents interest.}$$

(*Continued on Page 99*)

C 2

Cash (Dr.) Receipts Journal

Date	Accounts, Cr.	Explanation	L.F.	Cash Dr.	Cash Sales Cr.	Sundries Cr.
19— Nov 1	J. Whitman, Capital	Investment		10000 00		10000 00
3	Sales	R. Albert		400 00	400 00	
3	Sales	Norton & Hayes		375 00	375 00	
6	Notes Receivable	on above note		854 25		854 25
6	Interest Earned	on above note		4 27		4 27
10	Sales	Misc.		52 00	52 00	
10	R. Smith Co.	Apply on account		100 00		100 00
15	Sales	Misc.		350 00	350 00	
				1177 00	1177 00	1093 52
				12135 52	10958 52	10958 52
				12135 52	12135 52	

Cash, Dr.
Cash Sales, Cr.
Sundries, Cr.

C 3

Cash (Cr.) Payment Journal

Date	Accounts Dr.	Explanation	L.F.	Cr. Cash	Dr. Cash Purchases	Dr. J. Whitman Journal	Dr. General Expense	Dr. Sundries
19— Nov. 2	Purchases	J. Davis & Co.		1200 00	1200 00			
4	Rent	Paid Nov. rent		200 00				200 00
5	Machinery	Singer sewing mach.		400 00				400 00
6	Freight-on	Paid for freight		32 00				32 00
8	J. Whitman, Priv.			125 00		125 00		
9	General Expense	Petty cash		5 00			5 00	
12	Office Salaries			150 00				150 00
12	Wages			375 00				375 00
12	Note Payable			350 00				350 00
12	Interest Cost	On above note		3 50				3 50
15	Purchases	misc.		175 00	175 00			
15	J. Whitman, Pers.			375 00		375 00		
				375 00	1375 00	375 00	5 00	1510 50
				3390 50	1375 00	400 00	5 00	1510 50
				3290 50				
	Cash Purchases Dr.			1375 00				
	J. Whitman Pers. Dr.			400 00				
	General Expense Dr.			5 00				
	Sundries Dr.			1510 50				
	Cash, Cr.							

Transaction:

Mar. 12. Received from A. Brown a check for $490 in payment of his bill of Mar. 2, $500 terms 2% 10 days, net 30.

17. Received from A. Smith a check for $300 for his bill dated Feb. 15, terms 3% 10 days, net 30.

18. Received from C. Carver Co. check for $48.50 for his bill of $50 dated Mar. 8, terms 3% 10 days, net 30.

Entries:

(Cash (Dr.) Receipts Journal appears on Page 100)

Cash (1)

19— Mar 31		838 50	C2	8 3 8 50				

A. Brown (4)

		* 19— Mar 12		500.—	C2	5 0 0 00		

A. Smith (5)

		* 19— Mar 17		300.—	C2	3 0 0 00		

C. Carver Co. (6)

		* 19— Mar 18		50.—	C2	5 0 00		

* The debit entries are not shown in these transactions.

Sales Discount (12)

19—				11 50	C 2	11 50
Mar. 31						

Cash (Dr.) Receipts Journal   C 2

Date	Account, Cr.	Explanation	L.F.	Net Cash	Sales Disc.	Sundries
19—						
Mar. 12	A. Brown	Bill 3/1	4	490 00	10 00	500 00
17	A. Smith	Bill 2/15	5	300 00		300 00
18	C. Carver Co	Bill 3/8	6	48 50	1 50	50 00
				838 50	11 50	850 00
				838 50	11 50	850 00
	Cash, Dr.		1	838 50		
	Sales Discount, Dr.		12	11 50		
	Sundries, Cr.		✓		850 00	850 00

As illustrated on page 100, the customer receives a credit of the amount of his check *plus* the discount.

Note how only the *totals* of the Cash and Sales Discount columns are posted. Each individual item is posted from the Sundries column. However the total of the Sundries column is checked (√) because it is not posted since *every* item in the Sundries column is posted. Note the recording of the $300 from A. Smith.

Exercise 22:

Head up the Cash (Dr.) Receipts Journal as follows: Net Cash Dr., Sales Discount Dr., Cash Sales Cr., Sundries Cr.

Received cash for the following:

Apr. 2. T. Hanson $441 for bill of Mar. 23, $450 terms 2/10/30.

2/10/30 is the business man's way of saying 2% in 10 days, net 30 days.

    12. J. Wanamaker Co. $582 for bill of Apr. 2, $600 terms 3/10/30.
    15. Cash sales for the day $225.
    16. Cash sales for the day $210.
    18. D. Ascher and Co. $735 for bill of Apr. 8, $750 terms 2/10/30.
    20. J. Adams $100 for $100 note due today.
    21. P. James for refund on purchase of Mar. 2, $10.
    21. C. Sheffield $39.20 for bill of Apr. 11, $40 terms 2/10/30.
    25. Cash sale to T. Thompson $57.
    28. C. Braun $505 for $500 note, 6% interest, 60 days due to-day.
    30. Cash sales for the day $150.

Required: Make original entries, post to ledger.

(Cash (Debit) Receipts Journal appears on Page 102)

Cash (1)

Apr 30	3054.20	C2	3054.20		

Sales Discount (2)

Apr 30	42.80	C2	42.80		

(Ledger continued on Page 103)

C 2

Cash (Debit) Receipts Journal

Date	Account (Cr.)	Explanation	F.	Net Cash (Dr.)	Sales Discount (Dr.)	Cash Sales (Cr.)	Sundries (Cr.)
19— Apr. 2	J. Hansen	Bill 3/23	7	441 00	9 00		450 00
12	J. Wanamaker Co.	Bill 3/2	8	582 00	18 00		600 00
15	Sales		✓	225 00		225 00	
16	Sales		✓	210 00		210 00	
18	L. Archer & Co.	Bill 3/8	9	735 00	15 00		750 00
20	Notes Receivable	J. Adams	6	100 00			100 00
21	Purchase Returns	J. James bill 3/2	4	10 00			10 00
21	C. Sheffield	Bill 4/11	10	39 20	80		40 00
25	Sales	J. Thompson	✓	57 00		57 00	
28	Notes Receivable	C. Brown	6	500 00			500 00
28	Interest Earned		5	5 00			5 00
30	Sales	On above	✓	150 00		150 00	
				3054 20	42 80	642 00	2455 00

			F.		
Cash Dr.			1	3054 20	
Sales Discount Dr.			2	42 80	3097 00
Sales Cr.			3		642 00
Sundries Cr.			✓		2455 00
					3097 00

Solution for Exercise 22 continued:

Sales (3)

					19—					
					Apr	30	642.–	C2	642	00

Purchase Returns (4)

					19—					
					Apr	21	10.–	C2	10	00

Interest Earned (5)

					19—					
					Apr	28	5.–	C2	5	00

Notes Receivable (6)

					19—					
					Apr	20		C2	100	00
						28	600.–	C2	500	00
									600	00

J. Hanson (7)

					19—					
					Apr	2	450.–	C2	450	00

J. Wanamaker Co. (8)

					19—					
					Apr	12	600.–	C2	600	00

(Ledger continued on Page 104)

Solution for Exercise 22 continued:

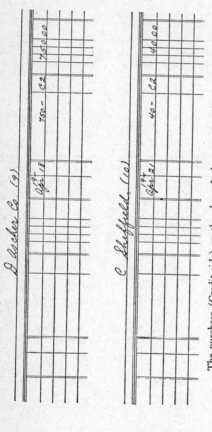

D. Archer Co. (9)

| | Apr. 18 | 750 - | C2 | 750 | 00 |

C. Sheffield (10)

| | Apr. 21 | 40 - | C2 | 40 | 00 |

The purchase (Credit side) on the above Ledger accounts is not shown.

(Entry of payment to S. Anderson—top Page 105)

Cash (Cr.) Payment Journal   C3

Date	Account, Dr.	Explanation	L.F.	Net Cash Dr.	Purchase Discount Cr.	Sundries Cr.
'9-_ Apr. 17	S. Anderson	Bill #7		196 00	4 00	200 00

Purchase Discount

When we pay for merchandise, we often receive an inducement to pay within a certain period of time. This deduction from our bill we call "Purchase Discount."

Transaction:

Paid $196 to S. Anderson for bill of Apr. 7, $200 terms 2/10, n/30.

(Entry for the above transaction appears on bottom of Page 104)

Exercise 23:

Open Cash (Cr.) Payment Journal with the following columns: Cash Cr.; Purchase Disc. Cr.; General Expense Dr.; S. Walen, Drawing Dr.; Sundries Dr.

June 1. Bought for cash merchandise $275.

2. Paid rent $250.

2. Paid D. Starr $291 for bill May 23 in amount $300, terms 3/10 n/60.

3. Paid R. Anderson $436.50 for bill of $450 dated May 24, terms 3/10 n/30.

3. Paid gasoline bill to local garage for our delivery truck $80. (Delivery Expense)

6. Bought new delivery truck $2650. Paid check on delivery.

7. Paid William Saunders $12 refund on sale made last week.

8. Paid $20 for painting all floors on our premises.

9. Paid fire insurance policy due today $168.

10. S. Walen drew $75.

12. Paid the following bills due today:

T. Ransome & Co. $480—terms 2/10 n/30 dated June 2.
J. Tomlinson & Sons $275—3/10 n/30 dated May 13.
B. Robinson $145—terms 2/20 n/30 dated May 23.
R. Anderson $435—terms 2/10 n/30 dated June 2.

13. Paid R. Hanscomb for note and interest due today. Face of note $150, 30 days, 6%.

15. Paid $13 for replacing window shades.

15. Paid $18 for wrapping paper.

15. Paid salaries: Bookkeeper $25, stenographer $20, errand boy $15.

15. S. Walen drew $150.

Required: Make original entries only.

(Solution on Pages 106 and 107)

Solution for

Cash (Cr)

Date		Account, Dr	Explanation
June 19—	1	Purchases	Misc.
	2	Rent	Paid June rent
	2	D. Starr	Paid invoice of 5/23
	3	R. Anderson	Paid invoice of 5/24
	3	Delivery Expense	Gasoline
	6	Delivery Equipment	Truck
	7	Sales Returns	Refunded to Wm. Saunders
	8	General Expense	Painting of floors
	9	General Expense	Fire Insurance
	10	S. Walen, Drawing	
	12	J. Ransome & Co.	Paid invoice of 6/2
	12	J. Tomlinson & Sons	Paid invoice of 5/13
	12	B. Robinson	Paid invoice of 5/23
	12	R. Anderson	Paid invoice of 6/2
	13	Notes Payable	R. Hanscomb
	13	Interest Cost	On above note
	15	General Expense	Replaced window shades
	15	General Expense	Wrapping paper
	15	Salaries	Bookkeeper
	15	Salaries	Stenographer
	15	Salaries	Errand boy
	15	S. Walen, Drawing	
		Sundries, Dr.	
		S. Walen, Drawing, Dr.	
		General Expense, Dr.	
		Purchase Discount, Cr.	
		Cash, Cr.	

Exercise 23

C 3

Payment Journal

L.F.	Cash Cr.	Purchase Discount Cr.	General Expense Dr.	J. Walen Drawing Dr.	Sundries Dr.
	275 00				275 00
	250 00				250 00
	291 00	9 00			300 00
	436 50	13 50			450 00
	80 00				80 00
	2650 00				2650 00
	12 00				12 00
	20 00		20 00		
	168 00		168 00		
	75 00			75 00	
	470 40	9 60			480 00
	275 00				275 00
	142 10	2 90			145 00
	426 30	8 70			435 00
	150 00				150 00
	75				75
	13 00		13 00		
	18 00		18 00		
	25 00				25 00
	20 00				20 00
	15 00				15 00
	150 00			150 00	
	5963 05	43 70	219 00	225 00	5562 75
	5562 75				
	225 00				
	219 00				
		43 70			
		5963 05			
	6006 75	6006 75			

Lesson XIV
DISCOUNTED NOTES
DISCOUNTED NOTES PAYABLE

The function of a bank is to receive money from those who have no need for it at the present time and to lend it to those who need it. The bank acts as a broker.

The depositor receives interest from the bank and the borrower pays a higher rate of interest on loans to the bank. The bank thus makes a profit of the difference for its services as banker.

Since the bank deals with other people's money, the State and Federal governments supervise its activities very rigidly. It must conform to every governmental regulation; e.g., it may not lend money except on a written promise, a note. The note may not run for more than four months in industrial communities, nor six months in agricultural communities.

The practice of borrowing money from a bank on a note is called "*Discounting* a note at the bank." It is customary for a bank to deduct the interest *in advance*. This interest *deducted in advance* is called "*Bank Discount*" or simply *Discount*.

Hence if we (A. Johnson) give our bank the following note:

$1000 $\frac{00}{100}$ New York, N.Y. March 10, 19 —
Sixty days after date I promise to pay to
the order of _National City Bank_
One Thousand and $\frac{no}{100}$ ——————— Dollars
at _National City Bank, 42 St. Branch_
Value received
No.——— Due May 9, 19-——— A. Johnson

The bank will charge us 6% interest for 60 days on $1000, or $10. The bank will deduct this amount and add $990 to our balance.

When the note is due on May 9, the bank will deduct $1000 from our account and return our note marked "Paid."

Entries:

When we borrow the money on March 10 we will record the following entry:

C.2.

Cash (Dr.) Receipts Journal

Date	Accounts, Cr.	Explanation	L.F.	Net Cash Dr.	Interest Cost Dr.	Sundries Cr.
19— Mar. 10	Notes Payable	National City Bank		990 00	10 00	1000 00

Notes Payable

						C.2 1000 00
			19— Mar. 10			

Interest Cost

19— Mar. 10		C.2 10 00	

Cash is debited for $990 because we received that amount. Notes Payable is credited for $1000 because that is the amount of the note. Interest Cost is debited for $10, the amount the bank charged us for the loan.

When the note falls due on May 9, the following entry is made.

Cash (Cr.) Payment Journal   C3

Date	Account Dr.	Explanation	L.F.	Net Cash Cr.	Sundries
19— May 9	Notes Payable	National City Bank 3/10		100000	100000

Observe that interest is not recorded because it was paid on March 10 when the note was discounted.

(Entries for transactions on top of Page 111)

Cash (Dr.) Receipts Journal   C2

Date	Accounts Cr.	Explanation	L.F.	Net Cash Dr.	Interest Cost Dr.	Sundries Cr.
19— June 12	Notes Payable	Nat. City Bank 1 mo.	2	99 50	50	10000
15	Notes Payable	Nat. City Bank 3 mos.	2	1477 50	2250	150000
17	Notes Payable	Nat. City Bank 90 days	2	19700	300	20000
20	Notes Payable	Nat. City Bank 120 days	2	166600	3400	170000
25	Notes Payable	Nat. City Bank 3 note	2	246250	3750	250000
				590250	9750	550000 00
				590250	9750	400000
						600000 00
	Cash, Dr.		1	590250		
	Interest Cost, Dr.		3	9750		
	Sundries, Cr.		1			600000
				600000	600000	600000

Transactions:

Discounted the following notes at our bank at 6%.

June 12. $100 payable 1 month.

15. $1500 payable 3 months.

17. $200 payable 90 days.

20. $1700 payable 120 days.

25. $2500 payable 3 months.

(Cash (Dr.) Receipts Journal appears on Page 110)

Cash (1)

June 30		5209.50	C2	5209 50							

Notes Payable (2)

June 12			C2	100 00							
15			C2	1500 00							
17			C2	200 00							
20			C2	1700 00							
25	6000.-		C2	2500 00							

Interest Cost (3)

June 30		97.50	C2	97 50							

Observe—

(1) Interest Cost is recorded in *total* at the end of the month.

(2) Notes Payable is recorded *daily, one line* for *each* note.

DISCOUNTED NOTES RECEIVABLE

Non-interest Bearing Note

When we receive a note from someone, we may either hold it until the due date or cash it (discount it) at the bank.

If we decide to discount it at the bank, we will sign our name on the back of the note in order to guarantee payment to the bank in case the maker of the note does not pay it on the due date. This practice is called "indorsing a note." We will then give it to the bank who will deduct the discount (interest) *for the time it will have to wait* until the date of maturity, and will add the balance to our account.

Transaction:

Jan.　4. Received a $1500 30 day note dated today from D. Norton on account.

　　　14. Discounted D. Norton's note at bank.

Entries:

(Cash (Dr.) Receipts Journal appears on Page 113)

General Journal　　　　　　　　　　　　　　　　　*J.*

	19—			L.F.	Dr	Cr
	Jan	4	Notes Receivable	2	1500 00	
			D. Norton	4		1500 00
			30 days - due Feb. 3			

Cash (1)

	19—						
	Jan	14		C2	1495 00		

Notes Receivable (2)

	19—						19—				
	Jan	4	D. Norton	J1	1500 00		Jan	14		C2	1500 00

(Ledger continued on Page 113)

C2

Cash (Dr.) Receipts Journal

Date	Accounts, Cr.	Explanation	L.F.	Net Cash Dr.	Interest Cost Dr.	Sundries Cr.
'19 Jan. 14	Notes Receivable	D Norton	2	149500	500	150000

Interest Cost (3)

'19 Jan. 14	C2	500		

D Norton (4)

'19 Jan. 14	J.	150000		

To obtain the interest, compute the time the bank has to wait. Find the interest for that time.

Thus we kept the note from January 4 to January 14—10 days. The bank will have to wait 20 days (30 — 10 = 20) until the due date.

$$\text{Principal} \times \text{Rate} \times \text{Time} = \text{Interest}$$

$$1500 \quad \times \quad \frac{6}{100} \times \frac{20}{360} = \$5.00$$

We debit Interest Cost because we pay the bank the interest even though D. Norton, the maker, pays no interest on this non-interest bearing note. In order to receive the money before the note is due, we are obliged to pay the bank the interest on the money advanced.

Rule: *Interest Cost* is debited when we discount a non-interest bearing Notes Receivable.

Summary:

When a non-interest bearing Notes Receivable is discounted we credit Notes Receivable through the Cash (Dr.) Receipts book. Interest Cost is debited. The net proceeds will be *less* than the face of the note.

Transactions:

Discounted the following notes at our bank at 6%:

May 10. E. Chase $1200 dated April 15, 60 days, receiving $1193 (Interest for 35 days).

Swift and Reed $1500 dated April 1, 90 days, receiving $1487.25 (Interest for 51 days).

Jones and Jones $350, dated April 20, 30 days, receiving $349.42 (Interest for 10 days).

Smith and Company $550 dated April 5, 60 days, receiving $547.71 (Interest for 25 days).

(Cash (Dr.) Receipts Journal appears on Page 115)

Cash (1)

May 31		e1	3577 38				

Interest Cost (5)

May 31		e1	22 62				

Cash (Dr.) Receipts Journal

Date	Accounts Cr.	Explanation	L.F.	Net Cash Dr.	Interest Cost Dr.	Sundries Cr.
'17 May 10	Notes Receivable	E. Chase	✓	1 192 00	7 00	1 200 00
10	Notes Receivable	Swift & Reed	✓	1 487 25	12 75	1 500 00
10	Notes Receivable	Jones & Saxe	✓	349 42	58	35 000
10	Note Receivable	Smith & Co.	✓	547 71	2 29	5 50 00
				3 577 38	22 62	3 60 00 0
	Cash, Dr.		1	3 577 38		
	Interest Cost, Dr.		5	22 62		
	Sundries, Cr.		1		3 60 00 0	3 60 00 0

Transaction:

Discounted the following non-interest bearing notes at our bank:

June 15. R. Harrison $1000 dated May 16, 60 days.

R. Carson Sons $1500 dated May 20, 90 days.

Eaton & Co. $1200 dated June 1, 30 days.

S. Perkins $850 dated June 10, 60 days.

Record entries into Cash (Dr.) Receipt Book headed same as in previous exercise.

(Cash (Dr.) Receipts Journal appears on Page 117)

Discounting of Interest Bearing Notes Receivable

If we had received an interest bearing note, kept it for some time and then discounted it at the bank *before* its due date—we would make the same entries we made when we discounted the non-interest bearing notes in the last chapter except for the difference of Interest.

Let us consider D. Norton's note on page 112. Face value $1500; time 30 days, dated Jan. 4, 19—.

It is a *non-interest* bearing note. Therefore D. Norton will pay $1500, the face value on the due date. If we wish to discount it, we will have to bear the cost, hence we debited Interest Cost for the interest charged by the bank.

Let us now assume that D. Norton gave us an *interest bearing* note at 6%, same face value $1500, and same time 30 days. On the due date D. Norton will pay $1500 plus $7.50 interest. The bank will receive $1507.50 from D. Norton on the due date. The bank must wait 20 days to receive this $1507.50. The bank thus lends us $1507.50. It therefore deducts $5.03—6% interest for 20 days on $1507.50. Our balance will be increased by $1507.50 minus $5.03 or $1502.47—the *present value* (proceeds) of the note.

It would be much easier if we could say that for each day the note runs the amount of interest increases daily. Since this note ran 10 days, it ought to be worth $1500 plus 10 days' interest at 6% or $1502.50. The bank, however, figures it differently. According to their method the present value is $1502.47. Accordingly, the bank figures it to its own advantage. The bank method is the accepted method.

(Cash (Dr.) Receipts Journal appears on Page 117)

C 2

Cash (Dr.) Receipts Journal

Date	Accounts, Cr.	Explanation	L.F.	Net Cash (Dr.)	Interest Cost (Dr.)	Sundries (Cr.)
19— June 15	Notes Receivable	P. Harrison		995.00	5.00	1000.00
15	Notes Receivable	P. Carson Lone		1484.00	16.00	1500.00
15	Notes Receivable	Eaton & Co.		1196.80	3.20	1200.00
15	Notes Receivable	S. Perkins		842.21	7.79	850.00
				4518.01	31.99	4550.00
				4518.01	31.99	4550.00
	Cash, Dr.			4550.00	4550.00	
	Interest Cost, Dr.					
	Sundries, Cr.					

C 2

Cash (Dr.) Receipts Journal

Date	Accounts, Cr.	Explanation	L.F.	Net Cash (Dr.)	Interest Earned	Sundries
19— June 14	Notes Receivable	D. Norton		1500.00		1500.00
14	Interest Earned	On above		2.47	2.47	

Exercise 24:

Discounted the following notes at our bank:

    July 15. B. Walker $300—6%—60 days—dated July 1.

             S. Hayes Co. $1500—6%—30 days—dated July 5.

             M. Burton $1000—0%—90 days—dated May 1.

0% Interest means non-interest bearing.

         Manley & Co. $500—0%—60 days—dated June 1.

         Singer Co. $1200—5%—60 days—dated June 15.

         Our own note $2000—0%—90 days—dated July 15.

         Our own note $1000—0%—30 days—dated July 15.

         D. Horton $1600—6%—60 days—dated June 1.

Required:

     Journalize and post.

         Head Cash (Dr.) Receipts book as follows:

             Net Cash Dr., Interest Cost Dr., Interest Earned Cr., Sundries Cr.

(See facing page for convenient mathematical table for Exercise 24)

(Cash (Dr.) Receipts Journal appears on Page 120)

Solution:

Notes Receivable (1)

					July 15	B. Walker	C2	300	00
					15	S. Hayes Co.	C2	1500	00
					15	M. Burton	C2	1000	00
					15	Manley Co.	C2	500	00
					15	D. Horton	C2	1600	00
					15	Singer Co.	C2	1200	00
						6,100—		6100	00

Notes Payable (2)

					July 15	National City	C2	2000	00
					15	National City	C2	1000	00
						3000—		3000	00

(Ledger continued on Page 121)

MATHEMATICAL TABLE FOR EXERCISE 24

To assist the student we list the following calculations necessary to obtain the figures in Exercise 24:

Maker	Note Face	Note Dated	Rate %	Time	Amount due on Maturity	Bank Interest (Discount)	Time to Maturity (Days)	Discount	Pres. Value Maturity Value less Bank Discount
B. Walker	$ 300.00	July 1	6	60	$ 303.00	6%	46	$ 2.32	$ 300.68
Hayes & Co.	1500.00	July 5	6	30	1507.50	6%	20	5.03	1502.47
M. Burton	1000.00	May 1	0	90	1000.00	6%	15	2.50	997.50
Manley & Co.	500.00	June 1	0	60	500.00	6%	16	1.33	498.67
Singer Co.	1200.00	June 15	5	60	1210.00	6%	30	6.05	1203.95
Ourselves	2000.00	July 15	0	90	2000.00	6%	90	30.00	1970.00
Ourselves	1000.00	July 15	0	30	1000.00	6%	30	5.00	995.00
D. Horton	1600.00	June 1	6	60	1616.00	6%	16	4.31	1611.69

C 2

Cash (Dr.) Receipts Journal

Date	Accounts, Cr	Explanation	L.F.	Net Cash Dr	Interest Cost Dr	Interest Earned Cr	Sundries Cr
July 15 '07	Notes Receivable	B. Walker	1	300 68		68	300 00
15	Notes Receivable	L. Haye & Co.	1	1502 47		2 47	1500 00
15	Notes Receivable	M. Burton	1	997 50	2 50		1000 00
15	Notes Receivable	Manley & Co	1	498 67	1 33		500 00
15	Notes Receivable	Singler Co	1	1503 95		3 95	1500 00
15	Notes Payable	National City	2	1970 00	30 00		2000 00
15	Notes Payable	National City	2	995 00	5 00		1000 00
15	Notes Receivable	D. Norton	1	1611 69		1 69	1600 00
				9079 96	38 83	8 79	9100 00
				9079 96	38 83	18 79	9100 00
	Cash, Dr			2079 96			
	Interest Cost, Dr			38 83	18 79		
	Interest Earned, Cr				9100 00		
	Sundries, Cr			9118 79	9118 79		

Solution for Exercise 24 continued:

Interest Cost (3)

July 31		3883	C2	38 83						

Interest Earned (4)

				July 31		1879	C2	18 79		

Cash (7)

July 31		8679 96	C2	8079 96						

Observe that on interest bearing notes the *Interest Earned* account is *credited*, but on non-interest bearing notes the *Interest Cost* account is *debited*.

In the Cash (Dr.) Receipt Book it is necessary to have a special column for each interest account (Interest Cost Dr. and Interest Earned Cr.).

Review:

HOW TO CALCULATE THE PRESENT VALUE OF A NOTE

A. *If non-interest bearing note—*

1. $\text{Face} \times \dfrac{\text{interest}}{100} \times \dfrac{\text{days still to run}}{360} = \text{Discount.}$

2. Face minus discount = Present Value.

B. *If interest bearing note—*
  1. Find Maturity Value of note

a. $\text{Face} \times \dfrac{\text{interest}}{100} \times \dfrac{\text{full time of note}}{360} = \text{Interest.}$

b. Face plus interest = Maturity Value.

2. $\text{Maturity Value} \times \dfrac{\text{interest}}{100} \times \dfrac{\text{days still to run}}{360} = \text{Discount.}$

3. Maturity Value minus Discount = Present Value.

Exercise 25:

The following notes are discounted at our bank:
Sept. 10 Maker R. Simon $150—6%—60 days—dated August 15.
         Maker J. Johnson $275—6%—30 days—dated Sept. 1.
         Maker M. Wiley & Co. $500—0%—60 days—dated August 1.
         Maker S. Rodgers $1000—0%—30 days—dated August 15.
         Maker Ourselves $5000—0%—60 days—dated Sept. 10.
         Maker Ourselves $1000—0%—90 days—dated Sept. 10.
         Maker R. Peterson $503—6%—60 days—dated August 18.

Required:
  Make the original entries:

(Solution for Exercise 25 appears on Page 123)

INDORSING NOTES RECEIVABLE TO CREDITORS

Non-Interest Bearing Notes Receivable Indorsed at Face Value—
If we make payment to a creditor we may pay:

        1. By cash.
        2. By our note (notes payable).
        3. By our customer's note (notes receivable).

Transaction:

May 1. We owe B. Jones $150. He agrees to accept at its face value a $100 note, dated April 1, time 60 days, which we received from T. Smith.

(Entry for the above transaction appears on Page 124)

Cash (Dr.) Receipts Book

C2

Date	Accounts, Cr.	Explanation	L.F.	Dr. Net Cash	Dr. Interest Cost	Cr. Interest Earned	Cr. Sundries
Sept. 10	Notes Receivable	R. Lemons note		150 64		64	150 00
10	Notes Receivable	J. Johnson note		275 41		41	275 00
10	Notes Receivable	W. Wiley & Co.'s note		498 33	1 67		500 00
10	Notes Receivable	S. Rodgers note		999 17	83		1000 00
10	Notes Receivable	Sundries		4950 00	50 00		5000 00
10	Notes Receivable	Sundries		985 00	15 00		1000 00
10	Notes Receivable	R. Pitman note		504 81		1 81	503 00
				8363 36	67 50	2 86	8428 00
				8363 36	67 50	2 86	8428 00
	Cash, Dr.			8363 36			
	Interest Cost, Dr.						
	Interest Earned, Cr.					2 86	
	Sundries, Cr.				8430 86		
					8430 86		

General Journal

				L.F.	Dr.		Cr.	
19—								
May 1	B Jones				100 00			
	Notes Receivable						100 00	
	T. Smith's 60 day note dated 4/1							

We debit B. Jones because we are decreasing his balance just as **we** would debit his account if we gave him our check.

Notes Receivable

					19—				
					May 1		J1	100 00	

B. Jones

	19—								
	May 1		J1	100 00					

Non-Interest Bearing Notes Receivable Indorsed At Present Value—

Suppose B. Jones refuses to accept T. Smith's note because he has to wait 31 days before he receives cash for it. Accordingly we agree to allow him to charge us interest at 6% for the time he has to wait for the cash. This is equivalent to saying that we give him T. Smith's note *at present value.*

The present value of the note is:

$$100 \times \frac{6}{100} \times \frac{31}{360} = \$.52 \text{ discount}$$

Face minus discount = Present Value
$$100 \quad - \quad .52 \quad = \$99.48$$

Entry:

8'

General Journal

			LF	Dr.	Cr.
19—					
May 1	B. Jones			99 48	
	Interest Cost			52	
	Notes Receivable				100 00
	T. Smith's 60 day note dated				
	4/1 at present value				

Interest Bearing Notes Indorsed at Present Value—

If T. Smith's note were an interest bearing note and B. Jones agrees to accept it at present value, the following entry would be made:

8'

General Journal

			LF	Dr.	Cr.
19—					
May 1	B. Jones			100 49	
	Notes Receivable				100 00
	Interest Earned				49
	T. Smith's 60 day note dated 4/1				
	at present value				

B. Jones is debited because he would be debited if we gave him cash.

Exercise 26:

Make the following entries:

May 15. Gave W. Jones, our creditor, A. Smith's $1,000 note, dated April 15, 60 days, 6%.

1. Make entry if W. Jones accepted it at face value.
2. Make entry if W. Jones accepted it at present value.
3. Make entry same as 2, assuming it to be a non-interest bearing note.

General Journal

			L.F.	Dr.	Cr.
1	W. Jones			1000 00	
	Notes Receivable				1000 00
	Gave A. Smith's note at face value				
2	W. Jones			1004 95	
	Notes Receivable				1000 00
	Interest Earned				4 95
	Gave A. Smith's note at present value				
3	W. Jones			995 00	
	Interest Cost			5 00	
	Notes Receivable				1000 00
	Gave A. Smith's note at present value				

Renewed Notes

We hold J. Thompson's note for $100 dated June 1; time, one month.
On July 1, he notifies us that he cannot pay this note but sends us
another note for $100 dated July 1, time, one month. We agree to *renew*
the note.

Entry:

J'

		General Journal	L.F.	Dr.	Cr.
19—					
July	1	Notes Receivable		100 00	
		Notes Receivable			100 00
		J. Thompson's note of 6/1			
		renewed for one month.			

It is necessary to make this entry because on the due date a note must
be removed from our books. It must either be paid, renewed, or the
maker will owe it on account. In any event the note *must* be taken off
the books.

Note Renewed in Part

If J. Thompson sent us a check for $25 and a note for $75, we would
make two entries—one for the check, the other for the note.

C2

	Date	Accounts, Cr	L.F.	Net Cash (Dr)	Sales Disc (Dr)	Sundries (Cr)
	July	1	Notes Receivable		25 00		25 00

General Journal J¹

	19		L.F.	Dr.	Cr.
July	1	Notes Receivable		75 00	
		Notes Receivable			75 00
		J. Thompson's note of 6/1			
		renewed in part			

INTEREST BEARING NOTES RENEWED

If Thompson's note were an interest bearing note, he may renew it by:

1. Paying the interest in cash and giving us a note for the same amount as the old note.

2. By giving us a new note for the sum of the old plus the interest.

In case 1, the cash is recorded in the Cash (Dr.) Receipts Book, credit Interest Earned for the interest. The note is renewed through the General Journal same as the non-interest bearing note renewed at the beginning of this chapter.

In case 2, we make the entry shown below:

General Journal J¹

	19		L.F.	Dr.	Cr.
July	1	Notes Receivable		100 50	
		Notes Receivable			100 00
		Interest Earned			50
		J. Thompson's note of 6/1			
		renewed with interest added.			

Transactions:

July 1. (1) We cannot pay our note for $100, time 30 days, due today. Burton Sheff agrees to have it renewed for a 30 day period.

(2) Assuming the above note to be interest bearing, we pay the interest in cash.

(3) Same as above, except that we increase the new note by the interest owing.

(4) We owe our bank a note for $1000, time 30 days, due to-day. The bank agrees to renew the note in part, we pay them $200 and give them a new note for the $800 for 30 days.

(5) The bank agrees to renew our $2000, 30 days note due to-day. We give them our new note for $2000, time 30 days.

Entries:

J1

General Journal

19—			L.F.	Dr.	Cr.
July	1	Notes Payable		100 00	
		Notes Payable			100 00
		Our note of 6/1 to B. Sheff			
		renewed for 30 days.			
	1	Notes Payable		100 00	
		Notes Payable			100 00
		Our note of 6/1 to B. Sheff			
		renewed, interest paid by cash.			
	1	Notes Payable		100 00	
		Interest Cost		50	
		Notes Payable			100 50
		Our note of 6/1 to B. Sheff renewed			
		with interest			

(Entries follow on Page 129)

Observe:

When our note is due at the bank and renewed, two transactions take place.

First, the old note is charged to our account. Use Cash (Cr.) Payment Book.

Secondly, the new note is discounted. Use Cash (Dr.) Receipts Book as above.

(Continued on Page 130)

C 2

Cash (Dr.) Receipts Book

Date	Accounts, Cr.	L.F.	Explanation	Net Cash (Dr.)	Interest Cost (Dr.)	Sundries (Cr.)
July 1	Notes Payable		Renewed part by National City for 30 days	776 00	4 00	800 00
1	Notes Payable		" Renewed in full by National City for 30 days	199 00	1 00	200 00

C 3

Cash (Cr.) Payment Book

Date	Accounts, Dr.	L.F.	Explanation	Net Cash (Cr.)
July 1	Interest Cost		Note of b/i to B. Sheff	50
1	Notes Payable		Part payment of b/i note due National City	200 00
1	Notes Payable		Balance of b/i note due National City	500 00
1	Notes Payable		b/i note due National City	200 00

PROTESTED NOTES

It is customary in business to place all notes for collection with our bank.

When a note is presented for payment and payment is not made, the bank messenger or any other person who presents the note for payment signs an affidavit that payment was not made. This affidavit is called a *Protest*. The note is said to be "protested" and the bank charges a small fee for the protest. This protest fee is charged back to the maker.

Transaction:

Aug. 1. Our bank informs us that J. Walter's note for $250 is uncollectible, protest fee $1.50.

2. Our bank informs us that Charles Braun's note for $175, which we discounted at our bank is not paid. The bank charges our account for $175 plus $1.35 protest fee.

3. Our note to M. Fleisher for $200 cannot be paid because we are temporarily short of cash. It is protested; fee $1.50. We promise to pay $201.50 before the end of the month.

Entries:

General Journal   J¹

			L F	Dr	Cr
Aug.	1	J. Walters		250 00	
		Notes Receivable			250 00
		Note protested			
	2	Charles Braun		175 00	
		Notes Receivable			175 00
		Note protested			
	3	Notes Payable		200 00	
		Protest Fee		1 50	
		M. Fleisher			201 50
		Our note protested			

C3

Cash (Cr.) Payment Book

Date	Accounts, Dr.	Explanation	L.F.	Net Cash, Cr.
Aug 1	J. Walters	Protest fees		1.50
2	Notes Receivable	Braun's protested note		175.00
2	Charles Braun	protest fee on above		1.35

Transaction:

Oct. 5. Our bank charges our account the following protest fees for these uncollected notes left with it for collection:

Donald Sheff note $300, fee $1.25
D. Adams   note $275, fee $1.50
D. Love   note $200, fee $1.25

8. The makers of the following endorsed notes did not pay their respective notes which were charged to our account.

Maker	Note	Indorsee	Fee
R. Halsted	$ 250	S. Horwitt	$1.10
L. Brown	$1000	A. Ash	$1.35
S. Fischer	$ 350	B. Glickenhaus	$1.25

Make the necessary entries.

J1

General Journal

Date			L.F.	Dr.	Cr.
Oct 8	S. Horwitt			251.10	
	Protest Fees				1.10
	Notes Receivable				250.00
	Note protested				
8	A. Ash			1001.35	
	Protest Fees				1.35
	Notes Receivable				1000.00
	Note protested				
8	B. Glickenhaus			351.25	
	Protest Fees				1.25
	Notes Receivable				350.00
	Note Protested				

L 3

Cash (Cr.) Payment Book

Date	Accounts, Dr.	Explanation	L.F.	Net Cash	Discount	Purchase Expense	Sundries
Oct 5	Donald Sheff	Protest fees		1 25			1 25
5	B. Adams	Protest fees		1 50			1 50
5	D. Lowe	Protest fees		1 25 / 4 00			1 25 / 4 00
	Sundries, Dr.			4 00		4 00	
	Cash, Cr						

SUMMARY CHART ON NOTES

1. When we receive a non-interest bearing note from a customer:

GENERAL JOURNAL

Notes Receivable	$100	
Smith (Customer)		$100

2. When we receive cash for a note:

Cash (Dr.) Receipts Book

July 1. Notes Receivable	$100

3. When we receive an interest bearing note:

GENERAL JOURNAL

Notes Receivable	$100	
Smith (Customer)		$100
Interest bearing note		

4. When we receive cash for an interest bearing note:

Cash (Dr.) Receipts Book

July 1. Notes Receivable	$100
July 1. Interest Earned	$ 1

5. When we give our non-interest bearing note to a creditor

GENERAL JOURNAL

Jones (Creditor)	$100	
Notes Payable		$100

6. When we pay our note:

Cash (Cr.) Payment Book

July 5. Notes Payable	$100

7. When we give our interest bearing note to a creditor:

GENERAL JOURNAL

Jones (Creditor)	$100	
Notes Payable		$100
Interest bearing note		

8. When we pay this interest bearing note:

Cash (Cr.) Payment Book

July 5. Notes Payable	$100
July 5. Interest Cost	$ 1

9. When we discount our non-interest bearing note at the bank:

Cash (Dr.) Receipts Book

Date	Cash Dr.	Int. Cost Dr.	Sundries Cr.
July 1. Notes Payable	$990	$10.00	$1000

10. When we pay our bank for above discounted note:

Cash (Cr.) Payment Book

Date	Net Cash Cr.	Sundries Dr.
Aug. 1. Notes Payable	$1000	$1000

11. When we discount at our bank a customer's non-interest bearing note:

Cash (Dr.) Receipts Book

Date	Net cash Dr.	Interest Cost Dr.	Sundries Cr.
Jan. 14, Notes Receivable	$1495	$5.00	$1500.00

12. When we discount at our bank a customer's interest bearing note:

Cash (Dr.) Receipts Book

Date	Net Cash Dr.	Interest Earned Cr.	Sundries Cr.
Jan. 14, Notes Receivable	$1500		$1500
14. Interest Earned	2.47	$2.47	

13. When we endorse a customer's non-interest bearing note at face value to a creditor:

GENERAL JOURNAL

Jones (Creditor)	$100	
Notes Receivable		$100

14. When we discount a customer's non-interest bearing note with a creditor at its present value:

GENERAL JOURNAL

Jones (Creditor)	$198.00	
Interest Cost	2.00	
Notes Receivable		$200.00

15. When we discount a customer's interest bearing note with a creditor at its present value:

GENERAL JOURNAL

Jones (Creditor)	$202.00	
Interest Earned		$2.00
Notes Receivable		$200.00

16. When a non-interest bearing note is renewed:

GENERAL JOURNAL

Notes Receivable	$100.00	
Notes Receivable		$100.00

17. When an interest bearing note is renewed and the new note contains the interest due on the old:

GENERAL JOURNAL

Notes Receivable	$202.00	
Interest Earned		$ 2.00
Notes Receivable		$200.00

18. When a non-interest bearing notes payable is renewed:

GENERAL JOURNAL

Notes Payable	$100.00	
Notes Payable		$100.00

19. When an interest bearing notes payable is renewed with interest on the old note added to the new:

GENERAL JOURNAL

Notes Payable	$100.00	
Interest Cost	2.00	
Notes Payable		$102.00

20. When a customer's note is protested:

GENERAL JOURNAL

Smith	$100.00	
Notes Receivable		$100.00

21. When a customer's note which we discounted at our bank is protested:

Cash (Cr.) Payment Book

Date	Cash Cr.
Jan. 10. Smith (Customer) For note protested	$100.00
10. Smith (Customer) Protest Fee	1.35

Lesson XV

PETTY CASH BOOK

In order to be certain that all receipts are accounted for, it is a definite rule in business that all money received either by cash or by checks must be deposited at the bank daily.

All payments are therefore made by check.

It is apparent however that we must have some cash to pay for small incidentals; e.g., 8 cents due postman for additional postage, 15 cents carfare for the errand boy, etc.

For this purpose we set up a Petty Cash Fund.

We will draw a check to the order of Petty Cash for $10. Our employer signs the check. We cash it at the bank. Then we put the money into a Petty Cash box, containing Petty Cash authorization slips, and a Petty Cash Book. The authorization slip will be signed for each cash withdrawal by the person who receives the money, and by the person responsible for the authorization of this disbursement. The reason for the withdrawal is clearly indicated on this slip.

When the fund is almost depleted, the bookkeeper will list all the amounts shown on the Petty Cash slips, and draw a check for the *total* of these slips. This type of fund is called the "Imprest Petty Cash Fund."

The Petty Cash Book will contain several columns for expense items and another column for the amount of the Petty Cash checks drawn to reimburse the fund.

At the end of the month the totals of the Expense columns are posted to the respective accounts.

No postings are made from the Cash Book for checks drawn for Petty Cash, except when the Petty Cash Fund is increased.

No posting is made from the "Checks Drawn" column, nor from the Petty Cash column because the credit to Cash is found in the net Cash column in the Cash (Cr.) Payment Journal when the fund is reimbursed, and the corresponding debit lies in the Expense columns in the Petty Cash Book.

The Imprest Petty Cash account receives only one posting—when the fund is set up.

Only when the Imprest Petty Cash Fund is added to or decreased will any additional postings be made to it.

(The Petty Cash Book will appear as shown on page 138)

The Cash (Cr.) Payment Book will look like this:

Date	Accounts, Dr.	Explanation	Check #	L.F.	(Cr.) Cash	(Dr.) Sundries
May 1	Imprest Fund		11	6	10 00	10 00
6	Petty Cash		72	✓	6 35	6 35
15	Petty Cash		84	✓	7 66	7 66
21	Petty Cash		98	✓	8 95	8 95
30	Petty Cash		105	✓	8 90	8 90
					41 86	41 86
	Sundries, Dr.			✓	41 86	
	Cash, Cr.		1			41 86

Petty Cash Book

Date	Item	LF	Checks Drawn	Petty Cash	General Expense Dr.	Selling Expense Dr.	Office Expense Dr.	Sundries Dr.
19— May 1	Electric bulbs			1.15	1.15			
1	Repairing desk			1.75			1.75	
2	Carfare			.20	.20			
3	Carfare			2.25	2.25			
6	Tip to truckman			1.00		1.00		
6	Check #72		6.35					
8	Theater tickets			6.00		6.00		
9	Picture wire			.25	.25			
11	Scratch pads			.60			.60	
13	Desk blotters			.75			.75	
14	Stamps			.06	.06			
15	Check #84		7.66					
16	Carfare			1.80	1.80			
19	Carfare			.40	.40			
20	J. Greene, Drawing	5		4.00				4.00
21	Replace window glass			2.75	2.75			
21	Check #98		8.95					
27	Chair repair			2.40	2.40			
30	Entertaining buyer			6.50		6.50		
30	Check #105		8.90					
			31.86	31.86	11.26	13.50	3.10	4.00
			31.86	31.86	11.26	13.50	3.10	4.00
	General Expense Dr.	8	11.26					
	Selling Expense Dr.	10	13.50					
	Office Expense Dr.	9	3.10					
	Sundries Dr.	1	4.00					
	Petty Cash Cr.	1	31.86					

NOTE: Observe how each item in the Sundries column is posted. The total is not posted. Petty cash (Cr.) is not posted, it is checked. In the Cash (Cr.) Payment Journal checks No. 72, No. 84, No. 98, and No. 105 are extended into the Sundries column and are also not posted but are checked.

Lesson XVI

CONTROLLING ACCOUNTS

Up to the present, we have used one ledger. All accounts for customers, creditors, and all miscellaneous accounts were kept in one ledger. Obviously such a ledger can become so bulky as to make it impractical to be used. Furthermore, a single error in posting to one customer's account will throw the Trial Balance out of balance, and necessitate every posting to every customer's, creditor's, and miscellaneous account to be checked.

Therefore, it is ordinarily customary to have three ledgers in business.

All customers' accounts will be kept in one ledger, called the Accounts Receivable Ledger.

All creditor's accounts are kept in another ledger, called the Accounts Payable Ledger.

The third ledger contains all the other accounts, such as Cash, Inventory, Sales, etc. It is called the General Ledger.

The General Ledger is the one from which we take a trial balance.

The other two ledgers, the Accounts Receivable and Accounts Payable; are called Subsidiary Ledgers.

When we take all customers' accounts out of our General Ledger to make up our Accounts Receivable Ledger we must replace these accounts with *one* account containing the *total* of *all* debits and the total of *all* credits of *all* customers' accounts removed. If we do not do this the Trial Balance will not balance, it will be short of all the debits and credits that have been removed.

This account is called Accounts Receivable Control. It is a summary account of all customers' accounts, just as if we kept all customers' accounts in one account. It replaces all the customers' accounts in the General Ledger.

Similarly, we have an Accounts Payable Controlling Account in the General Ledger containing a summary of all debit and all credit postings to all the creditors' accounts in the Accounts Payable Ledger. It replaces all creditors' accounts in the General Ledger.

Proving the Controlling Accounts

At the end of each month, we balance each customer's account, list up the balances on a sheet called "Schedule of Accounts Receivable," and total this schedule. This sum must equal the balance of the Accounts Receivable Controlling account in the General Ledger.

Similarly we balance each account in the Accounts Payable Ledger, list the balances on a sheet called "Schedule of Accounts Payable," and the sum of this schedule must equal the balance of the Accounts Payable Controlling Account in the General Ledger.

If the schedules agree with the controlling accounts, we are said to have Proved the Ledgers.

Errors in the General Ledger

If the Trial Balance does not balance, we need not concern ourselves with checking any items in the subsidiary ledgers.

Controlling Accounts Procedure

If an amount is to be posted to the debit side of a customer's account, place this amount in a column headed "Accounts Receivable Control Dr."

If an amount is to be credited to a customer's account, place this amount into a column headed "Accounts Receivable Control Cr."

If an amount is to be posted to the debit side of a creditor account, place this amount into a column headed "Accounts Payable Control Dr."

If an amount is to be posted to the credit side of a creditor's account, place it into a column headed "Accounts Payable Control Cr."

The individual items are posted to the subsidiary ledger, the totals to the Controlling Account.

Hence a controlling account contains the *totals* of all items posted *individually* to the subsidiary ledgers.

Rule: Place an amount into a column bearing the name and side of the ledger to which it is to be posted.

Obviously our journals must have these columns. Theoretically we should have a column for each debit and each credit for *each* ledger in *each* journal. However, there is no need placing an Accounts Payable column in the Sales (Cr.) Journal because we will never need it in that journal.

The next lesson presents a model set clearly illustrating the controlling account procedure.

Lesson XVII

MODEL BUSINESS SET

(Final Examination)

JANUARY TRANSACTIONS

Head up all books in the same manner as in the solution following this examination. In the ledgers set up three accounts on each page. Consult the Trial Balance in the solution for a list of all General Ledger accounts. Post from all books daily, except the totals which are posted monthly.

Jan. 2. J. Wilson began a jobbing stationery business investing $5000 cash and $1000 in merchandise.

2. Paid Cross & Brown rent $150 for the month.

3. Paid Atlas Insurance Company premium of $120 for $10,000 fire insurance on merchandise.

3. Paid by check for showroom equipment $700; office fixtures $250.

3. Bought the following merchandise dated today:

Campus Supplies Co.	$450 terms 2/10/30
Nufashion Stationery Company	275 terms 3/10/60
B. Richards Company	150 terms 2/30/90
S. Smithfield	400 terms 2/20/30

5. Sold merchandise to the following, shipped today:

R. H. Macy	$725 terms 8/10/30
Arnold Constable Company	400 terms 8/10/30
E. and F. Office Supplies Company	200 terms 3/10/60
Elegant Stationery Company	350 terms 2/20/60

6. Drew payroll check for $140 for the following: office salaries $55, shipping clerk $25, J. Wilson $60.

8. Bought G. M. delivery truck $1000. Gave a 30 day 6% note to Commercial Credit Corporation for same.

9. R. H. Macy returns $70 merchandise.

10. We return to Campus Supplies Co. merchandise $100.

11. We set up an Imprest Petty Cash Fund in amount $10. Drew check for same.

11. Sold and shipped today to:

R. H. Macy	$1200 terms 8/10/30
Ace Stationery Co.	150 terms 2/10/30

E. and F. Office Supplies Company   250 terms $\frac{1}{2}$ cash;
    bal. 30 day 6% note
Arnold Constable Company   275 terms 8/10/30

Jan. 12. Received the following invoices:

Campus Supplies Co. $250-2/10/30 dated Jan. 10.
S. Smithfield   105-2/20/30 dated Jan. 11.
B. Richards Company 275-60 day note—bill dated today

13. Received from E. and F. Office Supplies Co. check for $125, and a 30 day note dated Jan. 11 for $125.

13. Sent check to Campus Supplies Co. for $343 (discount $7-) in payment for bill of Jan. 3 less returns, less discount. Deduct returns before figuring discount.

13. Sent check to Nufashion Stationery Company $266.75 (discount $8.25) in full of 3rd less discount.

13. Sent our 60 day note dated Jan. 12 to B. Richards in full of Jan. 12.

13. Spent the following from Petty Cash Fund—twine 60 cents (Shipping Expense), tip to superintendent $5 (General Expense), carfare 20 cents (General Expense).

13. Draw check for payroll for $150 for office salaries $55, shipping clerk $25, J. Wilson $70.

13. Draw check for salesmen's commission $90.

15. Received the following checks:

R. H. Macy $602.60 discount $52.40
Arnold Constable $368.00 discount $32.00

15. E. and F. Office Supplies Co. sent us a 30 day note 6%—$194 discount $6.00. (Deduct returns before figuring the discount in every case.)

16. Cash Sales to date amounted to $103.45.

16. Paid out of Petty Cash for the following:

Telegram $ .35   (Gen. Exp.)
Postage   2.00   (Office Exp.)
Carfare   1.00   (Gen. Exp.)

16. Reimbursed the Petty Cash Fund for all disbursements to date $9.15.

17. Discounted at our bank our 30 day note for $1000.

18. Shipped the following sales today:

Arnold Constable $225 terms 8/10/30
R. H. Macy   550 terms 8/10/30

Elegant Stationery Company   175 terms 2/20/30

E. and F. Office Supplies Co.   450 terms 3/10/30

Jan. 18. R. H. Macy returns from merchandise sold on 11th—$250.

Arnold Constable returns from merchandise sold on 11th —$50.

19. The bill for repairing the delivery truck is paid, in amount $65 to G. M. Corporation.

20. Some of the stationery sold for cash is returned. Draw $12 check for refund to A. Wilson.

20. Paid Campus Supplies Co. bill due today $245, discount $5.

20. Draw check to payroll for $175 for office salaries $55, shipping $25, salesmen's commission $40, J. Wilson $55.

22. Received check from following:

R. H. Macy $874 discount $76

Ace Stationery Company $147 discount $ 3

Arnold Constable $207 discount $18

Allow the discount deducted because the bills were due on the 21st, which was Sunday.

23. Pay B. and O. Railroad $18.45 freight on purchases to date.

23. S. Smithfield's invoice for $400 is due today. We have arranged to pay this bill by note for 10 days with interest at 6%. They have agreed to allow us to deduct the 2% discount.

24. The following merchandise was received today:

Campus Supplies Company   terms 3/10/30—$560

Nufashion Stationery Company   terms 3/10/30—$400

B. Richards and Company   terms 2/10/60—$350

S. Smithfield   terms 2/20/30—$475

25. Elegant Stationery Company sends us their 30 day note with interest at 6% in amount $343, discount $7.

27. Drew payroll check for $190 as follows:

Office salaries $55, shipping clerk $25, salesmen's commissions $60, J. Wilson $50.

27. Paid out of Petty Cash:

Postage due	$ .08	(Office Exp.)
Stationery and supplies	2.64	(Office Exp.)
Removing rubbish	2.00	(Gen. Exp.)
Repairing truck	4.00	(Shipping Exp.)

Jan. 27. J. Wilson takes stationery home for his children. This stationery cost us $35.

28. Sent S. Smithfield our check for $102.90, discount $2.10, in full of bill of January 11.

28. Received check from R. H. Macy $506, discount $44.

31. Reimbursed Petty Cash $8.72.

Journalize, post, obtain Trial Balance. List Schedule of Accounts Receivable, and Accounts Payable. Prove controls.

FEBRUARY TRANSACTIONS

Feb. 1. Received the bank statement from our bank. The following checks were outstanding: $12, $18.45, $102.90 #12, #15, #17 respectively. The bank balance is $6015.43.
Reconcile the bank balance with our balance.

Make this statement on a separate sheet of paper.

1. Received the following invoices:
Nufashion Stationery Company, terms 3/10/30, $435, dated today.
Campus Supplies Company, terms 2/10/30, $645, dated today.

2. Our accountant instructs the bookkeeper to open a special journal for Sales Returns and Allowances, and a special journal for Purchases Returns and Allowances because of the increasing frequency of transactions of this type. Henceforth, do not use the General Journal for any Sales or Purchases returned or allowed. Use the respective special journal.

2. We returned to Campus Supplies Co. $75 merchandise bought on January 24 and $120 merchandise bought from S. Smithfield on January 24.

In posting from the Purchase Returns and Allowance Journal the ledger folio is PR1.

2. Paid our note due today $392, interest $.65.

2. B. Richards agrees to accept E. & F. Office Supplies Company's $125 note and the balance in cash in payment for his invoices of January 3. The note is accepted at its pres-

ent value. B. Richards allows us to deduct the 2% trade discount.

> Deduct the purchase discount from the bill first before deducting the present value of the note.

Feb. 3. Shipped the following merchandise today

Elegant Stationery Company	terms 3/10/60,	$530
E. & F. Office Supplies Company	terms 3/10/30,	$455
R. H. Macy Company	terms 8/10/30,	$965

3. Campus Supplies Co., agrees to accept our 10 day, 6% note, in payment of their invoice of January 24, less returns, less discount.

> Deduct the purchase returns before calculating the purchase discount.

5. We buy a delivery truck from Diamond T. Motor Corporation for $1275, terms $100 on the 5th and 20th of each month.

> Open an account with the Diamond T Motor Corporation in the General Ledger. Even though they are our creditor, we keep accounts in the Accounts Payable ledger only with those creditors from whom we buy merchandise to sell. Rule—If an account does not appear in our Purchase Journal, it cannot be kept in our Accounts Payable Ledger.

We send them our check for $100.

> Extend the amount into the General Ledger column. Why do we debit the creditor instead of charging this amount to Delivery Equipment?
> Answer. We are paying an indebtedness and are not buying $100 additional Delivery Equipment.

7. The total cash sales to date amount to $248.57.
7. Paid out of Petty Cash as follows:

Carfare	$ .40	(Gen. Exp.)
Repairs in showrooms	3.20	(Selling Exp.)

> All showroom expenses are charged to Selling Expense because the showroom is maintained to promote sales.

Dinner for office girls	2.30	(Office Exp.)

7. Paid Commercial Credit Company note due today with interest $1005.
8. R. H. Macy returns $240 merchandise sold on the 3rd. Arnold Constable returns $25 merchandise sold on January 18.

Elegant Stationery Company is permitted to deduct $15 from their bill of January 18 on account of inferior workmanship.

Feb. 8. Campus Supplies Co. agrees to allow us $15 on bill of January 24 on account of Elegant Stationery Company's complaint.

(Since this bill has been paid, deduct return from next bill.)

9. Shipped merchandise to the following:

E. & F. Office Supplies Co.	$235	terms 3/10/30
Ace Stationery Company	225	terms 2/10/30
Elegant Stationery Co.	175	terms 2/20/30

10. The following invoices were received:

B. Richards & Company	$250	terms 2/20/30 dated today
S. Smithfield	350	terms 2/20/30 dated Feb. 7
Nufashion Stationery Co.	300	terms 3/10/30 dated Feb. 9

10. Paid Payroll as follows $380—Office Expense $110, Shipping Expenses $50, Selling Expense $120, J. Wilson Drawing $100.

10. Paid the following bills:

New York Edison Co.	$16.43	(General Expense)
Hanover Wrapping Paper Co.	34.65	(Shipping Expense)
Corrugated Box Co.	46.35	(Shipping Expense)
Longacre Press, for printing	36.84	(Office Expense)
Longacres Press, for circulars	130.62	(Selling Expense)
Cross & Brown, Rent	150.00	(Rent)
New York Telephone Co.	35.42	(General Expense)

When we receive miscellaneous expense bills, we do not enter these bills ordinarily. It is customary to file these bills in a file captioned "Miscellaneous Bills Payable."

On or before the 10th of the following month we pay these bills and record these entries in the Cash Book.

11. Send check to Campus Supplies Co. for invoice due today.

Deduct the $15 charge before computing the discount. Since we have paid the bill against which this item is charged, we may deduct it from the next bill.

11. Richard Cox is employed as salesman. He will receive a drawing of $40.00 per week against commissions of 1% on all sales made by him. We will reimburse him for all expenses connected with his work. Make no entry.

Feb. 12. Reimburse Petty Cash for all disbursements to date.[14] $5.90. Paid the following from Petty Cash:

Replacing window pane	$2.00
Carfare	1.40
Taxi fare for delivery of order	3.20
Stamps	2.00

13. S. Smithfield agrees to accept at present value Elegant Stationery Company's note which we hold, in payment of invoice due today, less returns, less discount. We send them a check for the balance.

13. Received the following checks on bills due today:

E. & F. Office Supplies Company	$441.35
R. H. Macy	667.00

13. Our note to Campus Supplies Co. is due today. Inasmuch as our cash balance is low we arrange to renew this note by giving them a new note in exchange for the old, plus the interest due on the old note. The new note is to run for 10 days at 6% interest.

The Campus Supplies Co. account is not affected in this transaction.

14. Elegant Stationery Co. sends us S. Murphy's $100 30 day note, 6%, dated Jan. 25, at *face* value in payment of our bill of Jan. 18. We agree to allow them to deduct 2% discount. We receive their check for the balance.

14. We receive a check for $436.50, discount $13.50, from E. & F. Office Supplies Company in full of bill of Jan. 18.

Record in Cash Book exactly as stated above.

14. R. Cox reports the following sales, shipments are made today:

Sears & Co.	$1265.00 terms 2/10/30
Gimbel Bros.	1650.00 terms 2/10/30

14. Received check from E. & F. Office Supplies in payment of their $194.00 note and interest $.97 due today.

15. Received the following invoice dated today:

Nufashion Stationery Co.	$275.00 terms 3/10/30
Campus Supplies Co.	300.00 terms 3/10/30
B. Richards Co.	175.00 terms 2/20/30

Feb. 15. We returned merchandise to the following:

        Nufashion Stationery Co. $100.00 from bill of Jan. 24

        S. Smithfield   60.00 from bill of Feb. 7

        B. Richards Co.   75.00 from bill of Feb. 10

16. Our bank notifies us that they have charged our account $1000 for note due today.

17. The bank discounts our $500, 30 day note.

17. Received check from Arnold Constable in full of Jan. 18, $200.

18. We discover that E. & F. Office Supplies Co. was not entitled to the discount deducted by them in paying their bill of Jan. 18. Upon notifying them we receive their check for $13.50 today.

> Credit Sales Discount because the error lay in allowing the discount deducted.

18. R. Cox submits his expense account in amount $42.32. Draw check to reimburse him and include his weekly drawing of $40 in same.

> Charge Selling Expense for $42.32. Open an account entitled "R. Cox, Salesman." Debit this account with all money drawn by R. Cox against his commissions. At the end of the month credit this account for the commissions earned by him.

19. Reimburse Petty Cash, $8.60.

19. Paid out of Petty Cash the following:

        Stationery $2.10   (Office Exp.)

        Stamps   2.00   (Office Exp.)

        Carfare   .60   (Gen. Exp.)

19. Received from E. & F. Office Supplies Co. their 30 day note for $227.95 in full of the 9th, less discount. Ace Stationery Company send us their 60 day, 6% interest bearing note for $220.50 in full of the 9th, less discount.

20. Shipped the following today:

        R. H. Macy $625.00 terms 8/10/30

        Arnold Constable   265.00 terms 8/10/30

        E. & F. Office Supplies Co. 320.00 terms 3/10/30

        Elegant Stationery Co.   200.00 terms 2/20/30

        Ace Stationery Co.   325.00 terms 2/10/30

        Sears & Company   1850.00 terms 2/10/30

        Gimbel Brothers   2310.00 terms 2/10/30

        (R. Cox will be credited with commission at the end of

the month on all sales made to Sears & Company and to Gimbel Brothers.)

Feb. 20. Sent check to Diamond T. Motor Corporation for $100 as per contract.

21. Received the following invoices:

Modern Stationery Company $750, terms $\frac{1}{2}$ cash, balance 30 day note.

Acme Stationery Company   650, terms $\frac{1}{2}$ 30 days note. $\frac{1}{2}$ 60 day note.

S. Smithfield   490, terms 2/20/30

Campus Supplies Co.   1450, terms 2/10/30

B. Richards Company   650, terms 2/20/30

21. Sold for cash to date merchandise $246.00.

21. Send check to Modern Stationery Company for $375.00 and a 30 day note for $375.00.

21. Send Acme Stationery Company a 30 day note for $325.00 and a 60 day note for $325.00.

21. Fill out the State Unemployment Insurance Tax—3% on all payrolls for the month of January. Do not include money drawn by the proprietor.

Jan.	6	Payroll	$80.00
	13	Payroll	80.00
	20	Payroll	120.00
	27	Payroll	140.00
Total			$420.00 @ 3% = $12.60 Tax

Draw check to New York State Unemployment Insurance Fund for $12.60.

21. J. Wilson draws check for $125.

22. We discount at our bank S. Murphy's $100 note, and E. & F. Office Supplies Company's note for $227.95. The bank credits our account for $100.12 and $228.02 respectively for the present value of each.

23. Send check to B. Richards in full of January 24, in amount $350 and a check to Nufashion Stationery Co. in full of January 24, less returns. Amount of check $300.

Feb. 23. Our note for $476.09 and interest is due. Draw check in favor of Campus Supplies Co. for $476.88.

24. Draw payroll check for $420 for the following: Office salaries $110, shipping clerk salary $50, salesmen's salaries $150, J. Wilson drawing $110.

24. Received checks from Sears and Co. for $1239.70 and from Gimbel Bros. for $1617, in full of 14th less discount.

24. Our bank notifies us that S. Murphy's note has been protested and charges our account for $100 and $1.50 protest fee.

(Since Elegant Stationery Co. had given us the Murphy note, we charge their account $101.50. Observe this entry in the Solution. Note the circle around $101.50 in the Sundries Column. The "AR" means Accounts Receivable. Post a debit to Elegant Stationery and a debit to the control.)

25. Received a check for $101.50 from Elegant Stationery Co. for protested note and fee.

25. Sent check to Campus Supplies Co. for $291.00 in full of 15th, less discount.

25. R. Cox presents an expense account for $25. Reimburse him for same by check for $65 in order to include his drawing for the week of $40.

28. We list all sales made by R. Cox for the month. They total $7075. Give him credit for his commission on same at 1%.

28. Reimburse Petty Cash $4.70.

Journalize, post, obtain Trial Balance, Schedule of Accounts Receivable, and Schedule of Accounts Payable. Prove Controls.

(Solutions for Model Set appear on Pages 151-180)

Cash (Dr.) Receipts Journal   C2

Date	Account	Explanation	L.F.	Net Cash (Dr.)	Sales Discount (Dr.)	Interest Cost (Dr.)	Accounts Receivable (Cr.)	Sales (Cr.)	General Ledger (Cr.)
19— Jan. 2	J. Wilson, Capital	Investment	14	5000 00					5000 00
13	E & F Office Supplies Co.		3	125 00			125 00		
15	R. H. Macy & Co.		1	602 60	52 40		655 00		
15	Arnold Constable Co.		2	368 00	32 00		400 00		
16	Sales		✓	103 45				103 45	
17	Notes Payable	30 day City Trust Co.	13	995 00		5 00			1000 00
22	R. H. Macy & Co		1	874 00	76 00		950 00		
22	Ace Stationery Co		5	147 00	3 00		150 00		
22	Arnold Constable Co.		2	207 00	18 00		225 00		
28	R. H. Macy & Co		1	506 00	44 00		550 00		
				8928 05	225 40	5 00	3055 00	103 45	6000 00
				8928 05	225 40	5 00	3055 00	103 45	6000 00
	Cash, Dr.		1	8928 05					
	Sales Discount, Dr.		18	225 40					
	Interest Cost, Dr.		31	5 00					
	Accounts Receivable, Cr.		3				3055 00		
	Sales, Cr.		16				103 45		
	General Ledger, Cr.		✓				6000 00		
				9158 45			9158 45		

Cash (Cr.)

Date	Account	Explanation	check No.	L.F.	Net Cash	
19— Jan. 2	Rent	For January	1	23	150 00	
3	Insurance	$10,000 on mdse — fire	2	24	120 00	
3	Showroom Equipment		3	8	700 00	
3	Office Furniture		3	7	250 00	
6	Payroll		4	✓	140 00	
11	Imprest Petty Cash Fund		5	2	10 00	
13	Campus Supplies Co.		6	1	343 00	
13	Nufashion Stationery Co.		7	2	266 75	
13	Payroll		8	✓	150 00	
13	Salesmens Commission		9	✓	90 00	
16	Petty Cash		10	✓	9 15	
19	G M Corp.	Truck repair	11	✓	65 00	
20	Sales Returns & Allowances	A Wilson refund	12	17	12 00	
20	Campus Supplies Co.		13	1	245 00	
20	Payroll		14	✓	175 00	
23	Freight Inward	B & O. Railroad	15	22	18 45	
27	Payroll		16	✓	190 00	
28	S. Smithfield		17	4	102 90	
31	Petty Cash		18	✓	8 72	
					3004 59	
					3045 97	
	Accounts Payable, Dr.			12	980 00	
	Office Expense, Dr.			25	220 00	
	Shipping Expense, Dr.			27	165 00	
	Selling Expense, Dr.			29	190 00	
	J. Wilson, Drawing, Dr.			15	235 00	
	General Ledger, Dr.			✓	1278 32	
	Cash, Cr.			1	3068 32	
	Purchase Discount, Cr.			21		
					3068 32	

C 3

Payment Journal

Cr Purchase Discount	Dr Accounts Payable	Dr Office Expense	Dr Shipping Expense	Dr General Expense	Dr Selling Expense	Dr J. Wilson Drawing	Dr General Ledger
							150 00
							120 00
							70 00
							250 00
		55 00	25 00			60 00	
							10 00
7 00	350 00						
8 25	275 00						
		55 00	25 00			70 00	
					90 00		
							9 15
			65 00				
							12 00
5 00	250 00						
		55 00	25 00		40 00	55 00	
							18 45
		55 00	25 00		60 00	50 00	
2 10	105 00						
							8 72
22 35	980 00	220 00	165 00		190 00	235 00	1278 32
22 35	980 00	220 00	165 00		190 00	235 00	1278 32

3045 97
22 35
3068 32
3068 32

P1

Purchase (Dr) Journal

Date		Account	Terms	L.F.							
Jan 19–	3	Campus Supplies Co.	2/10/30	1		450 00					
	3	Nufashion Stationery Co.	3/10/60	2		275 00					
	3	B. Richards Co.	2/30/90	3		150 00					
	3	S. Smithfield	2/20/30	4		400 00					
	10	Campus Supplies Co.	2/10/30	1		250 00					
	11	S. Smithfield	2/20/30	4		105 00					
	12	B. Richards Co.	60 day note	3		275 00					
	24	Campus Supplies Co.	3/10/30	1		560 00					
	24	Nufashion Stationery Co.	3/10/30	2		400 00					
	24	B. Richards Co.	2/10/60	3		350 00					
	24	S. Smithfield	2/20/30	4		475 00					
						3690 00					
						3690 00					
		Purchases, Dr		19		3690 00					
		Accounts Payable, Cr.		12				3690 00			

S1

Sales (Cr) Journal

Date		Account	Terms	L.F.							
Jan 19–	5	R.H. Macy & Co.	8/10/30	1		725 00					
	5	Arnold Constable Co.	8/10/30	2		400 00					
	5	E.&F. Office Supplies Co	3/10/60	3		200 00					
	5	Elegant Stationery Co.	2/20/60	4		350 00					
	11	R.H. Macy & Co.	8/10/30	1		1200 00					
	11	Ace Stationery Co.	2/10/30	5		150 00					
	11	E.&F. Office Supplies Co.	1/2 cash, 1/2 30 day note, 6%	3		250 00					
	11	Arnold Constable Co.	8/10/30	2		275 00					
	18	Arnold Constable Co.	8/10/30	2		225 00					
	18	R.H. Macy & Co.	8/10/30	1		550 00					
	18	Elegant Stationery Co.	2/20/30	4		175 00					
	18	E.&F. Office Supplies Co.	3/10/30	3		450 00					
						4950 00					
						4950 00					
		Accounts Receivable, Dr.		3		4950 00					
		Sales, Cr.		16				4950 00			

General Journal

J^1

Dr. Accounts Payable	Dr. General Ledger	January 2, 19–	L.F.	Cr. General Ledger	Cr. Accounts Receivable
	1000 00	Inventory	5		
		J. Wilson Capital	14	1000 00	
		Investment			
		Jan. 8.			
	1000 00	Delivery Equipment	9		
		Notes Payable	13	1000 00	
		Purchased G.W. Truck & gave			
		30 day 6% note to the			
		Commercial Credit Corp.			
		Jan. 9			
	70 00	Sales Returns & Allowances	17		
		R.H. Macy & Co.	1		70 00
		Bill of Jan. 5.			
		Jan. 10			
100 00		Campus Supplies Co.	1		
		Purchase Ret. & Allow.	20	100 00	
		Bill of Jan. 3.			
		Jan. 13			
	125 00	Notes Receivable	4		
		C. & F. Office Supplies Co.	3		125 00
		60 day note in full of 1/11			
		Jan. 13			
275 00		B. Richards	3		
		Notes Payable	13	275 00	
		60 day note in full of 1/12			
		Jan. 15			
	194 00	Notes Receivable	4		
	6 00	Sales Discount	18		
		C. & F. Office Supplies Co.	3		200 00
		30 day-6% note in full of 1/5			
375 00	2395 00			2375 00	395 00

J²

General Journal

Dr. Accounts Payable	Dr. General Ledger		L.F.	Cr. General Ledger	Cr. Accounts Receivable
1375 00	2375 00			2375 00	395 00
	250 00	Sales Returns & Allowances	17		
		R. H. Macy & Co	1		250 00
		Ret. from Bill of 1/11			
		Jan. 18			
	50 00	Sales Returns & Allowances	17		
		Arnold Constable Co.	2		50 00
		Ret. from bill of 1/11			
		Jan. 23			
400 00		S. Smithfield	4		
		Notes Payable	13	392 00	
		Purchase Discount	21	8 00	
		10 day - 6% note in full of 1/3			
		Jan. 25			
	343 00	Notes Receivable	4		
	7 00	Sales Discount	18		
		Elegant Stationery Co.	4		350 00
		30 day - 6% note in full of 1/5			
		Jan. 27			
	35 00	J. Wilson, Drawing	15		
		Purchases	19	35 00	
		Stationery taken from stock			
775 00	3080 00			2810 00	1045 00
775 00	3080 00			2810 00	1045 00
	775 00	Accounts Payable, Dr.	12		
	3080 00	General Ledger, Dr.	✓		
		General Ledger Cr.	✓	2810 00	
		Accounts Receivable Cr.	3	1045 00	
	3855 00			3855 00	

PC 1

Petty Cash Book

Date	Particulars	L.F.	Checks Drawn	Petty Cash Cr.	Office Expense Dr.	Shipping Expense Dr.	Selling Expense Dr.	General Expense Dr.
19— Jan. 13	Sup't, Superintendent			60		60		
	Carfare			5 00				5 00
16	Telegram			20				20
	Postage			35				35
	Carfare			2 00				2 00
	Carfare			1 00				1 00
16	Petty Cash		9 15	9 15				
			9 15	9 15				
27	Postage			08	08			
	Stationery + Supplies			2 64	2 64			
	Repairing autotruck			2 00	2 00			
	Repairing truck			4 00		4 00		
31	Petty Cash		8 72					
			17 87	17 87	4 72	4 60		8 55
			17 87	17 87	4 72	4 60		8 55
	Office Expense, Dr.	25	4 72					
	Shipping Expense, Dr.	27	4 60					
	General Expense, Dr.	30	8 55					
	Petty Cash, Cr.	√		17 87				
			17 87	17 87				

Cash (Dr.)

Date		Account, Cr.	Explanation
Feb	7	Sales	
	13	E. & F. Office Supplies Co.	
	13	R. H. Macy & Co.	
	14	Elegant Stationery Co.	
	14	E. & F. Office Supplies Co.	
	14	Notes Receivable	
	14	Interest Earned	
	17	Notes Payable	
	17	Arnold Constable Co.	
	18	Sales Discount	To correct error of 2/14
	21	Sales	
	22	Notes Receivable	
	22	Interest Earned	
	22	Notes Receivable	
	22	Interest Earned	
	24	Sears & Co.	
	24	Gimbel Bros.	
	25	Elegant Stationery Co.	
		Cash, Dr.	
		Sales Discount, Dr.	
		Interest Cost, Dr.	
		Accounts Receivable, Cr.	
		Sales, Cr.	
		General Ledger, Cr.	

C4

Receipts Journal

L.F	Net Cash (Dr.)	Sales Discount (Dr.)	Interest Cost (Dr.)	Accounts Receivable (Cr.)	Sales (Cr.)	General Ledger (Cr.)
	11213	21		231		1122
✓	248 57				248 57	
3	441 35	13 65		455 00		
1	667 00	58 00		725 00		
4	56 80	3 20		60 00		
3	436 50	13 50		450 00		
4	194 00					194 00
34	97					97
13	497 50		2 50	500 00		
2	200 00			200 00		
18	13 50					13 50
✓	246 00				246 00	
4	100 00					100 00
34	12					12
4	227 95					227 95
34	07					07
6	1239 70	25 30		1265 00		
7	1617 00	33 00		1650 00		
4	101 50			101 50		
	6288 53	146 65	2 50	4906 50	494 57	1036 61
	6288 53	146 65	2 50	4906 50	494 57	1036 61
1	6288 53					
18	146 65					
31	2 50					
3		4906 50				
16		494 57				
✓		1036 61				
	6437 68	6437 68				

Cash (Cr.)

Date		Account, Dr	Explanation	Check No.	L.F.	Net	Cash
Feb	2	Notes Payable		19	13		392 00
	2	Interest Cost		19	31		65
	2	B. Richards		20	3		22 83
	5	Diamond T Motor Corp.		21	32		100 00
	7	Notes Payable		22	13	1000 00	
	7	Interest Cost		22	31		5 00
	10	Payroll		23	✓		380 00
	10	N.Y. Edison Co.		24	✓		16 43
	10	Hanover Wrapping Paper Co.		25	✓		34 65
	10	Corrugated Box Co.		26	✓		46 35
	10	Longacre Press		27	✓		167 46
	10	Rent		28	23		150 00
	10	N.Y. Telephone Co.		29	✓		35 42
	11	Campus Supplies Co.		30	1		617 40
	12	Petty Cash		31	✓		5 90
	13	S. Smithfield		32	4		3 81
	16	Notes Payable		–	13	1000 00	
	18	R. Cox, Salesman		33	10		82 32
	19	Petty Cash		34	✓		8 60
	20	Diamond T Motor Corp		35	32		100 00
	21	Modern Stationery Co.		36	5		375 00
	21	Unemployment & Ins. Fund		37	35		12 60
	21	J. Wilson, Drawing		38	✓		125 00
	23	B. Richards		39	3		350 00
	23	Nufashion Stationery Co.		40	2		300 00
	23	Notes Payable		41	13		476 09
	23	Interest Cost		41	31		79
	24	Payroll		42	✓		420 00
	24	Elegant Stationery Co.	M. Murphy's note protested	–	4/3		101 50
	25	Campus Supplies Co		43	1		291 00
	25	R. Cox, Salesman		44	10		65 00
	28	Petty Cash		45	✓		4 70
							6690 50
		Accounts Payable, Dr.			12	1991 74	
		Office Expense, Dr.			25	256 84	
		Shipping Expense, Dr.			27	181 00	
		General Expense, Dr.			30	51 85	
		Selling Expense, Dr.			29	467 94	
		J. Wilson, Drawing, Dr.			15	335 00	
		General Ledger, Dr.			✓	3437 83	
		Cash, Cr.			1		
		Purchase Discount, Cr.			21		
							6722 20

C 5

Payments Journal

Cr. Purchase Discount	Dr. Accounts Payable	Dr. Office Expense	Dr. Shipping Expense	Dr. General Expense	Dr. Selling Expense	Dr. J. Wilson Drawing	Dr. General Ledger
							39200
							65
300	2583						
							10000
							100000
							500
		11000	5000		12000	10000	
				1643			
			3465				
			4635				
		3684			13062		
							15000
				3542			
1260	63000						
							590
710	1091						
							100000
							4000
							860
							10000
	37500						
							1260
						12500	
	35000						
	30000						
							47609
							79
		11000	5000		15000	11000	
							Q.R. 10150
900	30000						
					2500		4000
							470
3170	199174	25684	18100	5185	46794	33500	343783

669050
3170
672220

P2

Purchase (Dr) Journal

Date		Account	Terms	L.F.							
Feb 19—	1	Nufashion Stationery Co	3/10/30	2	435	00					
	1	Campus Supplies Co	2/10/30	1	645	00					
	7	S. Smithfield	2/20/30	4	350	00					
	9	Nufashion Stationery Co	3/10/30	2	300	00					
	10	B. Richards & Co	2/20/30	3	250	00					
	15	Nufashion Stationery Co	3/10/30	2	275	00					
	15	Campus Supplies Co.	3/10/30	1	300	00					
	15	B Richards Co.	2/20/30	3	175	00					
	21	Modern Stationery Co.	½ cash, ½ 30 day note	5	750	00					
	21	Acme Stationery Co.	½ 30 day note, ½ 60 day note	6	650	00					
	21	S. Smithfield	2/20/30	4	490	00					
	21	Campus Supplies Co	2/10/30	1	1450	00					
	21	B Richards Co	2/20/30	3	650	00					
					6720	00					
					6720	00					
		Purchases, Dr		19	6720	00					
		Accounts Payable, Cr.		12				6720	00		

S2

Sales (Cr) Journal

Date		Account	Terms	L.F.							
Feb 19—	3	Elegant Stationery Co	3/10/60	4	530	00					
	3	E & F Office Supplies Co	3/10/30	3	455	00					
	3	R H Macy & Co	8/10/30	1	965	00					
	9	E & F Office Supplies Co	3/10/30	3	235	00					
	9	Ace Stationery Co.	2/10/30	5	225	00					
	9	Elegant Stationery Co.	2/10/30	4	175	00					
	14	Sears & Co.	2/10/30	6	1265	00					
	14	Gimbel Bros	2/10/30	7	1650	00					
	20	R H Macy Co	8/10/30	1	625	00					
	20	Arnold Constable Co	8/10/30	2	265	00					
	20	E & F Office Supplies Co	3/10/30	3	320	00					
	20	Elegant Stationery Co	2/20/30	4	200	00					
	20	Ace Stationery Co.	2/10/30	5	325	00					
	20	Sears & Co.	2/10/30	6	1850	00					
	20	Gimbel Bros	2/10/30	7	2310	00					
					11395	00					
		Accounts Receivable, Dr		3	11395	00					
		Sales, Cr		16				11395	00		

SR 1

Sales Returns & Allowances Journal

Date		Account	Return from bill of	L.F.									
Feb '19	8	R. H. Macy & Co.	2/3	1		240	00						
	8	Arnold Constable Co.	1/18	2		25	00						
	8	Elegant Stationery Co	1/18	4		15	00						
						280	00						
						280	00						
		Sales Returns & Allowances, Dr.		17		280	00						
		Accounts Receivable, Cr.		3						280	00		

P.R. 1

Purchase Returns & Allowances Journal

Date		Account	From bill of	L.F.									
Feb '19	2	Campus Supplies Co.	1/24	1		75	00						
	2	S. Smithfield	1/24	4		120	00						
	8	Campus Supplies Co.	1/24	1		15	00						
	15	Nufashion Stationery Co	1/24	2		100	00						
	15	S. Smithfield	2/7	4		60	00						
	15	B. Richards Co.	2/10	3		75	00						
						445	00						
		Accounts Payable, Dr.		12		445	00						
		Purchase Returns & Allowances, Cr.		20						445	00		

J3

General Journal

Dr. Accounts Payable	Dr. General Ledger		L.F.	Cr. General Ledger	Cr. Accounts Receivable
		Feb. 2, 19-			
124 17		B. Richards	3		
	83	Interest Cost	31		
		Notes Receivable	4	125 00	
		E.&F. Office Supply note due			
		March 14.			
		Feb. 3			
485 00		Campus Supplies Co.	1		
		Purchase Discount	21	9 70	
		Notes Payable	13	475 30	
		10 days - 6%			
		Feb. 5			
	1275 00	Delivery Equipment	9		
		Diamond T. Motor Corp.	32	1275 00	
		Bought truck, terms $100.			
		on the 5&20 of each month			
		Feb. 13			
344 09		S. Smithfield	4		
		Notes Receivable	4	343 00	
		Interest Earned	34	1 09	
		Elegant Stationery's note			
		Due Feb. 24.			
		Feb. 13			
	475 30	Notes Payable	13		
	79	Interest Cost	31		
		Notes Payable	13	476 09	
		Renewed old note by new			
		10 day, 6% note			
953 26	1751 92			2705 18	

General Journal

Dr. Accounts Payable	Dr. General Ledger			Cr. General Ledger	Cr. Accounts Receivable
953 26	1851 92			2905 18	
		Feb. 14			
	100 00	Notes Receivable	4		
		Elegant Stationery Co.	4		100 00
		I. Murphy's note - 30 day			
		6% dated Jan. 25			
		Feb. 19			
	227 95	Notes Receivable	4		
	7 05	Sales Discount	18		
		E & F. Office Supplies Co.	5		235 00
		30 days - due 3/21			
		Feb. 19			
	220 50	Notes Receivable	4		
	4 50	Sales Discount	18		
		Ace Stationery Co.	5		225 00
		60 day - 6%			
		Feb. 21			
375 00		Modern Stationery Co.	5		
		Notes Payable	13	375 00	
		30 days - due 3/23			
		Feb. 21			
650 00		Acme Stationery Co.	6		
		Notes Payable	13	325 00	
		Notes Payable	13	325 00	
		30 day note due 3/23			
		60 day note due 4/22			
		Feb. 28			
	70 75	Selling Expenses	29		
		R. Cox, Salesman	10	70 75	
1978 26	2382 67			3800 93	560 00
	1978 26	Accounts Payable, Dr.	12		
	2382 67	General Ledger, Dr.	✓		
		General Ledger, Cr.	✓	3800 93	
		Accounts Receivable, Cr.	3	560 00	
	4360 93			4360 93	

P C 2

Petty Cash Book

Date		L.F.	Check Drawn	Petty Cash (Cr.)	Office Expense (Dr.)	Shipping Expense (Dr.)	Selling Expense (Dr.)	General Expense (Dr.)
Feb '17	7	Carfare		40				40
		Showroom repairs		3 20			3 20	
		Dinner for office girls		2 30 / 5 90	2 30			
	12	Petty cash	5 90					
		Window pane		2 00				2 00
		Carfare		1 40				1 40
		Car fare		3 20			3 20	
		Stamps		2 00 / 8 00	2 00			
	19	Petty Cash	8 60					
		Stationery		2 10	2 10			
		Stamps		2 00	2 00			
		Carfare		60 / 4 70				60
	28	Petty Cash	4 70	19 20	8 40		6 40	
			19 20	19 20	8 40		6 40	
	25	Office Expense, Dr.	8 40					
	29	Selling Expense, Dr.	6 40					
	30	General Expense, Dr.	4 40					
	1	Petty Cash, Cr.	19 20	19 20				
			19 20	19 20				

ACCOUNTS RECEIVABLE LEDGER

R. H. Macy & Co. (1)

19—						19—					
Jan	5	8/10/30	S1	a	725 00	Jan	9	Ret. bill 1/5	J1	a	70 00
	11	8/10/30	S1	b	1200 00		15		C2	a	655 00
	18	8/10/30	S1	c	550 00		18	Ret. bill 1/11	J2	b	250 00
Feb	3	8/10/30	S2	d	965 00		22		C2	b	950 00
	20	8/10/30	S2		625 00		28		C2	c	550 00
					4065 00	Feb	8	Bill 2/3	SR1	d	240 00
							13		C4	d	725 00
											3440 00

Arnold Constable & Co (2)

19—						19—					
Jan	5	8/10/30	S1	a	400 00	Jan	15		C2	a	400 00
	11	8/10/30	S1	b	275 00		18	Ret. bill 1/11	J2	b	50 00
	18	8/10/30	S1	c	225 00		22		C2	b	225 00
Feb	20	8/10/30	S2		265 00	Feb	8	Bill 1/18	SR1	c	25 00
					1165 00		17		C4	c	200 00
											900 00

E. & J. Office Supplies Co (3)

19—						19—					
Jan	5	3/10/60	S1	a	200 00	Jan	13		C2	b	125 00
	11	1/2 cash-30 d. note	S1	b	250 00		13	By note	J1	b	125 00
	18	3/10/30	S1	d	450 00		15	By note	J1	a	200 00
Feb	3	3/10/30	S2	c	455 00	Feb	13		C4	c	455 00
	9	3/10/30	S2	e	235 00		14		C4	d	450 00
	20	3/10/30	S2		320 00		19	By note	J4	e	235 00
					1910 00						1590 00

Elegant Stationery Co. (4)

19—							19—					
Jan	5	2/20/60		S1	a	350 00	Jan	25	By note	J2	a	350 00
	18	2/20/30	535-/350-/175-	S1	b	175 00	Feb	5	Bill 1/18	SR2	b	15 00
Feb	3	3/10/60	525 00	S2		530 00		14	By note	J4	b	100 00
	9	2/20/30		S2		175 00		14		C4	b	60 00
	20	2/20/30		S2		200 00		25		C4	c	1 01 50
	24	murphy's protested note	1531.50 / 2336.50 / 905.-	J5	c	10 1 50						626 50
						1531 50						

Ace Stationery Co. (5)

19—							19—				
Jan	11	2/10/30		S1	a	150 00	Jan	22		C2	a	150 00
Feb	9	2/10/30		S2	b	225 00	Feb	19		J4	b	225 00
	20	2/10/30	700-/375-/325	S2		325 00						375 00
						700 00						

Sears & Co (6)

19—							19—				
Feb	14	2/10/30		S2	a	1265 00	Feb	24		C4	a	1265 00
	20	2/10/30	3115-/1465-/1850-	S2		1850 00						
						3115 00						

Gimbel Bros. (7)

19—							19—				
Feb	14	2/10/30		S2	a	1650 00	Feb	24		C4	a	1650 00
	20	2/10/30	3960-/1650-/2310-	S2		2310 00						
						3960 00						

ACCOUNTS PAYABLE LEDGER

Campus Supplies Co. (1)

Date		Item	Ref		Amount	Date				Ref		Amount
Jan	10	Ret. bill 1/3	J1	a	100 00	Jan	3	2/10/30		P1	a	450 00
	13		C3	a	350 00		10	2/10/30		P1	b	250 00
	20		C3	b	250 00		24	3/10/30	1360-/200-/560-	P1	c	560 00
Feb	2	Bill 1/24	PR1	c	75 00	Feb	1	2/10/30		P2	d	645 00
	3	By note	J3	c	485 00		15	3/10/30		P2		300 00
	8	Bill 1/24	PR1	d	15 00		21	2/10/30	3665-/3205-/7450-	P2		1450 00
	11		C5	d	630 00							3655 00
	25		C5	e	300 00							
					2205 00							

Nufashion Stationery Co. (2)

Date		Item	Ref		Amount	Date				Ref		Amount
Jan	13		C3	a	275 00	Jan	3	3/10/60		P1	a	275 00
Feb	15	Bill 1/24	PR1	b	100 00		24	3/10/30	675-/400-	P1	b	400 00
	23		C5	b	300 00	Feb	1	3/10/30		P2		435 00
					675 00		9	3/10/30		P2		300 00
							15	3/10/30	1485-/1010-	P2		275 00
												1685 00

B. Richards Co. (3)

Date		Item	Ref		Amount	Date				Ref		Amount
Jan	13	By note	J1	a	275 00	Jan	3	2/30/90		P1	b	150 00
Feb	2		C5	b	25 83		12	60 day note		P1	a	275 00
	2	By note at P.V.	J3	b	124 17		24	2/10/60	775-/325-/500-	P1	c	350 00
	15	Bill 2/10	PR1		75 00	Feb	10	2/20/30		P2		250 00
	23		C5	c	350 00		15	2/20/30		P2		175 00
					850 00		21	2/20/30	1850-/850-/1000-	P2		650 00
												1850 00

S. Smithfield (4)

Date		Item	Ref		Amount	Date				Ref		Amount
Jan	23	By note	J2	a	400 00	Jan	3	2/20/30		P1	a	400 00
	28		C2	b	105 00		11	2/20/30		P1	b	105 00
Feb	2	Bill 1/24	PR1	c	120 00		24	2/20/30	285-/455-	P1	c	475 00
	13	By note	J3	c	344 09	Feb	7	2/20/30		P2		350 00
	13		C5	c	10 91		21	2/20/30	1830-/980-	P2		490 00
	15	Bill 2/7	PR1		60 00							1820 00
					1040 00							

Modern Stationery Co. (5)

Feb.	21	By note	J4 a	375 00	Feb.	21	½ cash ½ 30 d. note	P2 a	750 00
	21		C5 a	375 00					
				750 00					

Ace Stationery Co. (6)

Feb.	21	By note	J4 a	650 00	Feb.	21	½ 30 d. note ½ 60 d. note	P2 a	650 00

GENERAL LEDGER

Cash (1)

Jan.	31	8928.05 / 304.97 / 5882.08	C2	8928 05	Jan.	31		C3	3045 97
Feb.	28	15216.58 / 716.97 / 5980.11	C4	6288 53	Feb.	28		C5	6690 50
				15216 58					9736 47

Imprest Petty Cash (2)

Jan.	11		C3	10 00

Accounts Receivable (3)

Jan.	31	4950- / 4100- / 850-	S1	4950 00	Jan.	31		C2	3055 00
Feb.	28		S2	11395 00		31		J2	1045 00
	24	16446.50 / 9806.50 / 6640-	C5	101 50	Feb.	28		C4	4906 50
				16446 50		28		J4	560 00
						28		JR1	280 00
									7846 50

Notes Receivable (4)

	19—								19—					
Jan	13	60d.– due 3/14	J1	a	125	00	Feb	2		J3	a	125	00
	15	30d.– 6% due 2/14	J1	c	194	00		13		J3	b	343	00
	25	30d.– 6% due 2/24	J2	b	343	00		14		C4	c	194	00
Feb	14	10d.– 6% due 2/24	J4	d	100	00		22		C4	d	100	00
	19	30d.– due 3/21	J4	e	227	95		22		C4	e	227	95
	19	60d.– 6% due 4/20	J4		220	50							

Inventory. (5)

	19—				
Jan	2		J1	1000	00

Office Furniture (7)

	19—				
Jan	3		C3	250	00

Showroom Equipment (8)

	19—				
Jan	3		C3	700	00

Delivery Equipment (9)

	19—					
Jan	8	G. M. Truck	J1	1000	00	
Feb	5	Diamond T motor	J3	1275	00	

R. Cox, Salesman (10)

	19—						19—				
Feb	18		C5	40	00	Feb	28		J4	70	75
	25		C5	40	00						

Accounts Payable (12)

19—					19—				
Jan 31		C3	980 00		Jan 31	3690—1335—1935—	P1	3690 00	
31		J2	775 00		Feb 28	19490—4340—	P2	6720 00	
			1755 00					10410 00	
Feb 28		C5	1991 74						
28		J4	1977 26						
28		PR1	445 00						
			6170 00						

Notes Payable (13)

19—					19—						
Feb 2		C5 a	392 00		Jan 8	30d.-6% due 2/7	J1 b	1000 00		
7		C5 b	1000 00		13	60d. due 3/13	J1	275 00		
13		J3 c	475 30		17	30d. due 2/16	C2 d	1000 00		
16		C5 d	1000 00		23	10d.-6% due 3/2	J2 a	392 00		
23		C5 e	476 09		Feb 3	10d.-6% due 2/13	J3 c	475 30		
			3343 39		13	10d.-6% due 3/23	J3 e	476 09		
					17	30d. City Trust, due 3/19	C4	500 00		
					21	30d. due 3/23	J4	375 00		
					21	30d. due 3/23	J4	325 00		
					21	60d. due 4/22	J4	325 00		
						5143 39 3343 39 1800 00		5143 39		

J. Wilson, Capital (14)

					19—					
					Jan 2	Investment	C2	5000 00		
					2	"	J1	1000 00		
								6000 00		

J. Wilson, Drawing (15)

19—						
Jan 27		J2	35 00		
31		C3	235 00		
Feb 28		C5	270 00		
			335 00		
			605 00		

Sales (16)

						19—							
						Jan.	31			C2		1 0 3 45
							31			81		4 9 5 0 00
											5 0 5 3 45
						Feb.	28			C4		4 9 4 57
							28			82		11 3 9 5 00
											16 9 4 3 02

Sales Returns & Allowances (17)

	19—							
Jan.	20			C3		1 2 00
	9			J1		7 0 00
	18			J2		2 5 0 00
	18			J2		5 0 00
					3 8 2 00
Feb.	28			SR1		2 8 0 00
					6 6 2 00

Sales Discount (18)

	19—								19—					
Jan.	15			J1		6 00	Feb.	18			C4		1 3 50
	25			J2		7 00						
	31			C2		2 2 5 40						
					2 3 8 40						
Feb.	19			J4		7 05						
	19			J4		4 50						
	28	396.60 −13.50 383.10		C4		1 4 6 65						
					3 9 6 60						

Purchases (19)

	19—							19—					
Jan.	31	3690.— −35.— 3655.—		P1		3 6 9 0 00	Jan.	27			J2		3 5 00
Feb.	28	10410.— −35.— 10375.—		P2		6 7 2 0 00						
						10 4 1 0 00						

Purchase Returns & Allowances (20)

						19–					
						Jan. 10		J1	100	00
						Feb. 28	545.–	PR1	445	00
									545	00

Purchase Discount (21)

						19–					
						Jan. 31		C3	22	35
						23	30.35	J2	8	00
									30	35
						Feb. 3		J3	9	70
						28	7125	C5	31	70
									71	75

Freight Inward (22)

19–										
Jan. 23		C3	18	45					

Rent (23)

19–										
Jan. 2		C3	150	00					
Feb. 10	300.–	C5	150	00					
			300	00					

Insurance (24)

19–										
Jan. 3	Mdse-Fire-10,000	C3	120	00					

Office Expense (25)

19—					
Jan	31		C3	220	00
	31	224.72	PC1	4	72
				224	72
Feb	28		C5	256	84
	28	489.96	PC2	8	40
				489	96

Shipping Expense (27)

19—					
Jan	31		C3	165	00
	31	169.60	PC1	4	60
				169	60
Feb	28	350.60	C5	181	00
				350	60

Selling Expense (29)

19—					
Jan	31		C3	190	00
Feb	28		J4	70	75
	28		C5	467	94
	28	735.09	PC2	6	40
				735	09

General Expense (30)

19—					
Jan	31		PC1	8	55
Feb	28		C5	51	85
	28	64.80	PC2	4	40
				64	80

Interest Cost (31)

	19–								
Jan.	31		C2		5 00				
Feb.	2		J3		83				
	13		J3		79				
	2		C5		65				
	7		C5		5 00				
	23		C5		79				
	28	15 56	C4		2 50				
					15 56				

Diamond T Motor Corp (32)

	19–										
Feb.	5		C5	1 00 00	Feb.	5	1375–300–1075–	J3	1 27 5 00
	20		C5	1 00 00					
				2 00 00					

Interest Earned (34)

					19–					
					Feb.	14		C4		97
						22		C4		12
						22		C4		07
						13	2 25	J3		1 09
										2 25

State Unemployment Insurance (35)

	19–					
Feb.	21		C5	12 60		

TRIAL BALANCE

January 31, 19—

L.F.

1. Cash	$5,882.08	
2. Imprest Petty Cash	10.00	
3. Accounts Receivable	850.00	
4. Notes Receivable	662.00	
5. Inventory	1,000.00	
7. Office Furniture	250.00	
8. Showroom Equipment	700.00	
9. Delivery Equipment	1,000.00	
12. Accounts Payable		1,935.00
13. Notes Payable		2,667.00
14. J. Wilson, Capital		6,000.00
15. J. Wilson, Drawing	270.00	
16. Sales		5,053.45
17. Sales Returns & Allowances	382.00	
18. Sales Discount	238.40	
19. Purchases	3,655.00	
20. Purchase Returns & Allow.		100.00
21. Purchase Discount		30.35
22. Freight Inward	18.45	
23. Rent	150.00	
24. Insurance	120.00	
25. Office Expense	224.72	
27. Shipping Expense	169.60	
29. Selling Expense	190.00	
30. General Expense	8.55	
31. Interest Cost	5.00	
	$15,785.80	$15,785.80

SCHEDULE OF ACCOUNTS RECEIVABLE

January 31, 19—

L.F.

2. Arnold Constable		225.00
3. E. and F. Office Supplies Co.		450.00
4. Elegant Stationery Co.		175.00
As per control		850.00

SCHEDULE OF ACCOUNTS PAYABLE

January 31, 19—

L.F.

3. B. Richards Co.		500.00
4. S. Smithfield		475.00
1. Campus Supplies Co.		560.00
2. Nufashion Stationery Co.		400.00
As per control		1,935.00

TRIAL BALANCE

February 28, 19—

L.F.

1. Cash	$5,480.11	
2. Imprest Petty Cash	10.00	
3. Accounts Receivable	6,600.00	
4. Notes Receivable	220.50	
5. Inventory	1,000.00	
7. Office Furniture	250.00	
8. Showroom Equipment	700.00	
9. Delivery Equipment	2,275.00	
10. R. Cox, Salesman	9.25	
12. Accounts Payable		4,240.00
13. Notes Payable		1,800.00
14. J. Wilson, Capital		6,000.00
15. J. Wilson, Drawing	605.00	
16. Sales		16,943.02
17. Sales Returns & Allowances	662.00	
18. Sales Discount	383.10	
19. Purchases	10,375.00	
20. Purchases Returns & Allowances		545.00
21. Purchase Discount		71.75
22. Freight—Inward	18.45	
23. Rent	300.00	
24. Insurance	120.00	
25. Office Expense	489.96	
27. Shipping Expense	350.60	
29. Selling Expense	735.09	
30. General Expense	64.80	
31. Interest Cost	15.56	
32. Diamond T Motor Corp.		1,075.00
34. Interest Earned		2.25
35. State Unemployment Insurance	12.60	
	$30,677.02	$30,677.02

February 28, 19—

L.F.

1.	R. H. Macy	$625.00
2.	Arnold Constable	265.00
3.	E. and F. Office Supplies Co.	320.00
4.	Elegant Stationery Co.	905.00
5.	Ace Stationery Co.	325.00
6.	Sears & Co.	1,850.00
7.	Gimbel Bros.	2,310.00
	As per control	$6,600.00

SCHEDULE OF ACCOUNTS PAYABLE

February 28, 19—

L.F.

3.	B. Richards Co.	$1,000.00
4.	S. Smithfield	780.00
1.	Campus Supplies Co.	1,450.00
2.	Nufashion Stationery Co.	1,010.00
	As per control	$4,240.00

Lesson XVIII

ACCOUNTING

The business executive has resources of various kinds which are directly under his supervision and management. It is his function to use these resources in such a manner that they may be employed most efficiently in the production of the service or commodity the business offers for sale.

Such control cannot be exercised intelligently unless the executive has at his command accurate and comprehensive information pertaining to every detail of his business. It is the duty of the accountant to provide a method by which this information is to be obtained.

It is just as essential for an executive to know the results of the past activities of the business, as it is to know the present. In this manner it will be possible for him to establish the probable results of the future.

Accountancy is therefore the method by which the executive compiles financial information from which he derives accurate and comprehensive information on all activities of the business. It is the duty of the accountant to exercise control over the assets, the liabilities, the earnings and the expenses of a business.

The results of the information so compiled is set forth in statements called the Balance Sheet and the Profit and Loss Statement.

It is customary to prepare these statements at the end of each year. However business conditions frequently necessitate the drawing up of statements semi-annually, quarterly, and occasionally monthly. Most frequently, however, semi-annual and annual statements are the rule.

A statement for the *calendar* year is one which begins January 1 and runs to December 31. A statement for the *fiscal* year runs from any day of the year to the end of one year from that date. For example, April 1 to March 31, of September 1 to August 31.

Inventory

At the end of each year it is necessary for us to prepare a list of all the merchandise on hand. This is called *inventory*.

Exercise 25:

John Jones
Trial Balance
Dec. 31, 19—

Cash	$4,000.00	
Accounts Rec.	2,000.00	
Notes Rec.	1,500.00	
Furniture & Fixtures	1,250.00	
Notes Payable		1,600.00
Accounts Payable		1,900.00
John Jones, Cap.		7,000.00
Sales		2,750.00
Purchases	3,500.00	
Expenses	1,000.00	
	$13,250.00	$13,250.00

REAL AND NOMINAL ACCOUNTS

There are three classes of accounts. Those representing assets and liabilities are called *real* accounts. If we were going out of business, all accounts representing salable items would be separated from all other accounts, these are the assets; all accounts representing *debts* of the business would be listed, these are the liabilities. All the remaining accounts would be listed separately; such as, (a) Purchases, Expense, Interest Cost, Rent, Sales Discount; (b) Sales, Purchases Discount, Interest Earned, etc. This last group of accounts (a and b) represent the "actions" of a business.

Let us consider the Sales account. This account merely represents a *record* of the sales *activity*. Could we sell the activity represented by this account? Of course, not. Sales is a record of what we *did,* not what we *have* or what we *owe*. This *activity* group of accounts are called *nominal* accounts. They represent the income (group a), and the cost of doing business (group b) of the business.

The third group is called the Proprietorship accounts, such as the capital and drawing accounts.

The *real* accounts (assets and liabilities) and the proprietorship accounts make up the Balance Sheet. The *nominal* accounts (cost and income accounts) make up the Profit and Loss Statement.

In order to make the Balance Sheet or Profit and Loss Statement, it is necessary to have complete records of every detail of our business. The Trial Balance has all these figures. Therefore all statements are made from the Trial Balance. To prepare the Trial Balance for these statements, write the letter "R" to the left of each real account in the Trial Balance; the letter "N" to the left of each nominal account, and the letter "P" before each proprietorship account. As each "R" and "P" is listed in the Balance Sheet, draw a circle around the "R" or "P", thus $\circledR$, $\circledP$; do the same with "N" when making the Profit and Loss Statement. In this manner we will avoid omitting any account from these statements.

BALANCE SHEET

The Balance Sheet is a statement which sets forth all the assets and liabilities of a business. The difference between these assets and liabilities results in the net worth (Proprietorship) of the business. This statement is also referred to as a "Statement of Assets and Liabilities."

BALANCE SHEET EQUATION

Assets equals Proprietorship

$$A = P \text{ (Net Worth)}$$

If the proprietor invests $1000 in cash in the business, the business is worth $1000.

$$A = P$$
$$\$1000 = \$1000$$

If he then borrows $500 in cash, his assets amount to $1500; his liabilities amount to $500, and his proprietorship still remains at $1000, because the net worth of the business has not changed. Thus:

$$A = L + P$$
$$\$1500 \text{ (\$1000 invested} + \$500 \text{ borrowed)} = \$500 \text{ (the debt)}$$
$$+ \$1000 \text{ (investment)}$$

The Balance Sheet Statement consists of placing the assets on one side, and the liabilities and proprietorship on the other side. The total of each side will be the same as illustrated in the above computation.

Given the following Trial Balance, prepare the Balance Sheet and the Profit and Loss Statement:

William Smith
Trial Balance
Dec. 31, 19—

Cash	$800.00	
Accounts Receivable	500.00	
Notes Receivable	900.00	
Machinery	800.00	
Furniture and Fixtures	400.00	
Accounts Payable		550.00
Notes Payable		750.00
William Smith, Capital		3,000.00
Sales		1,000.00
Purchases	1,800.00	
Expenses	100.000	
	$5,300.00	$5,300.00

Inventory on hand $1,200

The letter N will be placed before the Sales, Purchases, and Expense accounts. The letter P (Proprietorship) will be placed before William Smith, Capital account, and the letter R before all the other accounts.

The Balance Sheet will appear as follows:

William Smith
Balance Sheet
Dec. 31, 19—

Assets		*Liabilities*	
Cash	$800.00	Accounts Payable	550.00
Accounts Rec.	500.00	Notes Payable	750.00
Notes Rec.	900.00		
Inventory	1.200.00	Total Liabilities	$1,300.00
Machinery	800.00	*Proprietorship:*	
Furniture, Fixtures	400.00	William Smith, Capital	3,300.00
Total Assets	$4,600.00		$4,600.00

PROFIT AND LOSS STATEMENT

Do not refer to the Trial Balance for the figures in the following statement:

PROFIT AND LOSS STATEMENT

Sales (Selling Price of Goods Sold)	$1000
Cost of Goods Sold	600
Gross Profit	400
Expenses	100
Net Profit	$300

This is simple arithmetic.

Gross Profit = Selling Price minus Cost

Net Profit = Gross Profit minus Expenses

How to find the Cost of Goods Sold:

We have no account called Cost of Goods Sold. We must compute it.

The goods sold is no longer in our business, it is *missing*. Referring to the above Profit and Loss Statement, if we bought $1800 worth of merchandise during the year and had $1200 worth of merchandise on hand at the end of the year, we would be *missing* $600 worth of merchandise. Since the Purchases account represents the cost of the goods bought, and the Inventory (goods on hand) is figured at cost, the difference between the two is the *cost* of goods *missing* (cost of goods sold).

Form:

Cost of Goods Sold:		
Purchases	$1300	
Less New Inventory	700	
Cost of Goods Sold		$600

Now, referring to the Trial Balance given in this lesson, we will make the following Profit and Loss Statement:

William Smith
Profit and Loss Statement
December 31, 19—

Sales		$1000
Cost of Goods Sold:		
Purchases	1800	
Less New Inventory	1200	
	———	
Cost of Goods Sold		600
		———
Gross Trading Profit		400
Expenses		100
		———
Net Profit		300

Since the Balance Sheet must reflect the profit for the year, we must revise the proprietorship section and the Balance Sheet will appear as follows:

William Smith
Balance Sheet
December 31, 19—

Assets		*Liabilities*		
Cash	$ 800	Accounts Payable		$ 550
Accounts Receivable	500	Notes Payable		750
Notes Receivable	900	Total Liabilities		1300
Inventory	1200	*Proprietorship:*		
Machinery	800	William Smith, Cap.	3000	
Furniture & Fixtures	400	Profit	300	3300
	———			———
Total Assets	$4600			$4600

Exercise 26:

Using the Trial Balance of January 31 in Lesson XVII prepare a Balance sheet and Profit and Loss Statement. New Inventory $3500.

Solution:

J. Wilson
Balance Sheet
January 31, 19—

Assets

Cash	$5,882.08
Petty Cash	10.00
Accounts Receivable	850.00
Notes Receivable	662.00
Inventory	3,500.00
Office Furniture	250.00
Showroom Equipment	700.00
Delivery Equipment	1,000.00
Total Assets	$12,854.08

Liabilities

Accounts Payable			$1,935.00
Notes Payable			2,667.00
Total Liabilities			4,602.00
Proprietorship:			
J. Wilson, Cap.		6,000.00	
Profit	2,522.08		
Less:			
J. Wilson, Dr.	270.00	2,252.08	8,252.08
			$12,854.08

J. Wilson
Profit & Loss Statement
January 31, 19—

SALES		$5,053.45	
Less Sales Returns & Allow.	$382.00		
Sales Discount	238.40	620.40	
Net Sales			$4,433.05
COST OF GOODS SOLD			
Inventory beginning of year		$1,000.00	
Purchases	$3,655.00		
Less Purchases Returns & Allow. $100.00			
Less Purchase Discount	30.35	130.35	3,524.65
Freight Inward			18.45
Total		$4,543.10	
Less New Inventory		$3,500.00	
Cost of goods Sold			$1,043.10
GROSS TRADING PROFIT			$3,389.95
EXPENSES			
Rent		150.00	
Insurance		120.00	
Office Expense		224.72	
Shipping Expense		169.60	
Selling Expense		190.00	
General Expense		8.55	
Total Expense			$862.87
OPERATING PROFIT			$2,527.08
DEDUCTIONS FROM INCOME			
Interest Cost			5.00
NET PROFIT			$2,522.08

In the Balance Sheet, observe:

1. New Inventory is placed directly under Notes Receivable.

2. The proprietor's drawing is deducted from profit in order to obtain the increase in net worth.

In the Profit and Loss Statement, observe:

1. Deduct Sales Returns & Allowances, and Sales Discount from Sales to obtain the Net Sales.

2. Deduct Purchase Returns & Allowances, and Purchase Discount from Purchases to obtain the Net Purchases.

3. Old Inventory must be added to Purchases in order to ascertain the total cost of the goods to be accounted for.

4. Freight-Inward is a cost of the goods purchased, hence it is added to Purchases.

5. If we were to have Interest Earned in this exercise, we would need a new section called OTHER INCOME. Interest Earned would be listed here. All Income except Sales is listed in this section, such as Interest on Bonds, profits from investments, special non-operating profits, etc. The total will be added to "Operating Profit."

6. Interest Cost, as well as any non-operating loss such as losses on investments, cost of interests, etc., go into this section (Deductions from Income) of the Profit and Loss Statement.

7. The Net Profit in both Statements must agree.

For additional drill, we suggest that the student go back to any Trial Balance of any of the foregoing exercises and prepare a Balance Sheet and Profit and Loss Statement. Do not fail to provide the Inventory on hand in each case.

Summary:

Using the forms of Balance Sheet and Profit and Loss Statement as illustrated, it is essential to bear in mind the fact that Sales, Purchases, Expenses, and Earnings make up the Profit and Loss Statement. All other accounts make up the Balance Sheet.

In order to clarify this point, we suggest that the student bear this thought in mind: If we were going out of business we could sell any account that represents anything of salable value, such as Notes Receivable, merchandise, etc. We must also pay our debts. These accounts represent our assets and liabilities. Could we sell what is represented in our Sales Account, our Purchase Account, or the Expenses which our business incurred? Of course not! The latter accounts do not repre-sent things—they represent actions; hence they are used to ascertain our profit or loss.

All figures used in the statements are obtained from the Trial Balance.

The Inventory must be given in each case.

Lesson XIX

CURRENT ASSETS AND FIXED ASSETS

There are two main classes of assets—Current and Fixed. A Current Asset represents an asset which is either cash or is in the form of an asset which will be converted into cash within a brief period of time.

Examples: Cash, Merchandise Inventory, Accounts Receivable, Notes Receivable, Stocks and Bonds, etc.

A Fixed Asset represents a class of assets which we do not intend to convert into cash but has been purchased with the idea of its being used to conduct our business.

Examples: Office Furniture, Office Equipment, Machinery, Delivery Equipment, etc.

In considering the difference between these two kinds of assets, it will clarify the subject somewhat if we consider the Accounts Receiv-able or Notes Receivable account.

When we sell merchandise we expect to receive cash for it. It has become the custom, however, in business to promise payment either by note or by open account. This note or open account is an asset which we do not expect to remain as a note or open account permanently. Within a brief period of time we expect to receive cash for these assets. Therefore, current assets other than cash are temporary in nature and will be converted into cash in a short period of time.

On the other hand, the fixed asset account, such as Machinery and Office Equipment, represents assets which we intend to keep perma-nently as long as it is necessary to keep them in order to conduct our business. We surely do not expect to sell our office furniture because we are not in the office furniture business. We merely expect to *use* this furniture in order to conduct our business.

INVENTORY

In ascertaining the value of the merchandise on hand, the conservative accountant observes the following rule: *Cost or market price, whichever is lower.* If the market price is higher than the cost, we would be making a profit on our merchandise on which we would be compelled to pay federal and state taxes. However, we do not make a profit unless we have made a sale, therefore until the merchandise is sold, we must carry the merchandise at cost or market price, whichever is lower.

A statement showing the inventory, as of the end of the year, will be given to the accountant. He will record this inventory on our books.

ADJUSTING ENTRIES

In preparing the Balance Sheet it is essential that we look at our Trial Balance to see that every asset and liability is clearly set forth, which means, that every asset account must represent the *true* value of the asset, and that every liability represent the *true* liability. In addition, there are assets and liabilities which we do not keep a record of until they are paid, such as Interest Receivable, electric and telephone bills, etc. These items must be incorporated in our books.

DEPRECIATION

Let us consider the Office Furniture account.

Assuming that the office furniture is one year old. Is it worth as much now as when we bought it? Of course not. Wear and tear have depreciated it. It has lost value. How much? Experience has taught us the percentage of depreciation. The Federal Income Tax Department has established tables setting forth the percentage of depreciation on each kind of asset.

Referring to J. Wilson's business, let us accept the government's figure for the depreciation on office furniture.—10% per annum. The depreciation thus amounts to $25—(10% of $250). The Office Furniture account must be adjusted to reflect the depreciation. We must therefore decrease this account by $25 and record a loss—the depreciation—of $25 on this asset.

In view of the fact that we must keep a record of the cost of each asset, it is necessary for us to keep the asset account intact. The amount of depreciation will be recorded in *another* account called "Reserve for Depreciation on Office Furniture." The following entry will be made to adjust the Office Furniture account:

Depreciation on Office Furniture	$25.00	
Reserve For Depreciation on Office Furniture		$25.00

The Depreciation on Office Furniture account represents a loss to the business and will be included among the expenses in our Profit and Loss Statement.

The Reserve for Depreciation on Office Equipment will be listed in the Balance Sheet as follows:

Office Equipment	$250.00	
(less) Reserve for Depreciation on Office Equipment	25.00	
Net value of Office Equipment		$225.00

Therefore all Fixed asset accounts will be adjusted at the end of each year by debiting the depreciation account and crediting the Reserve for Depreciation of that asset. This entry will be recorded in the General Journal and will be listed under Adjusting Entries.

DEFERRED CHARGES

Whenever we buy anything to use, such as stationery, incidental supplies, wrapping paper, crates, etc., we debit the corresponding expense account. Thus our office expense account shows a total expenditure to date of $489.96. By looking into our supply closet, we find that we have not used up all the supplies. We take an inventory of these unused supplies and find that they amount to $30.00. The unused office supplies represent a deferred (left over) expense. Our Balance Sheet must show this left-over expense as a Deferred Charge and will list it among the assets. The entry will be as follows:

Deferred Charges	$30.00	
Office Expense		$30.00

The same adjustment will be necessary with the following accounts: Insurance, Shipping Expense, Selling Expense and General Expense.

If there are no unused items in any of these expenses, no adjustment will be necessary. However, if there are, the adjusting entry will have to be made through the General Journal by debiting the Deferred Charge account and crediting the respective expense account.

Adjusting Interest Earned

The Notes Receivable, which bear interest, earn interest daily. We do not record this interest, however, until the note is paid. At the end of the year it is necessary for us to calculate the interest earned on each note to date. The sum of the interest earned to date on all of the Notes Receivable is recorded as Deferred Interest. The following entry will be made:

Deferred Interest Earned	$20.00	
Interest Earned		$20.00

This entry will also be made through the General Journal.

Similarly, if there are any other earnings not yet recorded on our books it will be necessary to record them under Deferred Earnings. If we own real estate there may be rents due us. If we own stocks and bonds there may be interest or dividends owing to us. All earnings not on the books must be recorded.

Liabilities

There are two classes of liabilities—Current Liabilities and Fixed Liabilities.

A Current Liability is one representing a' debt which we must pay within a short period of time, such as Notes Payable, Accounts Payable, etc.

A Fixed Liability represents a debt which we owe but which will not have to be paid for a relatively long period of time. For example: Mortgages Payable and Bonds Payable.

Accrued Liabilities

Interest on notes payable not yet due accrues daily. We must ascertain the interest due on each note to date. Total these items and make an entry to record them as follows:

Interest Cost	$15.00	
Accrued Liabilities		$15.00

We must also list all unpaid bills and record same on our books— such as the electric and telephone bills, printer's bill and other miscellaneous bills which will be recorded only when they are paid. Total them up and debit the respective expense account and credit Accrued Liabilities.

Until we are fully assured that every account in the Trial Balance represents a true and accurate value, an adjustment will have to be made. Furthermore, each account must represent *one* of the following: an Asset, a Liability, an Expense or an Earning.

SUMMARY

To summarize, after a Trial Balance has been obtained as of the end of the year, adjusting entries must be made through the General Journal to correct all accounts which do not reflect the true and accurate value of the account it represents. These adjusting entries are made in the General Journal and posted to the respective accounts. A new Trial Balance will have to be made which we call the Adjusted Trial Balance. This Trial Balance will contain the true and accurate value of each account because the adjusting entries corrected any untrue values. From the Adjusted Trial Balance we make our Balance Sheet and the Profit and Loss Statement.

Exercise 27:

Make the following adjusting entries to the February 28 Trial Balance of J. Wilson, presuming it is dated December 31, 19—

Office Furniture	10%
Showroom Equipment	20%
Delivery Equipment	20%
Insurance Unexpired	$30.00
Office Supplies on Hand	$30.00
Shipping Supplies on Hand	$35.00
Interest Earned Accrued	$20.00
Interest Cost Accrued	$15.00

The following bills are owing and have not been recorded on our books:

New York Telephone Co.	$22.00
Consolidated Edison Co.	$15.00
Barry Press (for printing advertising circulars)	$40.00

Inventory on hand $4,265.00.

J5

General Journal

		L.F	Dr.	Cr.
Adjusting Entries – December 31, 19–				
Depreciation on Office Furniture			25 00	
Reserve for Depreciation on Office Furn.				25 00
Depreciation of Showroom Equipment			140 00	
Reserve for Dep. of Showroom Equip.				140 00
Depreciation of Delivery Equipment			455 00	
Reserve for Dep. of Delivery Equip.				455 00
Deferred Charges			95 00	
Insurance				30 00
Office Expense				30 00
Shipping Expense				35 00
Accrued Assets			20 00	
Interest Earned				20 00
Interest Cost			15 00	
Accrued Liabilities				15 00
Office Expense (N.Y. Telephone Co.)			22 00	
Office Expense (Consolidated Edison Co.)			15 00	
Selling Expense (Barry Press)			40 00	
Accrued Liabilities				77 00
Inventory, Dec. 31, 19–			4265 00	
* Trading Account				4265 00

* This entry will be fully explained in next lesson.

THE WORKING SHEET

It is customary for accountants to work on a sheet of analysis paper called the Working Sheet.

This paper will have ruling for the following: Name of Account, Trial Balance, Adjusting Entries, Adjusted Trial Balance, Profit and Loss, and Balance Sheet. There will be a debit and credit column for each money column.

The Trial Balance will be listed first. The adjusting entries will then be "posted" to the Adjusting Entries column as illustrated in the following Working Sheet. These two columns will then be combined into the next pair of columns headed Adjusted Trial Balance. The accounts in this last column are then divided into *real, nominal,* and *proprietorship* accounts. The nominal accounts will be extended into the Profit and Loss column, and the real and proprietorship accounts into the Balance Sheet columns. The *difference* between the debit and credit totals in the Profit and Loss column will equal the *same* amount as the difference between the debit and credit totals in the Balance Sheet column. This difference is the *profit.*

Exercise 28:

Make a Working Sheet using the February 28 Trial Balance of J. Wilson's Model Set, and the adjusting entries in Exercise 27.

(Solution for Exercise 28 appears on Pages 198 and 199)

Exercise 29:

Using the Working Sheet in Exercise 28, make the Balance Sheet and the Profit and Loss Statements.

(Solution for Exercise 29 appears on Pages 197 and 200)

Lesson XX

CLOSING THE BOOKS

At the end of each year it is necessary to "close the books," in order to start our new year with a clean slate.

What does this mean?

When we look at the Cash account, it tells us how much money we have *now*. If we were to look at any asset account, it would tell us the cost of that asset *from the very beginning* of our business up to the present. The liabilities accounts would show the money owing *from the very beginning* of our business up to the present. But when we look at the Sales account it tells us the total amount of Sales made for *this year* to date. All the nominal accounts will tell us the volume of their respective activity *for this year* to date. Hence the nominal accounts are kept *for the duration of one year only*. It is therefore necessary to "close them out" at the end of the year.

How is this done?

(Continued on Page 201)

J. Wilson
Balance Sheet
February 28, 19—

Assets

Current Assets:			
Cash		$5480.11	
Petty Cash		10.00	
Accounts Receivable		6600.00	
Notes Receivable		220.50	
Inventory		4265.00	
Total Current Assets			$16575.61
Deferred Assets:			
Deferred Charges		95.00	
Accrued Assets		20.00	
R. Cox, Salesman		9.25	
Total Deferred Assets			124.25
Fixed Assets:			
Office Furniture	250.		
Less Reserve for Deprec.	25.	225.00	
	700.		
Showroom Equipment	140.	560.00	
Less Reserve for Deprec.			
Delivery Equipment	2275.		
Less Reserve for Deprec.	455.	1820.00	
Total Fixed Assets			2605.00
Total Assets			19304.86

Liabilities

Current Liabilities:			
Accounts Payable		$4240.00	
Notes Payable		1800.00	
Diamond T. Motor Corp.		1075.00	
Total Current Liabilities			$7115.00
Deferred Liabilities:			
Accrued Liabilities			92.00
Total Liabilities			7207.00
Proprietorship:			
J. Wilson, Capital			6000.00
Profit	6702.86		
Less J. Wilson, Drawing	605.*		
Net Increase		6097.86	
Total Proprietorship			12097.86
			19304.86

*Observe how the drawing account is deducted from the profit and the remainder added to the capital account.

Solution for

J. Wilson

Working Sheet

Account	Trial Balance Dr.	Trial Balance Cr.	Adjusting Entries Dr.	Adjusting Entries Cr.
Cash	548011			
Imprest Petty Cash	1000			
Accounts Receivable	660000			
Notes Receivable	22050			
Inventory, Jan 1, 19–	100000			
Office Furniture	25000			
Showroom Equipment	70000			
Delivery Equipment	237500			
R. Cox, Salesman	925			
Accounts Payable		424000		
Notes Payable		180000		
J. Wilson, Capital		600000		
J. Wilson, Drawing	60500			
Sales		1694302		
Sales Returns & Allow.	66200			
Sales Discount	38310			
Purchases	1037500			
Purchase Returns & Allow.		54500		
Purchase Discount		7175		
Freight-Inward	1845			
Rent	30000			(g) 133
Insurance	12000		(d) 133	(d) 3000
Office Expense	48996		(g) 2200 / (g) 1500	(d) 3000
Shipping Expense	35060			(d) 3500
Selling Expense	73509		(g) 4000	
General Expense	6480			
Interest Cost	1556		(f) 1500	
Diamond T Motor Corp.		107500		
Interest Earned		225		(e) 2000
State Unemployment Ins.	1260			
	3067702	3067702		
Depreciation of Office Furn.			(a) 2500	
Reserve for Dep. of Off. Furn.				(a) 2500
Depr'n of Showroom Equip.			(b) 14000	
Res. for Dep. of Showroom Equip.				(b) 14000
Depr'n of Delivery Equip.			(c) 45500	
Res. for Dep. of Del. Equip.				(c) 45500
Deferred Charges			(d) 9500	
Accrued Assets			(e) 2000	
Accrued Liabilities				(f) 1500 / (g) 7700
Inventory, Feb. 28, 19–			(h) 426500	
Trading Account			(h) 509200	(h) 426500
Profit				509200
	3067702	3067702	509200	509200

Exercise 28:

Feb. 28, 19—

	Adjusted Trial Balance		Profit & Loss		Balance Sheet	
	Dr.	Cr.	Dr.	Cr.	Dr.	Cr.
	5480 11				5480 11	
	10 00				10 00	
	6600 00				6600 00	
	220 50				220 50	
	1000 00			1000 00		
	250 00				250 00	
	700 00				700 00	
	2275 00				2275 00	
	9 25	2353 11			9 25	231
		4240 00				4240 00
		1800 00				1800 00
		6000 00				6000 00
	605 00			121 11	605 00	
		16943 02		16943 02		
	662 00		662 00			
	383 10		383 10			
	10375 00		10375 00			
		545 00		545 00		
		71 75		71 75		
	18 45		18 45			
	300 00		300 00			
	90 00		90 00			
	496 96		496 96			
	315 60		315 60			
	775 09		775 09			
	64 80		64 80			
	30 56		30 56			
		1075 00				1075 00
		22 25		22 25		
	12 60		12 60			
	25 00		25 00			
		25 00				25 00
	140 00		140 00			
		140 00				140 00
	455 00		455 00			
		455 00				455 00
	95 00				95 00	
	20 00				20 00	
		92 00				92 00
	4265 00				4265 00	
	35674 02	4265 00	15144 16	4265 00	20529 86	670286
		35674 02		2184702		2052986
			670286			
	3567402	3567402	2184702	2184702	2052986	2052986

Solution for Exercise 29

J. Wilson
Profit and Loss Statement
February 28, 19—

Sales		$16943.02	
Less Sales Returns and Allowances	662.00		
Less Sales Discount	383.10	1045.10	
Net Sales			$15897.92
Cost of Goods Sold:			
Purchases		10375.00	
Less Purchases Returns and Allowances	545.00		
Less Purchase Discount	71.75	616.75	
Net Purchases		9758.25	
Freight-Inward		18.45	
Inventory January 1		1000.00	
Total merchandise to be accounted for		10776.70	
Less Inventory, February 28, 193—		4265.00	
Cost of Goods Sold			6511.70
Gross Trading Profit			9386.22
Expenses			
Rent		300.00	
Insurance		90.00	
Office Expense		496.96	
Shipping Expense		315.60	
Selling Expense		775.09	
General Expense		64.80	
Unemployment Insurance		12.60	
Depreciation on Office Furniture		25.00	
Depreciation on Showroom Furniture		140.00	
Depreciation on Delivery Equipment		445.00	
Total Expenses			2675.05
Operating Profit			6711.17
Other Income:			
Interest Earned			22.25
			6733.42
Deductions from Income:			
Interest Cost			30.56
Net Profit			6702.86

(Continued from Page 196)

We make closing entries in the General Journal at the end of each year and close out these accounts through a *Trading Account* which we must now open.

When is an account closed?

When the debit side of the account and the credit side of the account equal the same amount.

We reproduce the Trial Balance of Exercise 25.

John Jones
Trial Balance
Dec. 31, 19—

Cash	4000.	
Acc. Rec.	2000.	
Notes Rec.	1500.	
Furn. & Fix.	1250.	
Notes Payable		1600.
Accounts Payable		1900.
John Jones, Cap.		7000.
Sales		2750.
Purchases	3500.	
Expenses	1000.	
	13250.	13250.

Given:

Inventory	2500.

Since only the nominal accounts must be closed, let us consider the Sales Account. It shows a credit balance of $2750. To balance, it needs a debit of $2750. Let us close this into a Trading account as follows:

General Journal
December 31, 19—

Sales	2750	
Trading Account		2750 (a)

Let us do the same (debit a credit account, credit a debit account) with each nominal account.

Trading Account	3500	
Purchases		3500 (b)
Trading Account	1000	
Expenses		1000 (c)

Let us now post to these accounts.

Trading Account			Sales	
(b) 3500	(a) 2750		(a) 2750	2750 *
(c) 1000				

Purchases			Expenses	
3500 *	(b) 3500		1000 *	(c) 1000

* As per balances given in Trial Balance.

Observe how these entries balance off our nominal accounts.

Let us now look at our Trading account. Cost of doing business appears on one side, income on the other side. This would be entirely true if all the goods bought had been sold. Since we did not sell $2500 worth of these goods, it is necessary to offset this cost by placing $2500 on the credit side of the Trading Account because the purchases amount of $3500 appears on the debit side of the Trading account. The following journal entry is thus made to accomplish this:

Inventory   2500
    Trading Account   2500 (d)

Post this entry:

Trading Account	
b. 3500.	a. 2750.
c. 1000.	d. 2500.

Inventory	
d. 2500.	

The new inventory is incorporated into our books in this manner. (See footnote on page 195.)

Looking at our Trading Account now, we find that our income is on one side, our costs on the other. Thus the PROFIT is computed in the Trading Account.

We must now transfer this profit to our proprietorship account, because that account must show our true net worth at the end of each year.

To accomplish this, we close the Trading Account into the Capital Account; thus:

Trading Account   750
    John Jones, Cap.   750 (e)

Post this entry:

Our accounts now appear as follows:

Trading Account

b. 3500.	a. 2750.
c. 1000.	d. 2500.
e. 750.	

John Jones, Cap.

| | 7000.* |
| | e. 750. |

* As per balances given in Trial Balance.

Thus the closing entries accomplish the following:
1. Balance off all nominal accounts.
2. Incorporate the new inventory into our books.
3. Adjust the capital account to reflect the true net worth of the proprietorship.

Summary:

To close our books, we
1. Debit the Trading Account, and credit all nominal accounts which have a debit balance. (entry b and c above)
2. Credit the Trading Account and debit all nominal accounts which have a credit balance. (entry a)
3. Debit Inventory, and credit the Trading Account for the amount of the new inventory. (entry d)
4. Close the Trading Account into the capital account. (entry e)

Exercise 30:

Make closing journal entries to close J. Wilson's books.

Use the Adjusted Trial Balance in Exercise 28 since this Trial Balance shows the true status of J. Wilson's books.

Before making these entries observe:

1. That we have several new sales accounts—Sales Returns and Allowances, and Sales Discount. These two accounts must be closed into the Sales account first; then the Sales account, reflecting the true net sales, is closed into the Trading Account.

2. That we have several new Purchases accounts—Purchase Returns and Allowances and Purchase Discount. Close these into the Purchase account.

3. Freight-inward is a cost of merchandise bought and is also closed into the Purchase account. Then the Purchase account will reflect the true net purchases and will be closed into the Trading Account.

4. When all entries to the Trading Account have been made, the final entry to close this account will be the profit and will be closed into the J. Wilson, Drawing account because this drawing is made in anticipation of profits, and the drawing will be deducted from the profit to determine the net increase in proprietorship. The drawing account which will now reflect the net increase in proprietorship, will be closed into the capital account.

General Journal

J6

		L.F.	Dr.	Cr.
	Closing entries Dec. 31, 19—			
	Sales	16	1045 10	
	Sales Returns & Allowances	17		662 00
	Sales Discount	18		383 10
	To close Rets. and Allow. and			
	discount to Sales.			
	Sales	16	15897 92	
	Trading Account	36		15897 92
	To close Sales to Trading Account			

(Observe how the Sales Returns and Allowances, and the Sales Discount are first closed into the Sales account, then the *net sales* is closed into the Trading Account.)

Trading Account	36	2675 05				
Rent	23			300 00	
Office Expense	25			496 96	
Insurance	24			90 00	
Shipping Expense	27			315 60	
Selling Expense	29			775 09	
General Expense	30			64 80	
Unemployment Insurance	35			12 60	
Deprn of Office Furniture	37			25 00	
Deprn of Showroom Furniture	38			140 00	
Deprn of Delivery Equipment	39			455 00	
To close the Expenses to Trading Account					
Interest Earned	34	22 25			
Trading Account	36			22 25	
To close Int. Earned to Trading A/c.					
Trading Account	36	30 56			
Interest Cost	31			30 56	
To close Int Cost to Trading A/c					
Trading Account	36	6702 86			
J. Wilson, Drawing	15			6702 86	
To close Trading A/c to Drawing A/c					
J. Wilson, Drawing	15	6097 86			
J. Wilson, Capital	14			6097 86	
To close Drawing to Capital Account.					

		Purchase Returns & Allowances	20		545	00							
		Purchase Discount	21		71	75							
		Purchases	19					616	75				
		To close Rets. & All. and Disct.											
		into Purchases											
		Purchases	19		18	45							
		Freight-Inward	22					18	45				
		To close Freight-In to Purchases											
		Purchases	19	1000	00								
		Inventory (old)	5					1000	00				
		To close Inventory (old) to Purchases											
		Trading Account	36	10776	70								
		Purchases	19					10776	70				
		To close Purchases to Trading											
		Account.											
		Inventory (new)	5	4265	00								
		Trading Account	36					4265	00				
		To set up new Inventory.											

After these entries are posted rule off all the accounts that balance, and balance off all the accounts as per the following illustrations:

J. Wilson, Capital (14)

											19-								
								Jan	2	Investment	C2	5000	00		
									2	"	J1	1000	00		
								Dec	31	To close	J4	6047	86		
												12097	86		

J. Wilson, Drawing (15)

19-								19-						
Jan	27		J2		35	00	Dec	31	To close	J7	6702	86	
	31		C3	2335	00								
Feb	28		C5	2335	00								
Dec	31		J7	6097	86								
				6702	86						6702	86	

Sales (16)

19—					19—				
Dec	31	To close	J6	1045 10	Jan	31		C2	1 03 45
	31	To close	J6	15897 92		31		S1	4950 00
				16943 02					5063 45
					Feb	28		C4	494 57
				16943 02		28		S2	11395 00
									16943 02
									16943 02

Purchases (19)

19—					19—				
Jan	31	3690— 35— 3655—	P1	3690 00	Jan	27		J2	35 00
Feb	28	10,410— 35— 10375—	P2	6720 00	Dec	31	To close	J6	616 75
Dec	31	To close	J6	10,410 00 18 45		31	To close	J6	10776 70
Dec	31	To close	J6	1000 00					11428 45
				11428 45					
				11428 45					11428 45

Office Expense (25)

19—					19—				
Jan	31		C3	220 00	Dec	31	To adjust	J5	30 00
	31		P C1	4 72			To close	J7	496 96
Feb	28		C5	224 72 256 84					526 96
	28		P C2	8 40					
Dec	31	To adjust	J5	489 96 22 00					
	31	To adjust	J5	15 00					
				524 96 526 96					526 96

Interest Earned (34)

19—					19—				
Dec	31	To close	J7	22 25	Feb	14		C4	97
						22		C4	12
						22		C4	07
						13		J3	1 09
					Dec	31	To adjust	J5	2 25 20 00
				22 25					22 25

Trading Account (36)

19—					19—					
Dec 31	To close Pur.	36	10776	70	Dec 31	To close sales	36	15897	92	
31	To close	37	2675	05	31	To close	36	4265	00	
31	To close	37	30	56	31	To close	37		22 25	
31	To close	37	6702	86				20185 17		
			20185 17							
			20185 17					20185 17		

Summary:

To make closing entries, proceed as follows:

Step A—To close the (net) Sales account into the Trading Account:
  (1) Close Sales Returns and Allowances into the Sales account.
  (2) Close Sales Discount into the Sales account.
  (3) Balance Sales account, and close into Trading Account.

Step B—To close the (net) Purchases account into the Trading Account:
  (1) Close Purchases Returns and Allowances into the Purchases account.
  (2) Close Purchases Discount into the Purchases account.
  (3) Close Freight-Inward into the Purchases account.
  (4) Close (old) Inventory into the Purchases account.
  (5) Balance Purchases account, and close into the Trading Account.

Step C—Record (new) Inventory:
  (1) Debit Inventory (new), credit Trading Account.

Step D—To close all Expense accounts into the Trading Account:
  (1) Close all expenses accounts into Trading Account.

Step E—To close all "other Income" accounts into the Trading Account:
  (1) Close all "other Income" accounts into the Trading Account.

Step F—To close the Trading Account into the Drawing account:
  (1) Balance Trading Account, and close into Drawing account.

Step G—To close the Drawing account into the Capital account:
  (1) Balance Drawing account, and close into the Capital account.

II

BUSINESS ORGANIZATION AND PRACTICE

WHAT types of business firms are there? How is a typical business operated? What are the functions of each department of a business? The answers to these questions form an important foundation of knowledge which every student of business should possess. Such knowledge will provide you with a better understanding of your job, give your ambition wider scope, and help qualify you for a *better* job when the opportunity for advancement presents itself. It is therefore the purpose of this chapter to acquaint you with the essential principles of modern business practice.

TYPES OF BUSINESS CONCERNS AND THEIR FUNCTIONS

There are, of course, thousands of business concerns in the United States, large and small, supplying a seemingly endless variety of goods and services. To enumerate and describe them all might appear to be a very considerable task. Yet, despite their large number and diversity, they may be divided for purposes of study into a convenient number of distinct and familiar groups. Each of these groups of business concerns performs a special economic function; each contributes in a specific way to the production and distribution of goods and services. Let us see what these groups are:

a. Producers. Producers are the companies who extract and sell the raw materials used in manufacture; for example, iron and copper mining companies, growers of cotton, lumber, and so on. Farmers, too, are producers: they are producers of food, or of the basic ingredients used in the making of food, and may therefore be included in this economic group.

b. Manufacturers. There are several types of manufacturing concerns. The first type is the *converter*, who converts raw materials into finished materials which are not ready for use by the ultimate consumer, but are used in further manufacture. The second type is the manufacturer of consumer goods; his finished product is ready for consumer use. For example, the cotton mill *converts* raw cotton into textiles; the dress factory then buys these textiles for the manufacture of dresses. The dresses are ready to be worn; therefore it is a consumer product. Then there is a third kind of manufactured product—the kind designed as working equipment for factories and offices, such as machinery and tools, power and lighting equipment, office machines, and so on. In any case, a concern which fabricates any finished material or product, by hand or by machine, is known as a manufacturer.

c. Wholesalers. Wholesalers, or jobbers, are the intermediate link between manufacturers of consumer goods and the retail stores. They are located in the large cities and central trading areas. The manufacturer ships his product in large quantities to the wholesaler, who in turn distributes the product in smaller quantities to the retail stores in his territory. In many instances, however, manufacturers maintain their own local factory or distributing branches and sell their product direct to retailers, or to exclusive distributors, instead of through wholesalers. Manufacturers of automobiles and refrigerators generally adopt this latter method. Manufacturers of drugs, candy and cigarettes are among the users of the first method.

d. Retail Stores. There are five well-known types of retailers. The first is the neighborhood store, or "independent" store, specializing in a single line of goods, such as groceries, candy or drugs. Generally this type of store is managed and personally operated by the proprietor. Frequently, however, in big cities, it is a very sizable establishment with a full staff of employees. The second type of retail organization is the "chain-store," similar in operation to the neighborhood store, but consisting of branch stores in various localities, all under one ownershp and management. The third is the metropolitan department store, which is really a combination of many specialized stores housed in one building, each selling a different line of merchandise, but all controlled by a single management. The fourth type of retailer is the mail-order company, which sells goods to distant customers by means of periodical advertising, catalogs and circularizing. The final type of retailer is the exclusive distributor, or factory sales agency, which sells the products of only one or two manufacturers in a given line; a well-known example is the automobile dealer.

Thus far we have mentioned only the producers and distributors of material goods. Now we come to the special groups of business which serve all other business—and the general public as well. These are the groups which may be said to supply the motive power to our entire industrial and economic system:

e. Public Utilities. Typical public utilities are the electric companies, which supply light and power to factories, offices and homes; gas companies, and telephone and telegraph companies. Because such companies are organized to render services essential to the economic life of the public at large, their operation, financial structure and service rates are subject to a large measure of control by the government.

f. Transportation Companies. Transportation companies, or carriers, include the railroads, express companies, steamship, airplane and bus lines, local transit companies, and all other concerns engaged in carrying passengers and freight. Such concerns, in the public interest and welfare, are also, like the utilities, subject to considerable governmental regulation.

g. Banks. The banking system provides the financial "machinery" of the modern business world. Banks are a convenient depository for business funds; they facilitate the flow and exchange of credits; they provide checking accounts, collection service for notes and other instruments of credit, and loans for business financing. A special type of bank is the savings bank, the main function of which is to encourage thrift in small depositors and to invest the small savings of a community in sound interest-bearing bonds and building mortgages. Most depositors in a savings bank are wage-earners rather than business concerns.

h. Insurance Companies. Business concerns as well as individuals in private life are faced with many types of everyday risks. Protection against such risks is provided by insurance companies. Among the most common forms of insurance are fire, theft, workmen's compensation, personal injury, accident liability and life insurance. Insurance companies issue policies to the insured business concerns or individuals, providing for payment of specified sums in case of loss from a given cause. For this protection, the insured pays premiums to the insurance company at stipulated intervals.

Life insurance policies are issued by life insurance companies. They provide for the payment of a designated sum to a beneficiary in the event of death of the insured. Such policies, in addition, generally incorporate a personal savings feature: they accrue in cash or loan value and provide, if desired by the insured, an old-age retirement or pension fund.

There are two familiar types of insurance companies—the stock company and the mutual company. The *stock company* is owned by and operated for the profit of *stockholders* who receive annual dividends on their investments in the company; they are not necessarily policyholders. The *mutual company* is in effect owned by and operated for the profit of *policy-holders*; each receives a share of the annual profits of the company in the form of dividends, determined by the amount of annual premium which he pays for his insurance.

Most life insurance companies are mutual companies; most others are stock companies, although there is a growing number of "mutuals" in the general insurance field.

Insurance is sold either directly through an insurance company representative or through a "middleman" known as a general insurance broker or agency.

i. Service Companies. Among the major types of business is the group comprising the professional service, or brokerage type of concern. In this classification, we may include advertising agencies, real estate brokerage and management companies, and investment concerns as typical examples. Their function is somewhat like that of a wholesaler or retailer: the advertising agency is the middleman between the publisher and the advertiser; the real-estate company is the middleman between the builder or owner of property and the buyer or tenant; the investment concern is the middleman beween the company issuing stocks or bonds and the investor.

Service or brokerage concerns derive their profit from commissions and fees. Although their primary function is selling, the advisory service which they render their clients is frequently professional in character. Such service is based on long experience and specialized training and is often as valuable as the services of purely professional groups such as lawyers or accountants.

Another type of business service includes such activities as represented by laundries, contracting concerns, dry cleaning establishments, garages, and so on.

HOW IS A BUSINESS OPERATED?

The average business concern of any considerable size is divided, for purposes of efficiency, into specialized departments of work. The president, general manager, or proprietor of the business directs and co-ordinates the work of all these departments.

The departments most generally found in the average business concern are:

> The Purchasing Department
> The Receiving Department
> The Sales Department
> The Advertising Department
> The Stock Department
> The Factory Department
> The Shipping Department
> The Accounting Department

Let us now examine in detail the work of each of these divisions of business.

THE PURCHASING DEPARTMENT

The purchasing department buys all of the necessary materials, stock and equipment for a business concern. Upon the efficiency of this department—its judgment of quality, its bargaining ability, and its alertness to price and style trends—depends very considerably the profitable operation of the concern.

The head of the department is known as the purchasing agent, or head buyer. His is one of the most responsible executive positions in the firm. He must have broad experience in the line of business in which his firm is engaged. He must keep up to date on market conditions and must be able to appraise new styles and models with authority. He should be able, as far as possible, to anticipate price rises or decreases, and watch for opportunities to save money for his firm.

In the large organization there is generally a staff of assistant buyers who work under the supervision of the department head. In some cases, notably department stores and other large retail organizations, there are many special buyers, each of whom has an exceptionally complete knowledge of one or two particular lines of goods.

The principal duties of a buyer are to interview salesmen, inspect samples, and compile full information and prices covering all stock or equipment needed by the firm. In the large retail store, the buyers work closely with the Sales Department, in order to determine which retail items are most popular and sell most readily.

Generally, the Purchasing Department also buys the equipment and supplies necessary for the routine operation of a business, such as machinery, trucks, display equipment, office supplies and so on.

When stocks need to be replenished, or when a piece of equipment is needed, a requisition, or authorization to purchase, is sent to the Purchasing Department. The Purchasing Department then refers to its records for information on the sources of supply, latest prices and current varieties. Catalogs may be consulted. Or the supplying firms may be asked to submit quotations, or special estimates of cost if the item is to be manufactured to order. When the necessary information is in, and the buyer has decided where to make the purchase, the purchase order is made out and sent. A copy of this order is retained for the purchasing department's files; other copies are made for the receiving department, accounting department, and any other department to whom a record of the purchase will be useful.

When the order has been filled and shipped, an invoice is mailed in to the firm, and is routed to the purchasing department for checking of prices and terms. If approved, the invoice then goes to the Accounting Department for payment.

A position in the Purchasing Department is a desirable one because it offers the opportunity to learn an important branch of business and because it may lead to a position of high responsibility within the firm. Among the positions to be filled are those of secretary to the department head, purchase order writer, file clerk, typist and correspondent.

THE RECEIVING DEPARTMENT

All incoming stock, materials and supplies arrive at the Receiving Department. Here shipments are opened, checked for contents with a copy of the Purchasing Department's order, sorted and routed to the proper party, or stored with the Stock Department until needed. The arrival of each shipment is reported on special forms, sometimes called Receiving Tickets, to both the Purchasing Department and Accounting Department, so that the incoming invoice may be approved for payment. If there is any discrepancy in the goods ordered, or if there has been any damage in shipment, it is noted on the report so that a claim for adjustment can be entered at once.

THE SALES DEPARTMENT

The function of the sales department is to sell the goods or services of a business concern at a profit. Its principal duties are to supervise the work of salesmen, to plan general selling policies and to promote special campaigns. It keeps records of sales and of each salesman's expenses, orders and commissions.

Salesmen are paid in one of several ways: (1) salary (2) salary and commission (3) drawing against commission and (4) commission only. In some cases, especially where travelling is involved, they receive allowances for expenses, such as automobile costs, or railroad fares, meals, hotel rooms and entertainment.

The work of salesmen and of the sales department varies with the type of business. The factory salesman, or wholesale salesman, generally calls on his customers at their places of business to display his product and take orders, although frequently customers place orders by mail or telephone. Usually such orders do not call for cash payment; payment is made after receipt of an invoice. When the order is received, it goes to the Accounting Department for credit approval. If the credit information on hand is satisfactory, a copy of the order is passed on to the Stock or Factory Department to be filled. The Shipping Department then packs and forwards it and the Accounting Department mails the invoice to the customer. But if the credit information on hand is inadequate or unsatisfactory, the customer is expected to furnish more satisfactory information or to pay cash for his order.

The head of the Sales Department in any concern is, of course, the Sales Manager. He occupies one of the key positions in the firm, for on his experience and judgment, his inspirational qualities and enthusiasm, depends much of the progress of the business. Positions in the large sales department are numerous. In addition to the sales staff, there are positions for file clerks, tabulating machine operators, secretaries, stenographers, correspondents and typists, with a wealth of opportunity for learning a fascinating and lucrative branch of business.

THE RETAIL STORE

In the retail store and, in particular, the department store sales are handled differently. First, the majority of sales is made in the store. Second, although large stores have a great number of "charge-account" customers, the bigger part of its total sales is for cash.

When the customer makes a purchase in a department store, the sales clerk enters the purchase on a manifold sales pad which makes several carbon copies. One copy remains in the pad as a record of the clerk's sales. Another copy is placed in the package which the customer takes with him. If the purchase is to be delivered by the store, one portion of this copy serves as an address label for the package and the other portion serves as a guide for the stock and shipping departments in filling and packing the order. An additional copy is sent to the Accounting Department. If it is a charge purchase it is charged to the customer's account. If it is a cash purchase, it is entered in the record of total sales. In some stores, additional copies are made for the use of the sales and purchasing departments as a guide to what people are buying.

When a customer opens a charge account in a department store, he is given an identification card or coin which he shows to the clerk whenever he wishes to make a charge purchase. If the purchase is to be delivered, the number of the account is entered on the sales pad and the condition of the account is checked with the Accounting Department before the goods are shipped. If the purchase is to be taken out by the customer, the checking is done at once, while the package is being wrapped.

In addition to charge accounts, department stores also carry Installment, or Extended Payment Accounts. This is a convenient method of payment for purchasers of furniture, radio, refrigerators, jewelry and other expensive items. On such purchases a small initial payment is made and the balance is divided into a series of small weekly or monthly payments over an extended period of time, most commonly about one year.

In the smaller retail store, such as the neighborhood store, where the volume of sales is not large enough to require the attention of many departments, and where sales are almost exclusively for cash, the procedure, of course, is greatly simplified. The sales slip is made out with but one duplicate, which the proprietor retains for his own record. And in many small stores, the cash register alone provides all the sales record that is necessary.

THE MAIL-ORDER HOUSE

In the mail-order house orders are received, of course, entirely by mail. There are no salesmen; the medium of selling is the catalog, circular or periodical advertisement. The sales department and the advertising department function practically as one. As orders come in, clerks examine the items written on the order to see that catalog numbers and prices are correctly given. A copy of each order is then made and passed on for the attention of the stock and shipping departments. Copies of the order are also prepared for recording and analysis by the sales, advertising and purchasing offices.

The large general mail-order houses sell almost exclusively for cash, so that payment accompanies the order. But many mail-order houses also sell on the installment plan, so that a credit department is maintained for the collection of weekly or monthly payments.

THE ADVERTISING DEPARTMENT

Practically every business advertises in one form or another. Manufacturers of nationally distributed products owe their great mass sales to the powers of advertising. Advertising makes their goods known to the public and stimulates the desire to buy. The advertising department therefore plays an important role in the sales program of a large business concern. For that very reason, it is often organized as a special division of the sales department so that the work of both groups may be synchronized. The advertising department usually plans, writes and designs the sales promotion material used by the firm, such as sales letters, dealer helps, pamphlets, circulars and window displays. However—and this is a point worth remembering—the advertising department does not, usually, prepare the advertising which appears in magazines, newspapers or billboards, or which are heard on radio programs. This advertising is generally prepared by an advertising agency—an organization of expert planners and buyers of advertising, writers, artists, and other people especially trained in the making of advertisements and in placing them in the proper mediums. The advertising department does, however, work closely with the advertising agency, and all the work of the agency is subject to the supervision and approval of the advertising department. All orders for advertising go to the agency and all bills for advertising come from the agency. Thus the large advertiser saves a vast amount of bookkeeping detail and expense and at the same time is assured that his advertising money is being judiciously invested by competent specialists.

Several exceptions should be noted where the advertising agency is not an important factor in the advertising program of a business concern. One is the department store, where advertising must be prepared and published on short notice and where writers must be especially trained in the policies and merchandise of the store. Another exception, obviously, is the catalog mail-order house, where the chief selling effort goes into the making of the catalog, and where the thousands of detailed descriptions and illustrations of merchandise can best be prepared by the company's own specially trained staff. In both the department store and general mail-order house the advertising department looms large in importance and responsibility.

The head of the advertising department is the advertising manager. His job calls for broad experience in all phases of advertising work, as well as the ability to train and direct his assistants in the creation of advertising. He must prepare or assist in the preparation of advertising budgets and is responsible for the results obtained through advertising. His assistants comprise writers, artists, layout experts, and a general office staff of typists, checking clerks and filing clerks.

The Advertising Department of a large concern offers splendid opportunities to learn advertising and selling. Office positions in advertising agencies offer similar opportunities.

THE STOCK DEPARTMENT

The Stock Department is the division of a business concern in which materials, supplies and finished goods are stored. Its size and importance varies with the nature of the business. It may consist merely of a small room with a few rows of shelves, such as may be seen in the rear or basement of a small retail store. It may comprise an entire floor, as in the case of a wholesale business. Or it may, as in the case of a large manufacturer or department store, occupy an entire building known as a warehouse.

The work of the Stock Department is closely connected with that of the Receiving Department, Factory Department and Shipping Department. It both receives and disburses goods—in fact, it is more completely informed about the income and outgo of goods than any other department of the business. Accordingly one of its chief functions is the keeping of inventory records, which are records of stock on hand. This information is needed by the Accounting Department when it prepares statements showing the assets and liabilities of the business. It is also needed regularly by the Purchasing, Sales and Factory Departments, for on the size of inventories depends the amount of new buying to be done, the kind of selling effort needed, and the rate of production at which the factory is to operate.

In the large stock department there are positions for inventory clerks, calculating machine operators, typists and filing clerks.

FACTORY DEPARTMENT

In·a manufacturing business, the department where the finished product is made is, of course, the factory. The factory is in charge of a factory manager, superintendent or chief engineer. This executive is responsible for the efficient operation of his department and the uniform quality of the company's product. Sharing this responsibility with him are assistant engineers and factory foremen.

The finished products of the factory are stored with the Stock Department. When an order is received by the company, the Stock Department assembles the required items and sends them to the Shipping Department, which prepares the order for delivery.

Even in the factory department, seemingly remote from the office routine common to other departments of the business, there are office jobs to be filled. Factory reports must be made, information and correspondence exchanged and filed; hence, clerks, typists, and even bookkeepers are employed here as in other departments of business.

In the electric or gas company, the production department is centered in the power plants and service lines. The railroad company does not generally have either a factory or production department, but instead the railroad has its various operating departments—its traffic division, its track and signal maintenance, its operation of trains and stations. There are other types of business whose technical divisions might be difficult to classify, but generally speaking, we designate as the factory that department of a business which produces finished goods or services by means of power equipment, machinery or manual labor.

THE SHIPPING DEPARTMENT

The duties of the Shipping Department are to see that outgoing orders are properly packed, labeled and delivered. Retail store deliveries are generally made by the store's own trucks, and the supervision and daily routing of these trucks is one of the functions of the Shipping Department. Other types of business use express companies, freight, parcel-post and long-haul trucks. Whichever medium of delivery is employed, the responsibilities of all Shipping Departments are similar. They may be summed up as follows:

1. To determine the most economical and fastest methods of packaging and delivery.
2. To secure the lowest possible rates for shipments.
3. To verify and record all transportation bills.
4. To handle all necessary claims in case of damage or loss of shipments in transit, and to see that adjustments are made.

The large shipping department has positions for traffic clerks, claim and adjustment assistants, typists and file clerks.

THE ACCOUNTING DEPARTMENT

Every business needs to keep records of its transactions—its purchases, operating costs and sales; its payments and receipts; its profits and losses. The record-keeping division of a business is called the Accounting Department. This department has complete and up-to-date information about the financial condition of the concern—such as the amount of money on deposit in the bank; the current value of stock, fixtures and machinery; the amounts owed by customers and the amounts which the concern owes to others. All of this information is compiled from reports prepared by the other departments of the business. Periodically, the Accounting Department prepares financial statements summarizing the current worth of the company, which are furnished to the owners of the business, to banks and to credit associations.

Credit Division. Much business is done on credit. Goods are sold with the understanding that they are to be paid for after receipt of the invoice. Department stores, as we have seen, provide regular monthly charge accounts for customers. Purchases made by one business concern from another are payable within specified periods—10 days, 30, 60 or 90 days, or longer. Furniture, refrigerators, jewelry and so on, are generally sold on "installment" terms, which call for weekly or monthly payments over periods covering a year or more. The supervision of credit accounts is in the hands of the Credit Division of the Accounting Department.

Before credit is extended to a customer, approval must be given by the Credit Office. If the customer is new, his general credit reputation is investigated, either by inquiry from the references he has supplied, or through one of various types of "credit associations" to which business houses subscribe. These credit associations provide information about credit buyers for the common use of all its subscribers.

If the customer is not new, and has bought on credit from the same concern on previous occasions, the Credit Office simply refers to its own files to see if the customer's past bills were paid promptly and to determine if his current indebtedness is not excessive or past due.

Because credit work and collection work are so closely connected, the Credit Division is in charge of collections too. When payments are overdue, it sends out various reminders in the form of letters or statements, and makes every effort to bring the account up-to-date. Correspondents possessing great tact and persuasiveness are needed to carry on the work of credit and collection; their jobs carry considerable responsibility and pay good salaries.

Accounts Payable and Accounts Receivable. Bills incurred by a business concern are paid by the Accounts Payable Division of the Accounting Department. Incoming invoices are first checked by the purchasing department to see that the prices and terms conform with the original order. The receiving department notifies the Accounting Department that the goods have actually been received. With these O.K.'s in hand, the Accounting Department issues a check in payment, to be mailed on the date specified in the original terms of the purchase. There are, of course, other incoming bills for which purchase orders have not been issued, such as bills for rent, telephone, electricity, insurance and taxes. Such bills are approved by a responsible official and then passed on, like other bills, for payment.

Payments which come *into* the concern are handled by the Accounts Receivable, or Billing Division. When a sale is made by the firm, a copy of the order goes to this division. When the shipping department reports that the order has been shipped, a bill is made out. One copy goes to the customer, and another to the bookkeeper, who enters the amounts in his ledger. When payment comes in, the bookkeeper records the receipt.

Billing Procedure in the Department Store. The department store does not issue separate invoices for each credit sale. Instead, charges for each item purchased are itemized and printed directly on the customer's statement. All cash payments and credits are also posted directly to the statement. The statement is completely totaled at each posting, so that when the end of the month arrives there is nothing more to do but to mail it to the customer. A carbon copy of the statement is kept for the Accounting Department's ledger.

Installment Accounts. When a sale is made on installment terms, a ledger sheet is made out for the customer and the amount of his "down payment" is entered. Thereafter, as each weekly and monthly payment is made, it is credited on this sheet. Some concerns mail regular notices calling attention to the date when each payment is due; others provide the customer with a coupon book in which all the dates of payment are indicated, and the customer mails one of these coupons with each installment. Each coupon bears the customer's account number to insure proper crediting.

Billing Procedure in Public Utilities. The electric or gas companies issues many bills of comparatively small amounts. Once each month, meter readers examine the meters of the company's customers. They note the amount of electricity or gas consumed and record it in their meter books, in which there is a sheet for each customer. These are turned into the Billing Department, and clerks, operating special billing machines, compute the charges and enter them on bills. Each bill has two stubs; one stub is retained by the company and the other, attached to the original bill, is forwarded to the customer. The customer keeps his original bill for his own record, and detaches the stub and returns it with his payment. As each paid stub comes in it is paired with the stub in the company's file, thus assuring accuracy in crediting the customer's account.

Cost Accounting. In a factory it is necessary to know the exact cost of manufacturing a product so that a fair profit and selling price may be determined. The Cost Accounting Division assembles complete data showing the cost per unit of materials, labor, machinery, power and all other operating factors. This information is of vital importance to the factory manager, the sales manager and the purchasing agent.

Machine Operators. Modern accounting methods make increasing use of machines to save time and guarantee accuracy. There is a steady demand for operators of billing, tabulating, calculating and bookkeeping machines, and the student who wants to succeed in bookkeeping or accounting work should familiarize himself with the operation of these machines. In addition to machine operators, there are of course many other positions in the large Accounting Department—including bookkeepers, correspondents, filing clerks, stenographers and typists.

III

BUSINESS MATHEMATICS

By DAVID J. GLATZER

*Head of Clerical Department, Central
High School, New York City*

As business men and women, as consumers, workers and taxpayers, we experience arithmetic problems daily. The business man has to compute bills or prove extensions and totals. He has to figure mark-up and selling prices; sales clerks must compute the amount of purchases and make change; the manufacturer has to calculate factory costs; the investor figures cost of stocks and bonds, the yield on investments, etc.; the consumer figures purchases, taxes and budgets; in short, each one has his own peculiar problems which involve arithemetical calculations. In the civilization in which we live arithmetic problems are inescapable.

In this section the subject is organized according to business activities. The topics are arranged under the following titles:

1. Short Cuts.
2. Percentage.
3. Graphs.
4. Problems of the Retailer.
5. Problems of the Manufacturer.
6. Problems of the Commission Merchant.
7. Problems in Taxes.
8. Problems in Banking.
9. Problems in Insurance.
10. Problems in Investment.

Short cuts, percentage and graphs apply to all types of business and are therefore treated as separate units.

How to Solve Problems

1. *Interpretation*: Read the problem carefully. You must understand the problem before you attempt to solve it.
2. *List the facts* that are given.
3. *Determine* what you are required to find.
4. *Plan your solution* step by step.
5. *Prove* the result.

The following outline is suggested for arrangement of your work:
1. Facts given.
2. Information required.
3. Solution.
4. Proof.

A logical arrangement indicates clear thinking; therefore arrange your solution orderly and neatly.

Lesson I

SHORT CUTS

In this chapter short methods in multiplication and division are presented. They are valuable as aids in shortening and speeding up your arithmetical calculations. With practice, you will acquire skill in using them.

Vocabulary:

INTEGER—a whole number, like 1, 2, 3, etc.

FRACTION—a part of a unit, such as $\frac{1}{3}$.

NUMERATOR—the number above the line which indicates the number of parts.

DENOMINATOR—the number below the line which expresses the number of parts into which the unit is divided. In the fraction $\frac{3}{4}$, the numerator is three; the denominator is four.

DECIMAL—a fraction whose denominator is 10 or some power of 10. Example .06. The denominator which is omitted is indicated by the number of figures after the decimal point.

FACTORS—the multiplicand and multiplier.

PRODUCT—the result of multiplication.

DIVIDEND—the number which is to be divided.

DIVISOR—the number by which the dividend is divided.

QUOTIENT—the result of division.

ALIQUOT PART OF A NUMBER—a part by which the number is divisible without a remainder. For example, 25 is an aliquot part of 100 because the latter is exactly divisible by 25.

MULTIPLES OF AN ALIQUOT PART—numbers that contain the aliquot part without a remainder.

MULTIPLICAND—the number to be multiplied.

MULTIPLIER—the number by which the multiplicand is multiplied.

1. To multiply an integer by 10, 100, 1000, etc. Add as many zeros to the multiplicand as there are zeros in the multiplier.

$$765 \times 10 = 7,650$$
$$765 \times 100 = 76,500$$
$$765 \times 1000 = 765,000$$

If the multiplicand has a decimal, move the decimal point to the RIGHT as many places as there are zeros in the multiplier.

$$14.05 \times 10 = 140.5$$
$$14.05 \times 100 = 1,405$$
$$14.05 \times 1000 = 14,050$$

2. To multiply a number by 11, 101, 1001, etc.
First step: Multiply by 1, 100, 1000, etc.
Second step: Add the multiplicand to the product.

$76 \times 10 = 760$	$76 \times 100 = 7,600$	$76 \times 1000 = 76,000$
$76 \times 1 = 76$	$76 \times 1 = 76$	$76 \times 1 = 76$
$76 \times 11 = 836$	$76 \times 101 = 7,676$	$76 \times 1001 = 76,076$

3. To multiply a number by 9, 99, 999, etc., multiply by 10, 100, 1000, etc., then deduct the multiplicand:

$176 \times 10 = 1,760$	$176 \times 100 = 17,600$	$176 \times 1000 = 176,000$
$176 \times 1 = 176$	$176 \times 1 = 176$	$176 \times 1 = 176$
$176 \times 9 = 1,584$	$176 \times 99 = 17,424$	$176 \times 999 = 175,824$

4. To multiply a number by aliquot parts of 1, 10, 100, 1000, etc.
Problem: What is the cost of 32 yds. @ $62\frac{1}{2}\not\!c$ a yd.?

$$62\frac{1}{2}\not\!c \text{ is } \tfrac{5}{8} \text{ of } \$1.00$$
$$\tfrac{5}{8} \times \$1. \times 32 = \$20.00$$

By using the aliquot part instead of the given number, we simplify the work and frequently it becomes a mental problem. The aliquot parts which are commonly used are listed below. This table should be memorized in order that you may recognize the aliquot parts readily and use them efficiently.

Aliquot parts of 10

$1\frac{1}{4} = \frac{1}{8}$; $2\frac{1}{2} = \frac{1}{4}$; $5 = \frac{1}{2}$; $7\frac{1}{2} = \frac{3}{4}$

Aliquot parts of 100

Halves	*Thirds*	*Quarters*	*Fifths*
$50 = \frac{1}{2}$	$33\frac{1}{3} = \frac{1}{3}$	$25 = \frac{1}{4}$	$20 = \frac{1}{5}$
	$66\frac{2}{3} = \frac{2}{3}$	$75 = \frac{3}{4}$	$40 = \frac{2}{5}$
			$60 = \frac{3}{5}$
			$80 = \frac{4}{5}$

Sixths	*Eighths*	*Twelfths*	*Sixteenths*
$16\frac{2}{3} = \frac{1}{6}$	$12\frac{1}{2} = \frac{1}{8}$	$8\frac{1}{3} = \frac{1}{12}$	$6\frac{1}{4} = \frac{1}{16}$
$83\frac{1}{3} = \frac{5}{6}$	$37\frac{1}{2} = \frac{3}{8}$	$41\frac{2}{3} = \frac{5}{12}$	$18\frac{3}{4} = \frac{3}{16}$
	$62\frac{1}{2} = \frac{5}{8}$	$58\frac{1}{3} = \frac{7}{12}$	$31\frac{1}{4} = \frac{5}{16}$
	$87\frac{1}{2} = \frac{7}{8}$	$91\frac{2}{3} = \frac{11}{12}$	$43\frac{3}{4} = \frac{7}{16}$
			$56\frac{1}{4} = \frac{9}{16}$
			$68\frac{3}{4} = \frac{11}{16}$
			$81\frac{1}{4} = \frac{13}{16}$
			$93\frac{3}{4} = \frac{15}{16}$

5. Interchanging multiplier and multiplicand.
   Problem: Find 28% of $125.
   We may interchange the factors without changing the result.

$$125\% \text{ of } \$28.00 = \$35.00$$
$$(125\% = \tfrac{5}{4})$$

DIVISION

6. Division by 10 or by a multiple of 10. Move the decimal point in the dividend to the left as many places as there are zeros in the divisor.
   Problem: $6758 \div 1000 = 6.758$

7. Division by aliquot parts. Change the aliquot part to a fraction, invert and multiply.

Problem: Divide 150 by $8\frac{1}{3}$

$$8\frac{1}{3} = \frac{100}{12}$$
$$150 \times \frac{12}{100} = 18$$

EXERCISE 1

Make the following extensions mentally:

1.	60 hammers	@	.33⅓	11.	101 hammers	@	.49
2.	56 saws	@	.87½	12.	99 saws	@	.65
3.	88 locks	@	.62½	13.	16⅔ doz. bulbs	@	$1.20
4.	32 bolts	@	.06¼	14.	12½ doz. funnels	@	.96
5.	42 brushes	@	.83⅓	15.	99 knives	@	.27
6.	72 pliers	@	.37½	16.	25 strainers	@	.16
7.	36 planes	@	.50	17.	24 sockets	@	.06¼
8.	48 trowels	@	.25	18.	56¼ doz. locks	@	1.92
9.	74 knives	@	.99	19.	75 brushes	@	.40
10.	96 batteries	@	.06¼	20.	125 planes	@	.80

EXERCISE 2

Solve the following problems mentally:

1.	$ 21. ÷ .75	11.	300 ÷ 8⅓
2.	$200. ÷ 66⅔	12.	300 ÷ 37½
3.	$ 13. ÷ .50	13.	600 ÷ 75
4.	$150. ÷ 37½	14.	640 ÷ 66⅔
5.	$ 12. ÷ .80	15.	500 ÷ 6¼
6.	100. ÷ .33⅓	16.	400 ÷ 16⅔
7.	⅜ ÷ 9	17.	800 ÷ 66⅔
8.	36 ÷ .25	18.	900 ÷ 18¾
9.	60 ÷ .60	19.	490 ÷ 87½
10.	33 ÷ .75	20.	220 ÷ 91⅔

Lesson II

PERCENTAGE

To compare two things we must have a common measure. To compare quantities of liquids we use the units of liquid measure, pints, quarts, or gallons; to compare distances we use the units of linear measure, feet, yards, rods, or miles; to compare weights of articles we use the units of avoirdupois, ounces, pounds, hundredweight or tons, etc. To compare numerical quantities we use percentage, which means *hundredths*.

In business, comparisons are frequently made between sales of different periods, cost, expenses, gross profit and net profit. Percentage is a convenient method of expressing the relationship between numbers. It is used in every type of business and industry and is therefore presented as a special subject in this chapter. Skill in solving percentage problems is as essential as skill in the fundamental operations, addition, subtraction, multiplication and division.

What part of 28 is 7? The answer may be expressed as a fraction $\frac{7}{28}$ or $\frac{1}{4}$, .25, or as a per cent, 25%. It simplifies the comparison of two numbers or quantities when we use *hundredths* as a measure.

Each of the numbers used in the last problem has a name. The *base* is the number to which the other number is compared. The *percentage* is the number that is compared with the base. The rate or per cent indicates the relation between the *percentage* and the *base*. It usually has the "%" sign after the number. In the last illustration the base is *28*, the percentage is 7 and the per cent is *25%*.

Reading and Writing Per Cents

Is .15 more or less than 1? The decimal point indicates a quantity less than one unit. The decimal when used in connection with "%" expresses a quantity less than 1%; thus .5% is $\frac{1}{2}$ of 1%. .5 without the "%" sign means $\frac{50}{100}$ or 50%. Caution must be exercised in reading and writing fractions of a per cent.

Rule 1.—To convert a decimal to per cent form, move the decimal point two places to the right and use the "%" after the number.

Rule 2.—To convert a per cent form to a decimal form, move the decimal point two places to the left and drop the "%" sign.

Example 1. Change 35% to a decimal

$$35\% = .35$$

Example 2. Change .625 to a per cent

$$.625 = 62.5\%$$

Rule 3.—To change a fraction to per cent form.

Example 3. Change $\frac{73}{165}$ to a per cent

```
            .4424
   165 ) 73.0000
          660
          ---
          700
          660
          ---
          400
          330
          ---
          700
          660
          ---
           40
```

Rule 3.—To change a fraction to a per cent divide the numerator by the denominator and continue the division as far as required.

EXERCISE 3*

Read the following expressions as per cent:

1. $\frac{17}{100}$
2. .95
3. .9
4. .0775
5. $\frac{3}{4}$
6. .5%
7. $\frac{5}{1000}$
8. $\frac{1}{3}$
9. $.16\frac{2}{3}$
10. $\frac{7}{8}$

Change $\frac{42}{1.68}$ to a per cent

```
          .25
   168. ) 42.00
         336
         ---
         840
         840
         ---
```
$$.25 = 25\%$$

Rule 4.—To change a fraction to an equivalent per cent divide the numerator by the denominator.

* Answer to exercises and problems begin on page 305.

Write the following as a per cent:

1. .35	5. .8333	9. .0025
2. .12$\frac{1}{2}$	6. .875	10. 1.10
3. .065	7. .0625	11. 3.331$\frac{1}{3}$
4. .1525	8. .005	12. 1.625

Change the following to decimals:

13. 15%	17. 80%	21. 4.25%
14. 12$\frac{1}{2}$%	18. 93$\frac{3}{4}$%	22. 133$\frac{1}{3}$%
15. 75%	19. 13$\frac{1}{2}$%	23. 250%
16. 8$\frac{1}{3}$%	20. .5%	24. .005%

Change the following fractions to per cents: (Continue the division to the nearest thousandth)

25. $\frac{3}{4}$	29. $\frac{42}{168}$	33. $\frac{4.94}{26}$
26. $\frac{5}{8}$	30. $\frac{61.06}{172}$	34. $\frac{17.6}{44}$
27. $\frac{5}{6}$	31. $\frac{66}{165}$	35. $\frac{3.2}{9.6}$
28. $\frac{5}{12}$	32. $\frac{9.1}{13}$	36. $\frac{.20}{.75}$

PROBLEMS IN PERCENTAGE

To solve problems in percentage a knowledge of the fundamental principles of arithmetic is essential. Most of the problems are patterned after one of the following types.

Type 1.—What is 15% of $60.00?

Type 2.—What per cent of $60.00 is $9.00?

Type 3.—15% of what number is $9.00?

Type 4.—A number increased by 25% is 75. What is the number?

Type 5.—A number decreased by 10% is 54. What is the number?

When the type of the problem is determined, we group the given numbers accordingly and perform the operations which the solution of that type problem requires. These types and solutions are illustrated below.

Type 1.—Given the base and rate to find the percentage

Problem: A lamp is listed at $60.00 less 15%. What is the discount?

Given: The list price $60.00 (Base)

　　　　The rate of discount 15 % (Rate)

Find: The discount (Percentage)

Solution:

$$\begin{array}{r} \$60.00 \\ .15 \\ \hline \$\ 9.00 \end{array}$$

Explanation: Change 15% to a decimal and multiply

Proof: $\dfrac{\$9}{\$60} = \dfrac{3}{20} = 15\%$

Rule for type 1.　Base $\times$ Rate = Percentage

EXERCISE 7

Find the percentage at sight:

1.　80% of $45.
2.　75% of $240.
3.　$16\frac{2}{3}$% of $1800.
4.　$62\frac{1}{2}$% of $8000.
5.　$87\frac{1}{2}$% of $560.
6.　125% of $400.
7.　$112\frac{1}{2}$% of $1600.
8.　.5% of $660.
9.　$12\frac{1}{2}$% of $4000.
10.　$83\frac{1}{3}$% of $2400.

11.　27% of $3333.33
12.　45% of $2000.
13.　16% of $1250.
14.　66% of $1666.66
15.　56% of $125.
16.　32% of $250.
17.　36% of $2500.
18.　18% of $666.66
19.　40% of $750.
20.　35% of $6000.

Type 2. Given the base and percentage to find the rate.

　　　　$40. is what part of $120.?

　　　　What per cent of $120. is $40.?

　　　　$120. $\times$?% = $40.

　　　　The base is $120. The percentage is $40. Rate?

Solution: $40 ÷ $120

$\frac{40}{120} = \frac{1}{3} = 33\frac{1}{3}\%$

Proof: $120 $\times$ $33\frac{1}{3}$ = $40

Rule: To find the rate divide the percentage by the base.

Note: The number after "per cent of —" is the base.

What per cent of

1. $45.00 is $18?
2. $96.00 is $16?
3. $960.00 is $120?
4. $ .50 is $ .20?
5. $2.00 is $ .75?

6. $1.50 is $ .30?
7. $40.80 is $8.16?
8. $325.00 is $97.50?
9. $410.00 is $287.00?
10. $31.00 is $15.50?

Type 3. To find the base when the rate and percentage are given.

84 is $\frac{1}{3}$ of what number?

84 is $33\frac{1}{3}\%$ of what number? or ? $\times 33\frac{1}{3}\% = 84$

We are given the rate $33\frac{1}{3}\%$ and the percentage 84. The missing number is the *base*.

This is similar to type 2 of the problems in fractions.

Solution: $84 \div \frac{1}{3} = 252$ (in division by fractions, the denominator is the multiplier.)

Rule: The percentage divided by the rate equals the base.

Find the amount of which

1. $ 90.00 is 15%
2. 696.00 is 30%
3. 480.00 is $66\frac{2}{3}\%$
4. 735.00 is $87\frac{1}{2}\%$
5. 32.00 is $12\frac{1}{2}\%$
6. 96.00 is $6\frac{1}{4}\%$
7. 30.00 is 75%
8. 720.00 is 40%
9. 60.00 is 125%
10. 20.00 is $133\frac{1}{3}\%$

11. $ 45.00 is .5%
12. 90.00 is $\frac{3}{4}\%$
13. 777.00 is $.87\frac{1}{2}\%$
14. 20.00 is $\frac{1}{6}\%$
15. 6.90 is 23%
16. 7.20 is 18%
17. 168.00 is 42%
18. 10.80 is 12%
19. 16.50 is 33%
20. 11.20 is $6\frac{1}{4}\%$

Type 4. A. Per cent of Increase. A number increased by 25% equals 150. What is the number?

Solution: The missing number is the base or 100%. When we increase it by 25%, we get 125% of the number. Therefore the rate is 125%.

? $\times 125\% = 150$

$150 \div \frac{5}{4} = 120$

When the problem indicates an increase, be sure to add that increase and 100%.

Type 5. Per cent of Decrease.

A number decreased by 10% equals 810. What is the number?

Solution: The missing number is the base or 100%. Deducting 10% from the base we get 90%.

$? \times 90\% = 810$

$810 \div \tfrac{9}{10} = 900$

When the problem indicates a decrease, deduct the per cent of decrease from 100% and proceed in accordance with solution for type 2 problems.

EXERCISE 10

What number increased by

1. 25% of itself is 300?
2. 10% of itself is 242?
3. $33\tfrac{1}{3}$% of itself is 96?
4. 40% of itself is 9800?
5. 100% of itself is 36?

6. $62\tfrac{1}{2}$% of itself is 65?
7. $87\tfrac{1}{2}$% of itself is 900?
8. 5% of itself is 1050?
9. 30% of itself is 910?
10. 250% of itself is 1050?

EXERCISE 11

What number decreased by

1. 25% of itself is 9?
2. 10% of itself is 90?
3. $33\tfrac{1}{3}$% of itself is 120?
4. 40% of itself is 120?
5. 50% of itself is 45?

6. $62\tfrac{1}{2}$ of itself is 300?
7. $87\tfrac{1}{2}$% of itself is 14?
8. 15% of itself is 1700?
9. 30% of itself is 560?
10. $12\tfrac{1}{2}$ of itself is 56?

Five types of problems in percentage have been presented. To solve the problems that follow it is necessary to recognize the type. You will find it helpful to arrange your solution in this form:

a. Facts given.

b. Information desired.

c. Solution.

Each type of problem is illustrated below.

Type 1. Problem:—An investor realized a profit of 8% on his investment of $4850.00. What was his profit?

Facts given—Base, $4850.00; rate 8%

Find —Profit (percentage).

Solution —Base × Rate = Percentage.

$4850 × .08 = $388.

Proof: $\dfrac{\$388.}{\$4850.} = 8\%$

Type 2. Problem:—January sales were $10500. February sales were $787.50 less than January. What was the percentage of decrease?

Facts given—Base (January Sales).

Percentage (February decrease of sales).

Find —The rate (per cent of decrease).

Solution —Percentage ÷ Base = Rate.

$10500 ÷ $787.50 = 7½%

Proof: 7½% of $10500 = $787.50

Type 3. Problem:—The operating expenses of a retail store for 1965 were $10547. This is 26½% of the net sales. What were the sales?

Facts given—Percentage (operating expenses).

Rate (per cent of net sales).

Find —The base (net sales).

Solution —Percentage ÷ Rate = Base.

$10547 ÷ .265 = $39800.

Proof: .265 × $39800. = $10547.

Type 4. Problem:—A salesman's salary was increased from $60. to $70. per week. What was the rate of increase?

Facts given—Base (old salary).

Amount (new salary).

Find —The per cent of increase.

Solution —Increase ÷ Base = Rate.

The increase, $70. — $60. = $10.

The rate = $10. ÷ $60. = ⅙ or 16⅔%

Proof: .16⅔ × $60. = 10.00

$60. + $10. = 70.00

Type 5. Problem:—A suit marked $35. was reduced to $29.75. What was the mark down per cent?

Facts given—Base (original sales price).

Difference (marked down price).

Find —The per cent of decrease.

Solution —Decrease ÷ Base = Rate.

The decrease is $35. — 29.75 = $5.25

5.25 ÷ 35. = 15%

Proof: .15 × $35.00 = $5.25

$35.00 — $5.25 = $29.75

PROBLEMS IN PERCENTAGE

Solve the following problems,—and prove your results.

1. A wholesaler sold radios at $45. which was 40% less than the list price. What was the list price?

2. The 1950 census of a city was 165,440. The 1960 census was 173,-712. What was the rate of increase?

3. A retailer buys shirts @ $15.00 a dozen. He makes 40% gross profit on cost. What is the sale price per shirt?

4. In 1962 a building and lot were assessed at $18700, which represented an increase of 10% of the 1961 valuation. What was the assessed value in 1961?

5. After deducting a cash discount of 3% a customer paid $353.08. What was the invoice amount?

6. An employer cut all salaries 15%. One employee received $9.00 less because of this reduction. What was his salary before the reduction?

7. A lawyer's income in 1961 was 18% more than in 1960. If his income in 1961 was $7457.60 how much did he earn in 1960?

8. During March the operating expenses of a department store were 19% of the sales. If the expenses were $5440.84 what were the sales?

9. The sales were $4352 and the cost of sales, $2720. What was the per cent of gross profit on sales?

10. In problem 9 what was the per cent of the gross profit on cost?

11. A commission merchant made sales as follows:

>   1015 Bunches of Bananas @ $2.10
>   970 Bunches of Bananas @ $1.80
>   1425 Bunches of Bananas @ $1.50

His commission is $7\frac{1}{2}$% of sales. What were his commissions?

12. A salesman who works on a straight commission basis earned $3,600. If his rate is $7\frac{1}{2}$% on sales, what were his sales for the period?

13. Mr. Frohm sold a building for $126,500. The original cost to Mr. Frohm was $95,000. He spent $32,500 on permanent improvements and had a net income of $4,825 during the period of ownership. What was the per cent of profit or loss on cost in this transaction?

14. A and B are in the retail grocery business. A's average mark up is $33\frac{1}{3}$% on cost, while B's average mark up is 30% on sales. Assuming that each has net sales of $3000 for January, which one has a greater gross profit, and what was the difference?

15. Mr. Franklin purchased 100 motors for $10.00 less 5%. He sold 50% of them at a mark up of 50% on cost: 30% of the remainder at a mark up of 25% on cost and the rest of the lot at a loss of 15% on cost. What was his gross profit or loss on the entire lot?

Lesson III
GRAPHS

Graphs are used frequently in business and other activities to show essential data, because they convey the facts clearly, interestingly and convincingly. Statisticians and accountants use them to make comparisons, to show increases and decreases over a period of time, and to show component parts of a unit. The daily newspapers use them to show business trends. The purpose of this chapter is to explain how to read and construct three types of graphs:

> A—Circle graph
> B—Bar graph
> C—Line graph

Circle Graph.

Frank Payne earned $2400 in 1961. His living expenses were:

Rent	$ 720.00
Food	480.00
Clothing	408.00
Medical care	48.00
Recreation	168.00
Donations	48.00
Miscellaneous	168.00
Total	$2040.00

He deposited the balance in the savings bank. What per cent of his income did he spend on each item and what per cent did he save?

To find the per cent of income spent for rent, divide $720. by $2400, which equals 30%. Each item is divided by $2400 because this is the base. Since he spent $2040, he saved $2400 — 2040, or $360. The result of these calculations are tabulated thus:

Statement of Expenses and Savings

	1951	%
Rent	720.00	30.
Food	480.00	20.
Clothing	408.00	17.
Medical Care	48.00	2.
Recreation	168.00	7.
Donations	48.00	2.
Miscellaneous	168.00	7.
Savings	360.00	15.
Total	2400.00	100.

This information can be graphically expressed in a circular graph. Let the circle represent the entire income or 100%. A circle is divided into 360 degrees (written 360°) which are measured by an instrument called a protractor. We wish to show that 30% of the whole unit was spent for rent, 20% for food, etc. To construct the circular graph we perform the following calculations:

Step 1. Find what per cent of the whole amount is included in each part. This is shown in the tabulation. (Divide the amount of each item by the total.)

Step 2. Find the percentage based on 360°.

Rent ....30% of 360° = 108°
Food ....20% of 360° = 72°
Clothing ....17% of 360° = 61.2°
Medical care ...... 2% of 360° = 7.2°
Recreation .... 7% of 360° = 25.2°
Donations .... 2% of 360° = 7.2°
Miscellaneous ..... 7% of 360° = 25.2°
Savings ....15% of 360° = 54°

Total ... . 360°

Step 3. By means of a protractor, mark off the number of degrees on the circle.

Step 4. Label each part.

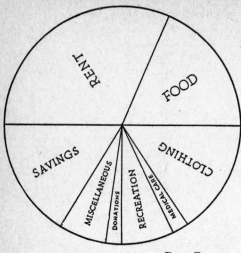

Circular graphs are used to show the relation of parts to the whole unit.

BAR GRAPHS

One of the commonly used graphs is the bar graph. Suppose you wish to compare the exports of the U.S. over a period of years, 1920-1930. This can be done very effectively by means of the bar graph.

The exports for the period were

	(in millions of dollars)		(in millions of dollars)
1920	$8,109	1927	$4,865
1922	$3,832	1928	$5,128
1924	$4,591	1929	$5,241
1925	$4,910	1930	$3,843
1926	$4,809		

The construction of the graph is as follows:

Step 1. Select a scale on which the quantities may be conveniently expressed and comparisons easily made. The largest number in the group is used as a basis for determining the markings on the scale. Exports were at the peak in 1920, when it reached a level of $8,109,000,000. Round off the numbers by using zeros for all digits following hundred million, in order to make the comparisons easy. The markings on the scale in the illustration are in units of billions. The bars may be made vertically or horizontally. In the illustration, horizontal bars are used.

Step 2. Indicate the scale of quantities in billions on the horizontal line, at the bottom.

Step 3. Indicate the years on the vertical line.

The space between bars should be at least as wide as the bars, to make the graph easy to read.

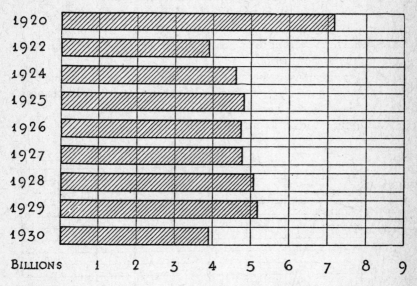

(Sometimes, the bars are arranged in order of size.)

LINE GRAPH

For showing increases or decreases or the trend of business the line graph is very effective. When the comparison covers a number of years, the line graph show when the changes were very marked either upward or downward.

Problem: The sales of the Art Metal Manufacturing Co. were as follows:

Year	Sales	Year	Sales
1948	$467,000	1953	$224,000
1949	480,000	1954	360,000
1950	275,000	1955	385,000
1951	248,000	1956	509,000
1952	197,000	1957	428,000

Construction of line graph.

Step 1. Select the divisions or scale according to the largest and smallest number. The best year was 1956, the poorest, 1952. The number of divisions should be reasonably small in order to simplify the graph. We can readily express all the amounts given by using 50,000 as the unit of the Scale.

Step 2. Show the scale of units (50,000—100,000—etc.) on the vertical line at the left.

Step 3. Show the years at the bottom, commencing at the left end with the earliest period.

Step 4. Directly above each year we place a dot on the level which indicates the amount of sales. When the number falls between the designated units, approximate the position.

Step 5. Connect the dots with a line.

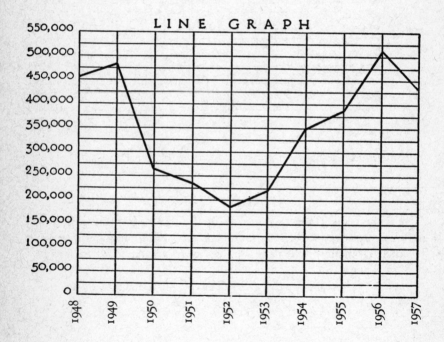

LINE GRAPH

PROBLEMS

Prepare a circular graph to show the following data:

1. Henry Philipps spends 28% of his income for rent, 20% for

clothing, 15% for recreation and health, 5% for education, 12% for miscellaneous items, 10% for life insurance, and saves the remainder.

2. The income from sales is applied as follows: 65% for merchandise, 10% for sales help, 5% for office help, 12% for expenses. The remainder is profit.

3. A town collected $150,000 for taxes. The expenditures are shown below.

Dept. of Education	$ 70,000.
Dept. of Sanitation	15,000.
Fire Department	8,000.
Health Department	6,000.
Roads	10,000.
Interest on Bonds	8,000.
Legal Department	5,000.
Executive Department	20,000.
Judicial Department	8,000.
Total	150,000.

Prepare a bar graph for the following problems.

4. Wolfsohn's Department Store sales for 1951 by months were:

Jan.	$150,000.	May	$175,000.	Sept.	$160,000.
Feb.	130,000.	June	160,000.	Oct.	180,000.
Mar.	160,000.	July	140,000.	Nov.	210,000.
Apr.	205,000.	Aug.	120,000.	Dec.	275,000.

5. The same department store showed gross profit for the same periods as follows:

Jan.	$45,000.	May	$54,000.	Sept.	$47,500.
Feb.	32,000.	June	52,000.	Oct.	60,000.
Mar.	47,000.	July	30,000.	Nov.	64,000.
Apr.	68,000.	Aug.	27,000.	Dec.	92,500.

6. Prepare a line graph for problem 4.

7. Prepare a line graph for problem 5.

8. The tabulation below shows the business index at the end of each month in 1951.

Jan.	101	May	110	Sept.	105
Feb.	108	June	107	Oct.	95
Mar.	107	July	107	Nov.	85
Apr.	108	Aug.	109	Dec.	78

Prepare a line graph.

Lesson IV

PROBLEMS OF THE RETAILER

Before the industrial revolution, people made or produced most of their needs in shelter, clothing and food for their own use. These needs were very simple and of limited variety. Today our wants and needs are as complex as life itself. It is the function of business to satisfy these varied wants and needs. The consumer purchases whatever he needs at a retail store. The retailer keeps a stock of merchandise on hand to be able to supply the needs of his customers. For this service he is compensated in the form of profits. The purpose of this chapter is to study the arithmetic problems of the retailer.

Vocabulary:

Study the following terms in order to understand the problems:

COST is the amount which the retailer pays for the merchandise.

SELLING PRICE is the price paid by the customer.

MARGIN or mark up is the difference between the cost and the selling price.

OPERATING EXPENSES include the expenses incurred in running a business, such as rent, taxes, light and heat, advertising, wrapping paper, twine, pay roll, etc.

NET PROFIT is the difference between gross profit and operating expenses.

CASH DISCOUNT is a deduction from the invoice amount which is allowed when the customer pays within the discount period.

DUE DATE is the day when an invoice is payable.

TERMS indicate the conditions of payment. It is shown in the invoice. The terms frequently used are as follows: 2/10 n/30 means 2% cash discount if payment is made within ten days; otherwise the full amount is due 30 days after the invoice date.

F. O. B. means freight is to be paid by the buyer.

R. O. G. means the discount and due dates are computed from the date when the goods are received.

C. O. D. means cash on delivery of goods.

C. I. F. means cost, insurance and freight are payable by the buyer.

K. D. means knocked down.

Finding the per cent of mark-up:

The mark-up per cent is usually based on selling price for several reasons.

First: the selling price is always known at the time of the sale whereas it may be necessary to refer to the purchase invoice or records to find the cost.

Secondly: expenses, gross profit and net profit are usually compared with sales.

Third: this agrees with sound business practice. However, since some retailers figure mark-up per cent on cost, both methods are illustrated. The problems indicate whether selling price or cost is used as the basis of comparison.

Finding the per cent of mark-up on selling price:

Example: What is the mark-up per cent on sales on an article that cost 65¢ and sells for $1.00?

Given: Cost and selling price.

Find: Per cent gross profit on sales.

Solution 1.
$$\begin{aligned} \$1.00 \quad &\text{selling price} \\ \underline{.65} \quad &\text{cost} \\ .35 \quad &\text{gross profit} \end{aligned}$$

2. $\dfrac{.35}{1.00} = \text{mark-up rate on sales.}$

3. $\dfrac{.35}{1.00} = 35\%$

Proof: 35% of $1.00 = $.35

Explanation:

1. The first step is to find the gross profit.
2. The second step is to form the fraction which indicates the mark-up rate on sales. The gross profit is the numerator and the *selling price* is the denominator.
3. The third step is to change the fraction to an equivalent per cent.
4. The fourth step is to prove the result.

Finding the per cent of mark-up on cost:

Example: What is the mark-up per cent on cost in the preceding problem:

Given: Cost and selling price.

Find: Per cent gross profit on *cost*.

Solution:

1. Gross profit .35

2. The mark-up rate on cost is $\dfrac{.35}{.65}$ or 53.84%

3.

$$
\begin{array}{r}
.5384 \\
65.\ \overline{)\ 35.00} \\
32\,5 \\
\hline
2\,50 \\
1\,95 \\
\hline
5\,50 \\
5\,20 \\
\hline
3\,00 \\
2\,60 \\
\hline
40
\end{array}
$$

Proof: 53.84% of $.65 = $.35

EXERCISE 12.

Fill in the blanks:

	Selling Price	Mark Up on S.P.	Gross Profit
1.	3.50	20 %	......
2.	24.00	$33\frac{1}{3}$%	......
3.	.65	20 %	......
4.	42.75	25 %	......
5.	9.00	$33\frac{1}{3}$%	......

	Cost	Mark Up on cost	Gross Profit
6.	95.00	15 %	......
7.	45.00	$33\frac{1}{3}$%	......
8.	180.00	$8\frac{1}{3}$%	......
9.	15.00	$16\frac{2}{3}$%	......
10.	22.50	40 %	......

Prove your results:

	Selling Price	Cost	Gross Profit	% Mark Up on Sales
11.	1.50	1.00	......	......
12.	12.50	11.25	......	......
13.	.72	.48	......	......
14.	1.60	1.20	......	......
15.	32.00	25.60	......	......

	Selling Price	Cost	Gross Profit	% Mark Up on Cost
16.	.44	.33	......	......
17.	1.50	1.20	......	......
18.	6.00	5.00	......	......
19.	1.68	1.47	......	......
20.	1.10	.99	......	......

2. *How to compute the selling price when the cost and mark-up per cent on cost are known.*

Example: Mr. Barnes operates on a mark-up of 25% on cost. Find the marked price of an article that cost $1.64.

Given: Cost and mark-up per cent on cost.

Find: The selling price.

Solution: 1. 25% of $1.64 = $.41
2. $1.64 + $.41 = $2.05

Proof: $\dfrac{.41}{1.64} = 25\%$

$$1.64 \overline{)\,41.00} \quad \begin{array}{r}.25\end{array}$$
$$\begin{array}{r}32\ 8 \\ \hline 8\ 20 \\ 8\ 20 \\ \hline \end{array}$$

Explanation:

1. Find the gross profit by multiplying the cost by mark-up per cent.
2. Add the gross profit and cost.

3. *How to find the selling price when the mark-up per cent on selling price and the cost are known*:

Example: A retailer buys hats at $24.00 a dozen. If his mark-up rate is $33\frac{1}{3}\%$ on sales, what is the resale price per hat?

Given: Cost and mark-up rate cn selling price.

Find: The selling price.

Solution: 1.   Let selling price $= \$1.00$

Mark-up	$.33\frac{1}{3}$
Cost	$.66\frac{2}{3}$

2. $\dfrac{33\frac{1}{3}}{66\frac{2}{3}} = \frac{1}{2}$ or 50% on cost

$\$24 \div 12 = \$2.00$, cost of 1 hat

3. 50% of $\$2.00 = \$1.00$

4. $\$2.00 + \$1.00 = \$3.00$ selling price

5. *Proof* $\dfrac{1.00}{3.00} = \frac{1}{3} = 33\frac{1}{3}\%$ of selling price

Explanation:

1. The selling price is the basis of comparison. Therefore the selling price is 100%. Since the mark-up is $33\frac{1}{3}\%$, the cost is $66\frac{2}{3}\%$ of the selling price.

2. The cost is known. Therefore we compute the equivalent mark-up per cent on cost.

3. To determine the gross profit we multiply the cost by the mark-up rate on cost.

4. Add the gross profit and cost to find the selling price.

5. Prove the result by computing the per cent of gross profit on sales. The calculation can be shortened by using the following formula:

$$\text{Selling Price} = \frac{\text{cost}}{100\% - \text{mark-up }\% \text{ on sales}}$$

Substituting the facts given, we get

$$\text{Selling Price} = \frac{\$24}{100\% - 33\frac{1}{3}\%} = \frac{\$24}{.66\frac{2}{3}}$$

$\$24 \times 3/2 = \$36.00$ per dozen

$\$36 \div 12 = \$3.00$ Selling Pr. per hat

Rule: Divide the cost by the difference between 100% and the mark-up rate on selling price.

4. *How to convert the mark-up rate on selling price to the equivalens mark-up rate on cost.*

Form a fraction using the given rate as a numerator and its complement as a denominator. (The complement of a per cent is the difference between 100% and the given rate.)

Illustration:

What is the equivalent mark-up rate on cost of 25% on selling price? The complement of 25% is 75%. $\frac{25\%}{75\%}$ is $\frac{1}{3}$ or $33\frac{1}{3}\%$.

The following table shows the equivalent mark-up rates of per cents that are frequently used.

Mark-up Rate on Cost	Mark-up rate on Selling Price
20%	$16\frac{2}{3}\%$
25%	20%
$33\frac{1}{3}\%$	25%
50%	$33\frac{1}{3}\%$
60%	$37\frac{1}{2}\%$
$66\frac{2}{3}\%$	40%

EXERCISE 13

Using the equivalent rates shown in the above table find the gross profit and selling price. Prove your results.

	Cost	Mark-up Rate on Selling Price	Equivalent Rate on Cost	Gross Profit	Selling Price
1.	$4.00	20%	......	......	......
2.	.75	40%	......	......	......
3.	$2.10	$33\frac{1}{3}\%$	......	......	......
4.	.65	$37\frac{1}{2}\%$	......	......	......
5.	$1.50	$16\frac{2}{3}\%$	......	......	......
6.	$18.00	25%	......	......	......
7.	$4.50	40%	......	......	......
8.	$5.00	$33\frac{1}{3}\%$	......	......	......
9.	$3.50	50%	......	......	......
10.	$8.00	$16\frac{2}{3}\%$	......	......	......

5. *How to find the per cent net profit, when the sales, cost and expenses are given.*

Example: F. Sloane's sales for June were $2400.00. If the cost of merchandise sold is $1600.00 and the expenses were $500.00 what was the per cent net profit?

Given: Cost, sales, and expenses.

Find: Per cent net profit.

Solution:

1. $2400.00 Sales
   1600.00 Cost of Sales
    800.00 Gross Profit
2.   500.00 Expenses
    300.00 Net Profit
3.   300.00 $= \frac{1}{8} = 12\frac{1}{2}\%$
  2400.00

4. *Proof:* $12\frac{1}{2}\%$ of $2400.00 $=$ $300.00

Explanation:

1. To find gross profit we deduct cost from sales
2. To find net profit, we deduct expenses from gross profit
3. To find the per cent net profit we divide the net profit by the sales.

6. *How to determine the selling price when the cost, per cent of operating expenses, and desired net profit rate on sales are known.*

Problem: A retailer buys tooth brushes at $1.80 per dozen. His operating expenses are 30% of sales. If he desires to make a net profit of 10%, at what price must he sell each?

Given: Cost per dozen, per cent of operating expenses and per cent of net profit desired.

Find: The selling price per brush.

Solution:

Cost + Expenses + Net Profit = Selling Price

1. $\frac{1.80}{12} = .15$ Cost of 1 tooth brush
2. $.15 + 30\% + 10\% = 100\%$ (selling price)
3. $.15 = 60\%$ of selling price
4. $.15 \div .60 = .25$ selling price of 1 tooth brush

Proof:

Cost	$=$	.15
Expenses	$= 30\%$ of .25 $=$	.075
Net Profit	$= 10\%$ .25 $=$	.025
Selling Price		.25

Explanation:

1. Selling price is the basis of all per cents and represents 100%.
2. Substitute the known facts in the formula.
3. After deducting the per cent for expenses and net profit, the remainder is 60%. That is, the cost is 60% of the selling price.
4. We know the cost. Since the cost is 60% or $\frac{3}{5}$ of the selling price, we divide .15 by 60% to determine the selling price.

EXERCISE 14

Find the selling price:

	Cost	Operating Expenses	Desired Net Profit	Selling Price
1.	$18.00	25%	15%	....
2.	1.50	37½%	12½%	....
3.	1.05	20%	10%	....
4.	.95	33⅓%	16⅔%	....
5.	1.60	12%	8%	....

7. Sometimes a retailer decides at what price level he must mark his merchandise, and then determines how much he should pay for the article in order to cover his expenses and get a desired net profit.

   Problem: Joseph Hahn decided to sell shoes at $6.50 a pair. If the expenses are 15% of sales, and he desires to make a net profit of 10%, how much should he pay for them?

   Given: Selling Price, per cent of expenses and desired per cent of net profit.

   Find: Cost

   Solution:

   1. Cost + Expenses + Profit = Selling Price
      Cost + 15% + 10% = 100%
   2. Cost = 75% of Selling Price
   3. 75% of $6.50 = $4.88 Cost per pair
   4. *Proof*: Cost   4.875
               Expenses 15% of 6.50   .975
               Net profit 10% of 6.50   .65
                                             ———
               Selling Price   6.50

Explanation:

1. We fill in the formula with all the given facts. The selling price represents 100%.
2. Deducting per cents of expenses and net profit from 100%, we find the per cent of cost on sales.
3. Multiply the selling price by the per cent of cost to find the cost.

	Selling Price	Expense	Desired Net Profit	Cost
1.	$7.50	25 %	15 %	....
2.	2.94	35 %	20 %	....
3.	1.80	15 %	10 %	....
4.	4.50	$27\frac{1}{2}$%	$12\frac{1}{2}$%	....
5.	5.00	$33\frac{1}{3}$%	$16\frac{2}{3}$%	....

PROBLEMS

1. An electric heating pad costs the retailer $1.65. At what price should he sell to make a gross profit of 40% on selling price?

2. A haberdasher sells ties at $1.25 which cost $ .75. What is his mark up rate on selling price?

3. A retailer buys saws at $1.75 less 20%. His operating expenses are 20% of sales. What should be the marked price to yield a net profit of 10%?

4. A furniture dealer desires to make a net profit of $12\frac{1}{2}$%. His operating expenses are $33\frac{1}{3}$%. What is the resale price of a dining room suite which cost $378.00?

5. An electric iron costs $4.50 less 40%. A retails it at 50% gross profit on cost, B retails it at 40% gross profit on selling price. Which one sells it cheaper? How much.

6. A retailer sells shoes at $8.75. If his operating expenses are $27\frac{1}{2}$% and net profit $12\frac{1}{2}$% of sales, what is the cost?

7. A department store buyer is planning a $33\frac{1}{3}$% reduction sale. He wants to purchase lamps to resell at $3.00 less $33\frac{1}{3}$%. What price should he pay for the lamps to realize a gross profit of 50% on cost?

8. Fill in the missing numbers:

		Per Cent on Sales
Sales	$200,000.00	100%
Cost of sales	136,000.00	.....
Mark up	....	.....
Operating Expenses	46,000.00	.....
Net Profit	....	.....

9. James Bohn who has been computing mark up on cost desires to change to mark up on selling price. If his mark up per cent is 40% on cost, what is the equivalent mark up rate on selling price?

10. Robert Fields is running a 20% reduction sale. Compute the mark down price of the following articles:

	Regular	*Mark Down Price*
Hat	$ 4.25	......
Coat	28.75	......
Gloves	.95	......
Shoes	12.50	......
Tie	1.75	......
Neckwear	1.40	......

Lesson V

PROBLEMS OF THE MANUFACTURER

Vocabulary:

FACTORY COST is the cost of producing an article and includes materials, direct labor and overhead.

RAW MATERIALS refer to the articles that are required to produce the finished goods.

INDIRECT LABOR is labor which is not directly connected with the manufacturing process, such as the foreman, time keeper, watchman, porter, etc. It is a part of the manufacturing expenses.

OVERHEAD includes all factory expenses, such as rent, heat, light power, factory supplies, indirect labor, repairs and maintenance of plant, etc.

List Price is the price shown in the catalogue.

Trade Discount is a deduction from the list price.

One of the elements of factory cost is labor. Wages are based on the hour system or piecework system. Under the former method the laborer is paid according to the number of hours of employment; under the latter, according to the number of units he produces. Usually overtime, the hours in excess of the fixed hours per day, is paid for on a basis of time and a half; that is for each hour of overtime, the employee is paid $1\frac{1}{2}$ times the rate per hour.

Under the hour rate system, an accurate record is kept of each employee's hours of service on a time card, a sample of which is shown below.

TIME CARD				
Weber Neckwear Co.　Employee's No. 4				
16 West 36th St., New York　Week ending				
July 15, 19—				
Employee　　　　Margaret Peruzzi				

	In	*Out*	*In*	*Out*	*Hours*
Monday	7:55	12:01	12:58	5:06	8
Tuesday	8:01	12:00	12:55	5:10	8
Wednesday	7:58	12:05	1:00	6:06	$9\frac{1}{2}$
Thursday	8:02	12:03	1:01	5:35	$8\frac{3}{4}$
Friday	9:00	12:01	12:59	5:02	7
Total					$41\frac{1}{4}$

Explanation: The schedule of hours are from 8 to 12 A.M. and from 1 to 5 P.M. making a total of 8 hours a day. Overtime commences after 5 P.M. and the overtime rate is one and a half times the regular rate. The first "In" column shows the time of arrival in the morning and the first "Out" column indicates the time when the employee went out for lunch. The next two columns show when the employee returned after lunch and when the employee left for the day. Time before 8 A.M. and 1 P.M. is not counted. Fractions of an hour less than $\frac{1}{4}$ are usually not considered. On Wednesday, the employee worked one hour overtime; therefore an hour and a half are added to the regular time. On Thursday the card shows a half hour overtime; therefore, three fourths of an hour are added to the regular time. On Friday the employee reported one hour late. The total hours of service are $41\frac{1}{4}$ hours.

When there is a large number of employees there is usually a time keeper who keeps the record of the employees' time. A time clock which punches the time is frequently used.

The next step is to prepare the pay roll sheet. Following is an illustration of a weekly pay roll.

Weber Neckwear Co. Pay roll for week ending July 15, 19—					
Employee No. Name	Hrs.	Rate $1.00	Total Wages	Social Security Tax	Amount Due
1. A. Peppone	46	$1.00	$46.00	.46	45.54
2. S. White	40	.75	30.00	.30	29.70
3. T. Wells	42	.60	25.20	.25	24.95
4. M. Peruzzi	41¼	.60	24.75	.25	24.50
5. M. Silver	32	.62½	20.00	.20	19.80
6. J. Brown	46	.50	23.00	.23	22.77
7. J. Marshall	46	.50	23.00	.23	22.77
8. G. Short	44	.60	26.40	.26	26.14
9. F. Lee	16	.40	6.40	.06	6.34
10. S. Block	40	.40	16.00	.16	15.84
Total			$240.75	$2.40	$238.35

The social security tax deduction at that time was 1% of the employee's wages. The time is taken from the time card.

Currency Breakdown

When the employees are paid in currency the exact amount of each one's pay is placed in an envelope. In order to have the necessary change the pay roll clerk computes the denominations required for the above pay roll in the following manner:

Currency Sheet Week ending July 15, 19—										
		Bills				Small change				
Employee	Amount	$10	$5	$2	$1	.50	.25	.10	.05	.01
1. A. Peppone	$45.54	4	1			1				4
2. S. White	29.70	2	1	2		1		2		
3. T. Wells	24.95	2		2		1	1	2		
4. M. Peruzzi	24.50	2		2		1				
5. M. Silver	19.80	1	1	2		1	1		1	
6. J. Brown	22.77	2		1		1		2	1	2
7. J. Marshall	22.77	2		1		1		2	1	2
8. G. Short	26.14	2	1		1			1		4
9. F. Lee	6.34		1		1		1		1	4
10. S. Block	15.84	1	1			1	1		1	4
Totals	$238.35	18	6	10	2	8	4	9	5	20

A pay roll check is drawn for the amount due the employees and a currency memorandum like the form below is presented to the bank teller to indicate the denominations required.

	Currency Memorandum	
	Number	*Amount*
Pennies	20	.20
Nickels	5	.25
Dimes	9	.90
Quarters	4	1.00
Halves	8	4.00
Ones	2	2.00
Twos	10	20.00
Fives	6	30.00
Tens	18	180.00
Total		238.35

EXERCISE 16

Compute the number of hours for the following employees allowing time and a half for overtime. The regular hours are 8-12 Saturday and 8-5 on every other day, with one hour for lunch.

1.
              2.

James Fields   Martha Jones

	A.M.	*P.M.*		*A.M.*	*P.M.*
M.	8:00–12:02	12:55–4:05	M.	7:58–12:05	....
T.	7:50–12:05	12:59–5:10	T.	7:57–12:02	12:57–6:05
W.	7:58–12:01	1:01–6:05	W.	8:05–12:05	12:57–5:03
Th.	8:02–12:05	12:57–6:36	Th.	7:59–12:04	12:55–5:05
F.	8:00–12:03	12:57–5:08	F.	7:58–12:03	1:00–6:35
S.	7:56–12:02	12:10	S.	....	....

3. Compute the amount due each employee and prepare the pay roll breakdown and currency memorandum.

KRAFT LUMBER COMPANY
Pay Roll Sheet
Week Ending Jan. 28, 19—

	Employee	Hrs.	Rate	Wages	S. S. Tax	Amount Due
No. 32.	R. Boles	44	.75	.....	.....	....
33.	S. Raphael	40	.62½	.....	.....	....
34.	T. Hart	48	.70	.....	.....	....
35.	A. Kobus	36	.75	.....	.....	....
36.	N. Freeman	44	.75	.....	.....	....
37.	M. Fields	40	.62½	.....	.....	....
38.	P. Fox	42½	.60	.....	.....	....
39.	G. Nomburg	38	.60	.....	.....	....
40.	J. Hopper	41¾	.50	.....	.....	....
	Total					

4.
DAISY DRESS COMPANY
Pay Roll Sheet
Week Ending Feb. 4, 19—

Employee	Units	Rate	Wages	S. S. Tax	Amount Due
S. Sanford	72	.60	.....	.....	....
J. Ober	56	.75	.....	.....	....
F. Hall	48	.87½	.....	.....	....
L. Stoller	32	.75	.....	.....	....
V. Whipple	56	.62½	.....	.....	....
J. Stewart	36	.75	.....	.....	....
N. Wheeler	42	.60	.....	.....	....
S. Mound	46	.90	.....	.....	....
Total					

Follow the same procedure as in 3.

DEPRECIATION

Every item of factory costs which is not a direct cost, such as raw materials and productive labor is included under overhead. When machinery is used, the wear and tear and obsolescense must be considered as factory expense item. This is called depreciation. There are several methods of computing depreciation.

A very simple method is to deduct the estimated junk value of the machine and divide the remainder by the estimated life. For example, a machine cost $1850.00. The estimated life is 10 years and the junk value $100.00. The annual depreciation is computed as follows:

$1850.00 Cost
100.00 Junk Value
$1750.00 Amount to be written off

$1750.00 ÷ 10 = $175.00 Annual Depreciation

DISTRIBUTION OF OVERHEAD

The overhead must be included in factory cost. The problem of computing raw materials and direct labor is a relatively simple matter, when compared with the problem of determining the amount of overhead to be charged to a unit of production. Cost accountants use various methods of distributing overhead. It is not within the scope of this book to present a detailed discussion of this complicated subject. One simple method is illustrated below:

Problem: The Fashion Clothes Company distributes overhead on the basis of cost of raw materials and direct labor, charging 15% of the total as overhead. If the materials for 48 suits cost $492.00, and the labor $295.20, what is the factory cost per suit?

Given: Cost of Raw Materials, direct labor, per cent of overhead on direct costs, and the number of suits.

Find: Factory cost of one suit.

Solution: Raw materials + Direct Labor + Overhead = Factory Cost.

1. $492.00 Raw Materials
     295.20 Direct Labor
    $787.20 Total Direct Cost of 48 Suits

2.   39.36 Overhead (15% of $787.20)
    $826.56 Factory Cost of 48 Suits

3.   826.56 ÷ 48 = $17.22 Cost of one suit

4. *Proof* $17.22 × 48 = $826.56

Find the factory cost per unit:

	Raw Materials	Direct Labor	Overhead Rate on Direct Costs	Number of Units	Factory Cost per Unit
1.	$456.25	$384.75	$12\frac{1}{2}\%$	100	......
2.	143.35	264.15	10%	50	......
3.	664.60	473.20	15%	40	......
4.	403.40	386.60	$8\frac{1}{3}\%$	144	......
5.	550.00	638.00	$16\frac{2}{3}\%$	250	......

Prove your results.

TRADE DISCOUNTS

In some industries like plumbing and hardware supplies, it is customary for the manufacturer to issue catalogues showing the items which he sells and the list prices. As the factory costs fluctuate upward or downward the prices change. In order to eliminate the expense of printing new catalogues every time the prices change, the list prices are made subject to trade discounts. To adjust the prices to higher or lower levels, the discounts are changed, while the list price remains the same.

A trade discount is a deduction from the list price. Sometimes a series of discounts are offered, such as 20%, 10% and 5%.

Trade discounts should not be confused with *cash* discounts. The latter is a deduction from the invoice amount offered for cash payments or for payments made within the discount period. Trade discounts are deducted from the list price and these deductions are made by the seller on the customer's invoice.

$75.00 less 40% and 10% is a trade discount.

2% ten days is a cash discount.

Problem 1.

An article is listed at $20.00 and the trade discount is 40%. What is the net selling price?

The list price is the base or 100%.

40% of $20.00 = $8.00 Trade Discount
$20.00 — $8.00 = $12.00 Selling Price

Proof $12.00 = 60% of $20.00

Problem 2.

The list price is $75.00 less 20%, 10% and 10%. Find the net selling price.

When there are two or more trade discounts, it makes no difference in what order the discounts are taken. To illustrate this point, we offer two solutions, one deducting the discounts in the order given, 20%, 10%, 10%, the other following the reverse order of discounts, 10%, 10%, and 20%.

Solution 1	*Solution 2*

The First Discount

20% of $75.00 = $15.00	10% of $75.00 = $ 7.50

The Price After the First Discount

$75.00 — $15.00 = $60.00	$75.00 — $ 7.50 = $67.50

The Second Discount

10% of $60.00 = $ 6.00	10% of $67.50 = $ 6.75

The Price After the Second Discount

$60.00 — $ 6.00 = $54.00	$67.50 — $ 6.75 = $60.75

The Third Discount

10% of $54.00 = $ 5.40	20% of $60.75 = $12.15

Net Selling Price

$54.00 — $ 5.40 = $48.60	$60.75 — $12.15 = $48.60

Note that after the first discount is deducted, the following discounts are computed on the last remainder or the price after the previous discount is deducted. In other words, each discount is based on a different amount.

EXERCISE 18

Find the net Selling Price.

	List Price				*Trade Discounts*
1.	$ 8.00	25%, 10%		6.	$ 4.40	25%, 12½%, 5%
2.	45.00	33⅓%, 10%, 5%		7.	30.00	50%, 10%, 3%
3.	16.00	40% and 12½%		8.	40.00	15%, 10%, 5%
4.	2.40	20%, 16⅔%		9.	6.00	12½%, 5%, 5%
5.	15.00	30%, 10%, 10%		10.	18.00	33⅓%, 16⅔%, 10%

TO FIND A SINGLE RATE OF DISCOUNT EQUAL TO A DISCOUNT SERIES

To shorten the calculation, we find a single rate of discount which is equivalent to a series of discounts.

Example: What single discount is equal to 15%, 10%, and 10%.

$$
\begin{aligned}
\text{Let} \quad \$1.00 &= \text{the list price} \\
\underline{.15} &= \text{the first discount, } 15\% \\
.85 &= \text{the remainder after deducting the first} \\
&\quad \text{discount} \\
\underline{.085} &= \text{the second discount, } 10\% \\
.765 &= \text{the remainder after deducting the second} \\
&\quad \text{discount} \\
\underline{.0765} &= \text{the third discount, } 10\% \\
.6885 &= \text{the net selling price}
\end{aligned}
$$

$$\$1.00 - .6885 = .3115 \text{ or } 31.15\%$$

EXERCISE 19

Find the single rate of discount equivalent to

1. 25% and 10%
2. $33\frac{1}{3}\%$, 10% and 5%
3. 40% and $12\frac{1}{2}\%$
4. 20% and $16\frac{2}{3}\%$
5. 30%, 10% and 10%
6. 25%, $12\frac{1}{2}\%$ and 5%
7. 50%, 10% and 3%
8. 15%, 10% and 5%
9. $12\frac{1}{2}\%$, 5% and 5%
10. $33\frac{1}{3}\%$, $16\frac{2}{3}\%$ and 10%

PROBLEMS

1. A watch is listed at $45.00 less 40% and 5%. What is the net selling price?

2. Refrigerators are invoiced at $225.00 less 30%, 10% and 5%. What is the net invoice cost?

3. Typewriters are listed at $85.00 less 20%, 10% and 10%. What is the net invoice price?

4. What should be the list price of a bathtub to yield $48.00 after deducting a discount of 40%?

5. Find the list price of a washing machine the net invoice price of which is $57.75 and the trade discount 45%?

6. A valise is to be sold for $16.20 net. If the manufacturer offers a trade discount of 40% and 10%, at what price should it be listed?

7. A bicycle listed at $40.00 less 15%, 10% and 10% was changed to $40.00 less $33\frac{1}{3}$%. Was the net selling price increased or decreased? How much?

Lesson VI

COMMISSION AND BROKERAGE

A commission merchant, broker, and buyer sell or buy for others. They bring together buyer and seller. The one who pays for their service is called the principal. For their service they receive a commission or brokerage.

Robert Fuller ships a carload of potatoes to Joseph Poggi to be sold on his account. Robert Fuller is the principal and Joseph Poggi the commission merchant. The commission is a percentage of the sales.

Study the following terms which are used in commission and brokerage:

A CONSIGNOR or SHIPPER is the principal who ships the goods.

A CONSIGNEE is the agent to whom the goods are forwarded.

A CONSIGNMENT or SHIPMENT refers to the goods to be sold by the commission merchant for the shipper.

A BROKER is an agent who buys or sells for the principal without handling the goods.

COMMISSION or BROKERAGE is the agent's compensation for his services.

NET PROCEEDS is the difference between the sales and charges.

An ACCOUNT SALES is an itemized statement of sales and charges which the commission merchant sends to his principal.

An ACCOUNT PURCHASE is an itemized statement of purchases and charges which the broker sends to his principal.

FINDING THE NET PROCEEDS

Problem: The Liberty Fruit Distributors received 800 bags of cocoanuts from the Mayaguez Trading Co. to be sold on their account. The consignee sold 400 bags @ $4.10; 300 @ $3.75; and 100 @ $3.25. Freight and insurance was .50 a bag, trucking .25 a bag, insurance and storage charges $40.00. Advertising costs were $15.00; commission 5%. What are the Net Proceeds?

Given: Consignment; sales; charges; rate of commission.

Find: Net Proceeds.

Solution:

Sales:	400 bags @ $4.10 = $1640.00	
	300 bags @ 3.75 = 1125.00	
	100 bags @ 3.25 = 325.00	
Total	800 bags	$3090.00	3090.00

Charges

Freight	.50 × 800 =	$400.00	
Trucking	.25 × 800 =	200.00	
Storage and insurance		40.00	
Advertising		15.00	
Commission	$3090 × .05 =	154.50	
Total Charges		809.50	809.50
Net Proceeds			$2280.50

EXERCISE 20

	Selling Price	Rate Comm.	Expenses	Net Proceeds
1.	1360.50	5%	148.25	......
2.	3471.00	2%	420.75	......
3.	546.40	7%	49.10	......
4.	2684.70	2%	328.50	......
5.	1965.15	3%	248.95	......
6.	4175.00	2%	816.30	......
7.	627.60	8%	59.10	......
8.	1382.40	5%	322.80	......
9.	916.25	7%	88.00	......
10.	1844.65	2%	428.35	......

PROBLEMS

1. The Liberty Fruit Company received a consignment of 3500 bunches of bananas from Jean Battista, Aguadilla, P. R. The consignee paid the following charges: freight $1070.80, dock labor $135.00, advertising $10.00. They sold 800 bunches @ $2.10; 1200 bunches @ $1.85; 500 bunches @ $1.90; 600 bunches @ $1.50; 400 bunches @ $1.25. The commission rate is $7\frac{1}{2}\%$. Find the net proceeds.

2. N. Nagleberg & Co. received a consignment of 2500 boxes of oranges from Henry Baccardi. He sold 925 boxes @ $3.75; 650

boxes @ $3.50; 700 boxes @ $3.60; 225 boxes @ $3.40. The consignee advanced the following expenses: Freight 70¢ a box, insurance $12.50; dock labor $35.00; cartage 15¢ a box. The commission is 5%. Find the net proceeds.

3. In problem 1, what was the percentage of expenses (include commission) on the Sales? (Continue to two decimal places.)

4. A commission merchant whose rate is 5% received $45.00 commission. What were the sales?

5. In problem 1, the shipper's cost averaged 70¢ a bunch. What was his profit or loss?

6. John Langford shipped 1960 boxes of grapefruit to the Washington Fruit and Produce Co. to be sold on their account. The commission merchants advance $1000 to the shipper, paid for freight 90¢ a box, insurance $14.75, cartage 10¢ a box, advertising $7.50, repacking $35.00, storage charges $39.20. 14 boxes were lost in repacking. The commission rate is 5%. Fruit was sold @ $3.75 per box. Find the net proceeds.

7. Frank Richardson sold through a commission merchant 3500 bushels of wheat @ 95¢ a bushel. The commission rate was $2\frac{1}{2}\%$ and the freight was 20¢ per hundred pounds. What were the net proceeds? (1 bushel of wheat weighs 60 lbs.)

8. A lawyer was given for collection a claim of $160.00. He collected 75% of the claim and charged his client 15% for his services. How much does the lawyer owe his client?

Lesson VII

PROBLEM IN REAL ESTATE TAXES

The money required to operate state, county and city governments is derived chiefly from taxes on real estate. The procedure for levying taxes is as follows:

1. The executive branch prepares a budget which lists the appropriations for each subdivision of the government.

2. The legislative branch adopts the budget and levies taxes in amounts which according to estimates will yield sufficient sums to meet the government requirements for the period.

Let us assume that Rosedale Manor has adopted a budget of $50,000 for next year. How much shall be levied against each property owner? In order to distribute the tax on an equitable basis, each lot and building is valued for tax purposes. This value is known as an assessed valuation, and is usually less than the resale value of the property. Let us further assume that the total valuation of all real estate in Rosedale Manor is $2,000,000. The tax rate is computed by dividing the budget total by the assessed valuation.

$$\$50,000 \div \$2,000,000 = .025$$

This rate may be expressed as

$2\frac{1}{2}$ mills per dollar, or
$2.50   per hundred dollars, or
$25.00   per thousand dollars

To change the tax rate from per dollar to per hundred dollars, move the decimal point in the tax rate two places to the right. Why?

To change the tax rate from per dollar to per thousand dollars, move the decimal three places to the right. Why?

A's property (which is situated in Rosedale Manor) is assessed at $15,000. What is the amount of tax levied against him?

Given: Assessed valuation and the tax rate.

Find: The tax.

Solution: Base × Rate = Tax

$15,000 × .025 = $375.00

Proof: $375.00 ÷ .025 = $15,000.

Care must be exercised to point off the correct number of decimal places in the result. In this problem, there are three decimal places in the rate; therefore, we point off three decimal places to the left in the result. When the rate is per hundred dollars, divide the assessed valuation by 100 and proceed as above. When the rate is per thousand dollars, divide the assessed valuation by 1000 and proceed as above.

EXERCISE 21

Find the tax rate

	Assessed Valuation	Amount of Tax	Rate Per Dollar	Rate Per $100	Rate Per $1000.00
1.	$ 8,000,000	$ 120,000	......	......	......
2.	70,000,000	350,000	......	......	......
3.	40,000,000	700,000	......	......	......
4.	200,000,000	2,500,000	......	......	......
5.	100,000,000	3,000,000	......	......	......

Change the tax rates per dollar to equivalent tax rates per hundred and per thousand dollars.

Rate Per Dollar	Rate Per $100	Rate Per $1000.00
1. .03½	......	......
2. 35 mills	......	......
3. 20 mills	......	......
4. 2¾ cents	......	......
5. 27.5 mills	......	......
6. 18.64 mills	......	......
7. 82.25 mills	......	......
8. 75 mills	......	......
9. .075	......	......
10. .01864	......	......

Note 1 mill is $\frac{1}{10}$ of a cent and may be decimally expressed as .001 or .1¢

Compute the tax

	Assessed Valuation	Tax Rate	Tax
1.	$ 6,500	27.5 mills	......
2.	12,000	$ 1.758 per $100	......
3.	25,000	$ 8.254 per $1000	......
4.	14,600	25 mills	......
5.	10,500	$ 1.952 per $100	......
6.	30,000	$12.581 per $1000	......
7.	5,000	$ 1.5724 per $100	......
8.	7,500	$14.079 per $1000	......
9.	8,000	26.9 mills	......
10.	6,000	$ 1.426 per $100	......

The formulas explained in the chapter on Percentage may be applied to tax problems, if you substitute the terms used in property taxes for the terms used in percentage.

Percentage	*Taxes*
Base	Assessed Valuation
Rate	Tax Rate
Percentage	Tax

The type problems illustrated below indicate how the percentage formulas are applied.

Type 1. Assessed Valuation $\times$ tax rate = Tax
  This *type has already been* illustrated.

Type 2. Tax $\div$ assessed valuation = Tax Rate.
  Problem: The tax levied on a building assessed at $6500 was $178.75
      What was the tax rate?
  Solution: 178.75 $\div$ $6500 = .0275 or 2¾%
  Proof: $6500 $\times$ .0275 = $178.75

Type 3. Tax Rate $\div$ Tax = Assessed Valuation
  Problem: At 1.426 per hundred dollars the tax amounts to $85.56.
      What is the assessed valuation?
  Solution: 1.426 $\div$ $85.56 = $6000
  Proof: $\dfrac{\$6000 \times 1.426}{100} = \$85.56$

EXERCISE 24

Fill in the missing number in the following problems.

	Assessed Valuation	*Tax Rate*	*Tax Levy*
1.	$14,500	. . . . . .	$253.75
2.	. . . . .	17.5 mills	560.00
3.	125,500	1.875 per 100	. . . . . .
4.	1,500,000	. . . . . .	1,875.00
5.	. . . . . .	12.582 per 1000	10,694.70

Lesson VIII

PROBLEMS IN BANKING AND LOANS

What service does the retailer offer? the manufacturer? the middle man? the bank? There are times when everyone needs funds or credit. The retailer may need it in order to carry a more complete stock of merchandise. The manufacturer may require additional funds to expand his plant, to replace obsolete machinery or to tide him over the period required to convert raw materials into finished goods. The commercial bank makes loans to its depositors providing the financial statements submitted meet its requirements. In this chapter we shall consider the following problems connected with banking and loans:

1. Simple Interest—Cancellation Method
2. 60 day method
3. Bank discount—non-interest bearing notes
4. Bank discount—interest bearnotes

Vocabulary:

Commercial credit instruments are written evidence of debt and can be transferred by endorsement and delivery, such as promissory notes, drafts and bonds.

The MAKER OR DRAWER is the one who signs the note.

The PAYEE is the one to whom the money is due.

MATURITY DATE is the day when the note falls due.

TERM OF DISCOUNT is the number of days from the date of discount to the maturity date.

The FACE VALUE of the note is the principal.

MATURITY VALUE is the principal and interest.

NET PROCEEDS is the difference between maturity value and discount.

ENDORSER is the one who signs his name on the back of a credit instrument. He thereby guarantees payment.

SIMPLE INTEREST—CANCELLATION METHOD

In percentage problems we learned that *Base* times *Rate* equals *Percentage*. Interest problems have very much in common with percentage problems. Study the following table of comparison.

Percentage	Interest
Base	Principal
Rate	Rate
......	Time
Percentage	Interest

What is the new factor in interest? It is obvious that interest on $1500.00 at 6% for 6 months is less than the interest on the same amount at the same rate for one year. The formula to find interest is

$$P \times R \times T = I.$$

Compare the formula with the one for percentage.

Problem:

Thomas Brown borrowed $1000.00 from Henry Lyons for 60 days at 6% per annum.

$1000.00 is called the principal, 60 days is the time, 6% per annum is the rate.

To compute the interest we multiply the principal by the rate by time, expressed as a fraction of a year. Sixty days equals $\frac{60}{360}$ of a year.

EXERCISE 25

Find the interest:

	Principal	Time	2%	3%	4%	6%
1.	$500	1 year	......	......	......	......
2.	800	90 days	......	......	......	......
3.	600	60 days	......	......	......	......
4.	2400	30 days	......	......	......	......
5.	240	75 days	......	......	......	......
6.	1000	$2\frac{1}{2}$ yrs.	......	......	......	......
7.	400	180 days	......	......	......	......
8.	4800	15 days	......	......	......	......
9.	720	10 days	......	......	......	......
10.	160	45 days	......	......	......	......

THE 60-DAY METHOD

Bankers and business men compute interest on the basis of 360 days to the year. While this method does not give results that are exact it is used because 360 is an easier number to work with. Short term bank loans are generally made for 30, 60, or 90 days. $\frac{30}{360}$, $\frac{60}{360}$, or $\frac{90}{360}$ are reducible to simple fractions. For the same reason business men figure 30 days to every month regardless of the calendar days. Banks however figure calendar days when computing the number of days of a loan. July 15-Oct. 15 would be counted as 3 months or 90 days, according to the methods of business men, whereas the banks would figure 92 days for the same period: Why?

The 60-day method is a short-cut for computing interest for periods less than a year. The basis of this method is 60 days $= \frac{1}{6}$ of a year. When the interest is 6% for one year, we multiply the $\frac{6}{100}$ by $\frac{1}{6}$ to find the equivalent rate for 60 days.

$$\tfrac{6}{100} \times \tfrac{1}{6} = 1\%$$

Rule: To find the interest on any sum of money for 60 days at 6% take 1% of the principal.

Example: What is the interest on $1328.25 for 60 days at 6%.

Answer: $13.28 (1% of $1328.25)

Proof: $1328.25 $\times \frac{6}{100} \times \frac{60}{360} =$ $13.28

If the period of time is a multiple of 60 days find the interest for 60 days and multiply the result by the multiple of 60 days.

For Example: 120 days $= 60 \times 2$
180 days $= 60 \times 3$
240 days $= 60 \times 4$

For periods less than 60 days we use an aliquot part of 60, thus:

6 days $= \frac{1}{10}$ of 60
15 days $= \frac{1}{4}$ of 60
20 days $= \frac{1}{3}$ of 60
30 days $= \frac{1}{2}$ of 60

Illustrations:

a. What is the interest on $400.00 for 240 days at 6%?
Interest for 60 days $=$ $4.00
Interest for 240 days $=$ $4.00 \times 4 =$ $16.00

b. What is the interest on $400.00 for 15 days at 6%?
Interest for 60 days $=$ $4.00
Interest for 15 days $=$ $4.00 \times \frac{1}{4} =$ $1.00

c. What is the interest on $400.00 for 90 days at 6%?
Interest for 60 days $=$ $4.00
Interest for 30 days $=$ 2.00
Interest for 90 days $=$ 6.00

d. What is the interest on $400.00 for 18 days at 6%?
Interest for 60 days $=$ $4.00
Interest for 6 days $=$ .40
Interest for 12 days $=$ .80
Interest for 18 days $=$ 1.20

To shorten the calculation, break up the time into periods which are aliquot parts of 60, thus:

$72 = 60 + 12$
$54 = 60 - 6$
$24 = 30 - 6$
$36 = 30 + 6$
$80 = 60 + 20$ etc.

Find the interest at 6% on $1500.00 for

1. 66 days	5. 90 days	9. 60 days	13. 39 days
2. 120 days	6. 6 days	10. 45 days	14. 72 days
3. 180 days	7. 36 days	11. 20 days	15. 90 days
4. 240 days	8. 10 days	12. 50 days	16. 18 days

EXERCISE 26

Break up the following into periods which are multiples or aliquot parts of 60:

1. 66 days	5. 90 days	9. 70 days	13. 39 days
2. 40 days	6. 3 days	10. 76 days	14. 150 days
3. 36 days	7. 10 days	11. 57 days	15. 186 days
4. 75 days	8. 96 days	12. 21 days	16. 42 days

THE 60-DAY METHOD AT OTHER RATES

When the interest rate is more or less than 6% the interest can be computed in the following manner:

a. First compute interest at 6%. Divide the interest at 6% by 6 and multiply by the required rate.

Example: Find the interest on $1800.00 for 30 days at 4%.

Interest for 60 days @ 6% = $18.00
Interest for 30 days @ 6% =   9.00
Interest for 30 days @ 1% = $9.00 ÷ 6 = $1.50
Interest for 30 days @ 4% = $1.50 × 4 = $6.00

EXERCISE 27

Find the interest by using the 60-day method.

	Principal	Time	6%	5%	7%	4%	2%
1.	$ 900.00	60 days	......	......	......	......	......
2.	$1500.00	72 days	......	......	......	......	......
3.	$2400.00	120 days	......	......	......	......	......
4.	$ 300.00	36 days	......	......	......	......	......
5.	$ 800.00	66 days	......	......	......	......	......
6.	$ 600.00	90 days	......	......	......	......	......
7.	$1600.00	45 days	......	......	......	......	......
8.	$1000.00	180 days	......	......	......	......	......
9.	$2000.00	180 days	......	......	......	......	......
10.	$9000.00	80 days	......	......	......	......	......

BANK DISCOUNT

Non-Interest Bearing Notes.

John Doe needs money to pay for his purchases. He applies at his bank for a loan of $1500.00 for three months. The bank having agreed to make the loan asks John Doe to fill in a promissory note. John Doe fills in the note as follows:

No. 52   New York, March 15, 1965

Three months after date I promise to pay
to the order of MYSELF $1500.00
Fifteen hundred ....dollars

John Doe

Promissory Note

John Doe endorses the note and gives it to the bank.

Banks usually deduct from the face value of the note the charge for their services. In this case, the bank will charge John Doe interest on $1500.00 for the period of the loan. This charge is called "Bank Discount." It is customary for banks to figure the exact number of days from the date of discount to the maturity date of the note.

This interval is called the "Term of Discount."

HOW TO COMPUTE THE TERM OF DISCOUNT

The discount date in the above transaction is March 15, 1965. The note will become due three months after March 15, which is June 15. The exact number of days from March 15 to June 15 is arrived at in the following manner:

March 15-31—16 days
April has   —30 days
May has   —31 days
June has   —15 days
Total (term
of discount)—92 days

The interest on the bank discount on $1500.00 for 92 days at 6% is $23.00. After deducting the bank discount from the face value of the note, you get the net amount which will be credited to John Doe's account.

$1500.00 — $23.00 = $1477.00. This is called the net proceeds.

EXERCISE 28

(Feb. 28 days)

	Date of Discount	Maturity Date	Term of Discount
1.	Jan. 5	March 5	....
2.	Feb. 10	May 10	....
3.	March 20	Apr. 19	....
4.	Apr. 2	June 1	....
5.	May 25	July 10	....
6.	June 9	Sept. 9	....
7.	July 17	Aug. 16	....
8.	Aug. 5	Nov. 3	....
9.	Sept. 30	Dec. 5	....
10.	Oct. 1	Nov. 30	....

How to Compute the Date of Maturity.

a. When time is expressed in months.

A note dated April 10, becomes due three months after date. What is the date of maturity?

April 10 plus three months equals July 10. The number of months is added to the date of the note. If the maturity date is on Saturday, Sunday or a legal holiday, the note falls due on the next business day.

b. When the time is expressed in days.

A note dated April 10, falls due 90 days after date. What is the date of maturity?

Number of days left in April (Apr. 30 — 15 = 15 days)

May	31
June	30
	$\overline{76}$ days
July	14

Total number of days from April 10-July 14 is 90.

Note: we took a total after June 30 because we approached the required number of days. Fourteen additional days are required in July to bring the total up to 90.

EXERCISE 29

Find the Maturity Date:

No.	Date of Note	Time	Maturity Date
1.	Jan. 5	60 days	....
2.	Feb. 10	90 days	....
3.	Mar. 20	20 days	....
4.	Apr. 2	60 days	....
5.	May 25	90 days	....
6.	June 9	90 days	....
7.	July 17	40 days	....
8.	Aug. 5	50 days	....
9.	Sept. 30	90 days	....
10.	Oct. 1	80 days	....

INTEREST-BEARING NOTES

No. 10   New York, N. Y., May 20, 1965.

Ninety days after date I promise to pay to the order of William Strauss................$1000.00
One Thousand 00/100..................Dollars

Value received with interest at 6%

John Henderson

Payable at Commercial Bank and Trust Co.
150 Broadway, New York.

Compare this note with the preceding illustration of a note. Are there any points of difference? How much should the holder of the above note collect from John Henderson on the date of maturity? Since the note bears interest at 6% the drawer must pay in addition to the face value the interest on $1000.00 for ninety days. The amount is computed thus:

Face Value $1000.00
Interest (on $1000 for 90 days) 15.00
Maturity Value $1015.00

Note that if this were a non-interest bearing note, the drawer would pay $1000.00.

Let us assume that on June 19, the payee, William Strauss, is in need of funds. If his credit standing is satisfactory, he can discount the note at his bank. To transfer the note to the bank, William Strauss endorses his name. The endorsement guarantees to the bank that the signature of the drawer is bona fide, and that the note will be paid by the endorser if the drawer fails to pay. What are the net proceeds, if the bank charges at the rate of 6%?

Given: The face value, time of note, date of discount, interest rate, discount rate.

Find: Discount, and Net Proceeds.

Solution: $P \times T \times R =$ Interest
$P + I =$ Maturity Value
$M.V. \times$ Term of Discount $\times R =$ Discount
$M.V. - D =$ Net Proceeds

Banks compute the discount on the maturity value of the note. They figure the exact number of days from the date of discount to the maturity date. The routine for computing the net proceeds is as follows:

1. Find the Date of Maturity.

May 20 + 90 days ....August 18

May (31 − 20) ... 11 days	
June .... 30 days	(If August 18 falls on Saturday, Sunday or a legal holiday,
July .... 31 days	the note matures on the following business day ....)
August .... 18 days	
Total .... 90 days	

2. Compute the Maturity Value.
Principal $1000.00 + Interest, $15.00 = $1015.00
(The interest is computed for the time of the note at the specified rate of interest.)

3. Find the term of Discount.

From the date of discount, June 19, to the maturity date, August 18, there are 60 days.

$$\text{June } (30-19)\ 11 + \text{July } 31 + \text{August } 18 = 60 \text{ days}$$

4. Compute the Discount (on the maturity value).
   Interest on $1015.00 for 60 days at 6% $10.15
5. Compute the Net Proceeds.

Maturity Value	$1015.00
Discount	10.15
Net Proceeds	$1004.85

When the time of the note is expressed in months, the date of maturity is computed by adding the specified number of months to the date of the note.

EXERCISE 30

Find the maturity value of the following notes bearing interest at 6%.

	Face of Note	Time		Face of Note	Time
1.	$1500.00	90 days	6.	$4400.00	30 days
2.	$4500.00	3 mos.	7.	$280.00	60 days
3.	$500.00	60 days	8.	$441.00	90 days
4.	$5000.00	2 mos.	9.	$720.00	6 mos.
5.	$3600.00	1 mo.	10.	$800.00	4 mos.

EXERCISE 31

Find the term of Discount.

	Date of Note	Time	Date of Discount		Date of Note	Time	Date of Discount
1.	Jan. 15	60 days	Jan. 25	6.	June 8	2 mos.	June 20
2.	Feb. 1	90 days	Mar. 15	8.	July 3	3 mos.	Aug. 31
3.	Mar. 30	30 days	Apr. 9	8.	Aug. 25	4 mos.	Aug. 31
4.	Apr. 10	60 days	May 15	9.	Sept. 20	2 mos.	Oct. 10
5.	May 5	90 days	May 15	10.	Oct. 3	3 mos.	Oct. 10

Find the discount and Net Proceeds. The interest rate and discount rate are 6%.

	Date of Note	Face Value	Time of Note	Date of Discount	Discount	Net Proceeds
1.	April 3	$1000.00	90 days	April 3	....	....
2.	May 10	$600.00	60 days	June 10	....	....
3.	June 20	$1230.00	3 mos.	July 8	....	....
4.	July 25	$900.00	2 mos.	Aug. 10	....	....
5.	Aug. 5	$450.00	60 days	Aug. 10	....	....
6.	Sept. 10	$1470.00	90 days	Nov. 5	....	....
7.	Oct. 20	$762.00	30 days	Oct. 20	....	....
8.	Dec. 5	$2000.00	3 mos.	Jan. 4	....	....

Lesson IX

INSURANCE

The purpose of all insurance is to protect the insured against financial losses. The property owner generally carries fire insurance to protect himself against losses resulting from fire. The owner of an automobile usually carries public liability, property damage, fire and theft insurance. Insurance policies are available for nearly every type of risk. Some forms of insurance are compulsory by law, such as Compensation, Unemployment Insurance and Social Security.

The agreement between the insurance company and the insured is called a *policy*. The insured should read his policy carefully to make sure that he has proper coverage. The rates are based on the nature of the risk involved. The *premium* is the cost of the policy to the insured. The face of the policy is the highest amount which the insurance company will pay for losses in accordance with the terms of the policy. Percentage formulas apply to insurance problems. The terms explained in the preceding paragraph are compared with the terms of percentage.

Percentage	Insurance
Base	Face of Policy
Rate	Insurance Rate
Percentage	Premium

Problems in Fire Insurance

Finding the Premium: Unless otherwise specified, fire insurance policies are for one year. The rates are quoted on the basis of one year. For periods greater than a year, the rate charged is computed by adding 75% of the annual rate for each additional year.

Problem 1: A retailer insured his fixtures and merchandise for $7500.00 for one year. The annual rate was 95¢ per $100.00. What is the premium?

Given: Amount of insurance, and annual rate.

Find: The premium.

Solution: *Explanation*

$$\frac{\$7500}{100} \times .95 = \$71.25$$

The rate is quoted per $100
Therefore divide $7500 by 100
Face of Policy × Rate = Premium

Proof: $71.25 ÷ .95 = $75
$75 × 100 = $7500

Problem 2: In the above policy, the policy was written for 3 years. What is the premium?

Solution:

	.95	Rate for first year
¾ of .95 =	.7125	Rate for second year
	.7125	Rate for third year
	2.375	Rate for three years

$$\frac{\$7500}{100} \times 2.375 = \$178.13 \text{ Premium for three years}$$

The rate for the second and third years is ¼ less than the annual rate. Therefore the three year rate is $2\frac{1}{2}$ times the annual rate. The calculation can be shortened by using $2\frac{1}{2}$ times the annual rate.

80% Co-Insurance Clause

Experience has shown that fire rarely destroys 100% of the property. It is therefore unnecessary to insure property for its full value. Furthermore to encourage property owners to carry adequate insurance, the companies issue policies containing an 80% co-insurance clause. If property is valued at $10,000.00, the owner is required to insure it for $8,000.00 if he wants full coverage, thereby saving 20% on the premium. In the event of a fire loss, the company pays the full amount of the loss up to $8000.00, under the 80% co-insurance clause. However, if the amount of insurance carried on this property is less than $8000.00, the owner is a co-insurer for the difference between $8000.00 and the face of the policy.

Illustration 1:

The owner insured property valued at $15000.00 for $12000.00 with an 80% co-insurance clause. The fire loss is $8000.00. How much can the owner collect from the insurance company? $\dfrac{\$12000}{\$15000} = 80\%$

The owner had full coverage up to $12000.00. The loss is less than the face of the policy. Therefore $8000.00 is the amount collectible.

Illustration 2:

In the preceding problem, the owner insured the property for $9000.00. How much can he collect?

$\dfrac{9000}{15000} = 66\tfrac{2}{3}\%$ The owner did not have full coverage, because the amount of insurance is less than 80%.

80% of $15000 = $12000   The amount of insurance required under the 80% co-insurance clause is used as a basis for computing the amount collectible.

Insurer's share of fire loss

$\dfrac{9000}{12000} = \tfrac{3}{4}$ The face of the policy divided by 80% of the property valuation gives the part of the loss collectible from the insurer. (The owner was a co-insurer for the difference, $\tfrac{1}{4}$ of the loss.)

$\tfrac{3}{4}$ of $8000 = $6000   Amount collectible.

Under the 80% co-insurance clause, when the property is insured for an amount less than 80% of its full value, the formula for computing the amount of collectible insurance is

$$\frac{\text{Face of Policy}}{80\% \text{ of full value of property}} \times \text{Fire Loss} = \text{Collectible Insurance}$$

Illustration 3:

The Excelsior Realty Company carried $40,000.00 insurance on a building which was 80% of its value. The insurance was distributed among three companies as follows:

Fidelity & Casualty	$20000.00
The Mutual Indemnity	$10000.00
The U. S. Casualty	$10000.00

The property damage resulting from fire was $8,000.00. What is each company's share of this loss?

Given: Amount of insurance carried with three insurance companies and the fire loss.

Find: The loss shared by each company.

Solution: Since the property was insured for 80% of the value, the insurance companies should pay the full amount of the loss.

Loss to U. S. Casualty $\quad \dfrac{\$10000}{\$40000} \times \$8000 = \$2000$

Loss to Fidelity and Casualty $\dfrac{\$20000}{\$40000} \times \$8000 = \$4000$

Loss to Mutual Indemnity $\quad \dfrac{\$10000}{\$40000} \times \$8000 = \$2000$

The fraction of the loss shared by each company is formed by using the face of the policy as a numerator and the total amount of insurance carried as a denominator.

EXERCISE 33

Find the premium:

	Amount of Insurance	Rate per $100	Period of Insurance
1.	$15,000	.85	1 year
2.	25,000	.90	2 years
3.	3,000	.735	3 years
4.	18,000	.65	3 years
5.	7,500	1.02	1 year

Find the amount of insurance to be carried under the co-insurance, 80%, clause:

	Value of Property	Amount of Insurance Required
1.	$ 5,000	....
2.	12,500	....
3.	16,000	....
4.	25,000	....
5.	60,000	....

Find the fraction of the loss which the insurance company is liable for:

	Value of Property Insured	Amount of Insurance Carried	Amount of Insurance Required Under 80% Insurance Clause	Fraction of Loss Insurer Must Pay
1.	$ 5,000	$ 2,000	....	....
2.	12,500	8,000	....	....
3.	16,000	9,600	....	....
4.	25,000	15,000	....	....
5.	60,000	24,000	....	....

PROBLEMS

1. The Excelsior Manufacturing Company owns a plant valued at $50000.00 which was insured for $40000.00 under an 80% co-insurance clause. A fire damaged the building to the extent of $10000.00. What amount does the insurance company have to pay?

2. Referring to problem 1, the building was insured for $25000.00. If the same fire loss is sustained, how much is the insurance company liable for?

3. The Excelsior Manufacturing Company had a fire which damaged property to the extent of $42000.00. How much does the insurance company pay if the building was insured for $40000.00?

4. The same company insured the building for $25000.00. The fire

loss was estimated at $25000.00. How much does the insurance company pay?

5. William Johnson insured his store and merchandise valued at $37500.00 with two companies; Co. A $15000.00 and Co. B $10000.00. There is a fire loss of $25000.00. How much will each company pay?

6. A building valued at $35000.00 was insured for $28000.00 with an 80% co-insurance clause. The fire loss was $20000.00. Find the amount which the insurance company should pay.

7. In problem 6, the building was insured for $21000.00. How much should the insurer pay?

8. The merchandise in a factory was fully insured for $35000.00. The insurance was divided among four companies.

Company A	$5000.00
Company B	$5000.00
Company C	$15000.00
Company D	$10000.00

What share of a fire loss of $7000.00 should each company pay?

9. The fire loss on a building valued at $75000.00 was $10000.00. If the building was insured for $50000.00 how much can the owner recover from the insurer?

10. A building is insured for $15500.00 and the contents for $5000.00 at .625 per $100.00 for the building and 8.725 per $1000.00 for contents. Find the premium for a three year policy.

Lesson X

PROBLEMS IN INVESTMENTS

Vocabulary:

CERTIFICATES, SHARES, STOCK are written evidence of ownership in a corporation.

PREFERRED STOCK carries a fixed dividend rate when as and if the profits for the year are sufficient to meet the dividend requirements.

COMMON STOCK entitles the owner to dividends when as and if the board of directors of the corporation declare them. There is no fixed rate specified in the stock.

BONDS are credit instruments issued under seal, generally secured by a mortgage. The maturity date, interest rate and time when interest is payable is specified in the bond. Bonds and stocks have the characteristics of negotiable instruments.

DIVIDENDS are profits of a corporation distributed among the stockholders.

PAR VALUE STOCK has a definite value expressed on the face of the instrument.

NO PAR VALUE STOCK has no designated value expressed on the face of the stock.

MARKET VALUE is the value at which the security is quoted on the stock or recognized exchanges.

EX DIVIDEND means that the stock is quoted without the dividend rights.

A BROKER is one who buys and sells securities for the public.

BROKERAGE is the charge for executing orders to buy or sell securities.

A "BULL" is a trader who operates for a rise in prices.

A "BEAR" is a speculator who operates for a fall in prices.

FULL OR ROUND LOTS are lots of 100 shares or multiples thereof.

ODD LOTS are lots less than 100 shares.

BID PRICE is the price at which the buyer will buy.

OFFER is the price at which the owner will sell.

BUYING ON MARGIN is a transaction in which the buyer pays only a part of the purchase price. The broker lends him the balance and retains the stock as security of the loan.

CORPORATIONS. The proprietorship of a business may be vested in an individual, two or more partners or in stockholders. In the first case we have the form of individual ownership; in the second case, a partnership; in the third case, a corporation. Organized under the laws of the state in which its main office is located, a corporation operates under a charter or certificate of incorporation issued by that state. The capital is divided into shares of stock. In par value stock, the value per share is designated on the certificate. It may range from $1.00 to $100.00.

A par value of $100.00 does not necessarily mean that the stock is worth $100.00. If the corporation operates at a profit the stock may sell above par value; if it operates at a loss, the stock may sell below par value. Book value, which is based on capital and surplus is a better indication of the value of stock. In no par value stock the book value is determined by dividing the capital and surplus by the number of shares outstanding. Thus if a corporation has 2500 shares outstanding and its capital and surplus total $25000.00, the book value per share is $10.00.

STOCK EXCHANGE. The stock exchange is an institution organized to create a market for buying and selling securities. The orders to buy and sell are executed through its members. No one else may trade on the exchange. The largest stock exchange in the world is the New York Stock Exchange. Only those stocks and bonds which meet the requirements of the stock exchange and the Securities Exchange Corporation (a federal government bureau) are listed and may be traded in on the stock exchange. The technical rules and machinery for trading cannot be detailed in this limited space but these can be readily obtained through a broker or brochures published by the stock exchanges.

STOCK QUOTATIONS. The prices of securities fluctuate according to the economic law of supply and demand. The opening price at the beginning of the day is determined according to the orders to buy and sell received by the brokers prior to 10 A.M., the hour at which trading commences. The prices of each sale are printed on a ticker sent out by the stock exchange during the business day. Quotations are expressed without the dollar sign; cents are usually indicated as a fraction of a dollar. Thus "$84\frac{7}{8}$" means the price is \$84.87$\frac{1}{2}$.

The financial page of the daily newspaper shows the prices of stocks and bonds traded. On page 284 appears a section of the New York Stock Exchange quotations from the financial page of *The Wall Street Journal*. The following information is listed across the page (from left to right):

1. The year's high.
2. The year's low.
3. Name of the stock and dividend rate per share where applicable.
4. Number of shares sold (in hundreds).
5. Opening price.
6. Highest price (for yesterday).
7. Lowest price (for yesterday).
8. Closing price (for yesterday).
9. Net change—the difference between yesterday's closing price and that of the day before yesterday.

Thus, the first security listed gives Abacus, 500 shares sold; the stock opened at $45\frac{5}{8}$; the highest price was 46 and the closing was 46, which is $\frac{3}{4}$ above the closing price of the preceding day.

Active stocks are generally traded in "round lots" of 100 shares or multiples thereof. Any quantity traded of less than 100 shares is called an "odd lot" and is handled through an odd-lot dealer who executes the order. For shares selling at \$40.00 or more per share, there is a charge

New York Stock Exchange Quotations

1 (19—) High	2 Low	3 Stocks Div.	4 Sales in 100s	5 Open	6 High	7 Low	8 Close	9 Net Chg.
47⅛	40¼	Abacus 3.61f	5	45⅝	46	45⅝	46	+ ¾
52¾	38¼	Abbott Lab 1	88	46½	47¼	46¼	47¼	+1¼
26⅜	16¾	ABC Con .80	57	23⅜	23¾	23¼	23¾	+ ⅛
48⅝	39⅛	ACF Ind 1.80	71	48¾	49¼	48⅝	48⅞	+ ½
73½	49½	Acme Mkt 2b	23	56¼	56¾	56⅛	56¾	+ ½
31⅞	26¼	AdamE 1.84e	3	29½	29¾	29½	29½	......
18¼	12½	Ad Millis .40a	4	14¾	15	14¾	15	+ ⅛
67	41⅛	Address 1.40	98	59	59	58	58	+ ¼
96⅞	15⅝	Admiral	639	91	93⅜	90¾	91	−3⅝
37	25⅜	Aeroquip .70b	18	36	36¼	35¾	36	− ⅛
81⅜	51⅛	Air Prod .20b	23	80	80	79¼	79½	− ½
75¾	53¾	Air Red 2.50	33	75⅜	76¼	75¼	76¼	+ ¾
3¾	2⅜	AJ Industries	56	3½	3½	3½	3½	......
39⅜	34½	Ala Gas 1.80	8	36⅝	36⅞	36⅝	36⅞	+ ⅛
25¾	13⅛	AlbertoCu .28	114	14⅞	14⅞	14¼	14½	− ½
14½	8¾	Alleg Corp.	623	14½	14⅞	14½	14¾	+ ⅜
51	27½	Alleg 6pf .60	23	51¼	51¾	51¼	51¾	+1⅜
55	39¾	Allegh Lud 2	36	53⅛	53¼	53⅛	53⅛	......
31	26½	Alleg Pw 1.14	29	28	28	27½	27¾	+ ⅛
31¾	27¾	AllenIn 1.40a	12	30⅞	31⅝	30¾	31⅝	+1⅛
58¼	46⅛	Allied C 1.90b	142	51⅞	52	51½	51½	− ⅛
20⅞	14⅞	AlliedKid .85	20	18	18⅜	18	18⅛	......
38½	10⅛	Allied Pd .50	183	39	39¾	38¼	38½	+ ¾
89⅞	68⅝	Allied Strs 3	18	80	80⅞	80	80⅜	− ⅛
17	12⅝	AlliedSup .60	46	15⅛	15⅛	15	15⅛	+ ⅛
35⅜	18½	AllisChal .75	203	34⅜	34¾	34⅛	34⅛	− ¼
120½	92	AllisCh pf4.20	8	116½	116½	116	116	− ¼
120	94	AllisCh pf4.08	1	116½	116½	116½	116½	......
15⅛	10⅞	AlphaPC .50	46	12½	12½	12¼	12⅜	......
14⅛	9¼	Alside .20a	51	13⅞	14	13⅝	13¾	+ ⅛
34⅛	25¼	Alum Ltd .90	336	34	34¼	33¾	33¾	− ⅜
79⅝	60½	Alcoa 1.40	141	79⅝	80	79½	79⅞	+ ⅜
26⅞	19¼	AmalSg 1.20a	1	26⅜	26⅜	26⅜	26⅜	......
29¾	23	Amerace 1b	5	25⅞	26	25⅞	26	+ ½
87½	69⅛	Amerada 2.80	x88	75⅜	75¾	75¼	75½	+ ¼
45⅜	29½	AAirFiltr1.40	4	40¾	40⅞	40⅝	40⅞	+ ⅛
69¾	44⅛	AmAirlin 1.25	166	61½	61⅞	61⅛	61⅛	+ ⅛
27½	20	Am Baker 1	14	21¼	21⅜	21¼	21⅜	+ ⅜
28	23½	AmBk Note 1	2	24	24⅜	24	24⅜	+ ⅜
30⅜	15½	A Bosch .50g	57	29⅛	29⅝	29⅛	29¼	+ ¼
69	56⅝	Am Brk Sh 3	30	67⅛	69	66¾	69	+1½
76¾	48	AmBdcst 1.60	97	75	75	74	74⅝	− ⅜
59	42⅛	Am Can 2.20	48	56⅞	57⅜	56⅞	57⅜	+ ⅞
43	39½	ACan pf 1.75	6	39¾	39⅞	39¾	39⅞	+ ⅛
13⅜	10½	Am Cem .60	19	12¼	12⅜	12¼	12⅜	+ ⅛
40⅜	29½	AmChain 1.40	9	37½	37⅝	37⅛	37⅛	− ⅝
52	38	AmCom 1.60b	5	48	48¾	48	48¾	+1⅛
22⅜	16	AmConsum 1	4	17	17	17	17	− ¼
21½	16½	AmCrySug 1	12	20⅜	20¾	20⅛	20¾	+ ½
91	85½	ACry pf 4.50	z120	86⅝	86⅝	86½	86½	−1½
90⅜	67⅝	AmCyan 2.30	56	91⅛	91⅛	89¾	90⅛	......
34½	29¼	AmDist 1.40a	6	31⅝	31¾	31½	31⅝	− ⅛
47⅝	40⅞	AmElPw 1.32	217	41⅞	42½	41⅞	42	......
48⅜	33	A Enka 1.10a	56	38⅝	39	38⅝	38⅞	+ ⅛
38⅞	23⅝	AmExp Isbrn	7	31¾	31⅞	31¾	31¾	− ¼
96⅜	88¼	AExIsbrn pf6	5	93	93	92¼	92¼	+ ½
20	16½	Am FPow 1	13	19⅞	20	19⅞	20	+ ⅜
31	22¾	AmHoist 1.20	5	28⅜	28⅞	28⅜	28⅞	+ ¼
90½	64⅞	AHome 1.80a	64	87½	87⅞	86⅞	86⅞	+ ⅛
74½	62¼	AmHome pf2	104	73¼	73⅜	73	73	− ¼
46½	22⅞	Am Hosp .40	223	45⅞	46	45½	45¾	− ¼
24⅜	20	AmInvCo 1.10	14	20⅝	20¾	20⅝	20⅝	+ ⅛
21⅞	16⅛	Am MFd .90	171	19½	19⅝	19⅜	19⅜	− ⅛
54¼	40⅜	AMet Cl 1.90	84	51⅞	52	50¾	51⅜	− ¼

Rates of dividends (following the name of the stock) are annual disbursements based on the last quarterly or semi-annual declaration. Dividends or payments not designated as regular are identified as follows:

a—also extra or extras; b—annual rate plus stock dividend; e—declared or paid this year; f—payable in stock during the past year, estimated cash value on the ex-dividend, or ex-distribution date; g—paid last year.

Also, symbols before the number of shares sold indicate the following:

x—ex-dividend; z—sales in full.

(courtesy, *The Wall Street Journal*)

of $\frac{1}{4}$ of a point (dollar) below the next round-lot sale; if the shares are selling for less than $40.00 per share, the charge is $\frac{1}{8}$ of a point below the next round lot sale. Thus, if Mr. Jones sells 40 shares of American Motors quoted at $8\frac{5}{8}$, he receives $8\frac{1}{2}$ per share less transfer taxes and brokerage. If Mr. Jones buys 40 shares of the same stock at the same quotation, he pays $8\frac{3}{4}$ per share plus brokerage.

BROKERAGE. Brokers charge commissions on all orders to buy or sell according to a schedule of rates followed by member brokers of the various exchanges throughout the country (with the exception of certain minimum rates on the Boston, Detroit, and Los Angeles Exchanges). The table of rates applying to each round- or odd-lot unit of stocks selling at $1 per share or more is:

Money Involved	Commission	For each round lot		For each odd lot
$100 to $399	2% plus	$3	or	$1
$400 to $2,199	1% plus	7	or	5
$2,200 to $4,999	$\frac{1}{2}$% plus	19	or	17
$5,000 and above	$\frac{1}{10}$% plus	39	or	37

A quick reference table of New York Stock Exchange commission rates follows.

Price of Shares	Rate/100 Shares	Price of Shares	Rate/100 Shares
$ 1	$ 6.00	$ 60	$45.00
5	12.00	70	46.00
10	17.00	80	47.00
15	22.00	90	48.00
20	27.00	100	49.00
25	31.50	125	51.50
30	34.00	150	54.00
40	39.00	200	59.00
50	44.00	250	64.00

When a transaction involves multiples of 100 shares, multiply the rate per 100 shares by 2, 3, 4, or whatever amount is applicable in order to find the commission. There is also a separate schedule for stocks selling below $1.00, which varies from $.10 to $5.25 per hundred shares.

Minimum and Maximum Charge Per Transaction. In addition to the above rates, when the amount involved in a transaction is less than $100, the commission shall be mutually agreed upon by the broker and the customer. The minimum commission shall be not less than $6; the maximum is $1.50 per share or $75 per single round-lot transaction.

Transfer Taxes. The federal and state governments levy taxes on the sale of stocks. These taxes are payable by the seller. Transfer taxes are exacted by the federal government and by the states of Florida, New York, South Carolina, and Texas. In addition, the Securities and Exchange Commission imposes a fee on sales of securities on any registered exchange.

TABLE OF FEDERAL AND STATE TAX RATES AND S.E.C. TRANSFER FEE

Federal Tax:

4¢ per $100 (or major fraction) of market value not exceeding a maximum of 8¢ per share; a minimum of 4¢ per transaction is imposed.

State Taxes:

Florida—15¢ per $100 par value or fraction thereof
15¢ per share on par value stock regardless of selling price

New York—1¢ per share for stock selling under $5
2¢ per share for stock selling between $5 and $9.99
3¢ per share for stock selling between $10 and $19.99
4¢ per share for stock selling over $20

South Carolina—4¢ per $100 par value or fraction thereof
4¢ per share on no par value stock regardless of selling price

Texas—3.3¢ per $100 par value or fraction thereof regardless of selling price
3.5¢ per share on no par value stock regardless of selling price

S.E.C. fee—1¢ on $500 or fraction thereof of the money involved in the transaction.

Problem 1: James Stanley bought 200 shares of American Tel. and Tel. @ 60. What is the cost?

Solution:

1. 200 × $60...................... $12,000.00 Cost of Shares
    2 × $45...................... 90.00 Brokerage
    $12,090.00 Total Cost

Problem 2: James Stanley sold in New York 100 shares of Bethlehem Steel @ 40. What were the net proceeds?

Solution:

1. 100 × $40...................... $4,000.00 Sales Price

    1 × 39.....$39.00 Brokerage
    40 × 4¢.....$ 1.60 Federal Tax
    100 × 4¢.....$ .40 State Tax
    8 × 1¢.....$ .08 S.E.C. fee..... 41.08 Total Deductions
    $3,959.92 Net Proceeds

Problem 3: James Stanley bought 300 shares of American Can @ $42\frac{1}{4}$ and sold them in New York @ $56\frac{3}{4}$. What was his net profit on the transaction?

Solution:

1. 300 × $42\frac{1}{4}$ .... $12,675.00 Cost
2. .001 × 12675 + 3 × 39 .... 129.68 Brokerage
    $12,804.68 Total Cost

3. 300 × $56\frac{3}{4}$................ $17,025.00
4. .001 × 17025 + 3 × 39...... $ 134.03 Brokerage
5. 170 × .04 .... $ 6.80 Federal Tax
6. 300 × .04 .... $ 12.00 N.Y. State Tax
7. 34 × .01 .... $ .34 S.E.C. fee
    $ 153.17 Total Deductions
    $16,871.83 Net Proceeds
    12,804.68 Cost
    $ 4,067.15 Net Profit

PROBLEMS

In the following problems use the "close" stock prices shown on page 284 where applicable, and consult the brokerage and transfer tax rates listed in the accompanying tables:

1. What is the total cost of 200 shares of Admiral (brokerage included)?

2. What is the cost of 50 shares of Air Reduction?

3. What are the net proceeds from the sale of 100 Allegheny Corporation (including Federal and N.Y. State Taxes and S.E.C. fee)?

4. In problem 2, a Texas seller sold the shares @ 80¼. What was his net profit on the transaction (assuming no par value)?

5. Bought 125 Alcoa. What is the total cost?

6. Sold 200 American Airlines in Florida. Assuming there is no par value, what are the net proceeds?

7. Sold 150 Abacus in Ohio. Find the net proceeds.

8. In problem 1, the buyer later sold his shares @ 92 in New York. What was the net profit or loss?

9. Mr. Henry Willingsworth bought 100 Amerace @ 23; 50 @ 24½; 100 @ 25½. What was his average cost per share including broker's fee?

10. Mrs. J. P. Jones sold in South Carolina 100 U.S. Smelting preferred @ 89 (par value 100). Find the net proceeds.

Dividends

Sound business practice requires an annual statement of profit and loss. When a corporation shows profits, the board of directors decide what portion, if any, shall be distributed among the stockholders. These sums paid to the stockholders are called dividends. The directors usually declare dividends annually, semi-annually or quarterly. The dividend is generally expressed as a specified amount per share.

Problem 4: The XYZ Corporation has outstanding 8000 shares par value $25.00. The directors decide to distribute $6000.00 as a dividend. What is the rate of dividend?

$$8000 \times \$25 = \$200,000 \text{ Capital Stock}$$
$$\$6000 \div \$200,000 = 3\% \text{ Dividend Rate}$$
$$\textit{Proof}: \$200,000 \times .03 = \$6000 \text{ Dividend}$$

Problem 5: In problem 4, how much should a stockholder who owns 500 shares receive?

$$\$25 \times .03 = \$.75 \text{ Dividend on One share}$$
$$500 \times .75 = \$375 \text{ Dividend on 500 shares}$$

Rule: To find the amount of dividend multiply the dividend rate by the par value of the total shares.

EXERCISE 36

Determine the rate of dividend:

	Capital Stock	Amount of Dividend		Capital Stock	Amount of Dividend
1.	$50,000	$5,000	5.	$100,000	$1,250
2.	$150,000	$4,500	6.	$1,000,000	$27,500
3.	$500,000	$40,000	7.	$400,000	$9,000
4.	$250,000	$15,000	8.	$2,500,000	$125,000

EXERCISE 37

Determine the dividend amount received *annually* by the stockholder per share.

	Par Value per Share	No. of Shares	Annual Div. Rate		Par Value per Share	No. of Shares	Annual Div. Rate
1.	$100	300	5%	5.	$50	1,000	10%
2.	$50	250	8%	6.	$5	2,000	4%
3.	$25	100	$4\frac{1}{2}\%$	7.	$25	800	7%
4.	$10	1000	9%	8.	$75	400	8%

BONDS

When the national, state or city government wishes to borrow money it usually issues bonds, which specify the face value, interest rate and maturity date. In the same manner, a corporation may borrow large sums of money for a long period of time by selling its bonds. These have the characteristics of promissory notes. They are evidence of indebtedness. Unlike a note, however, a bond is a formal document issued under the corporation seal, and when issued by a private corporation, it is generally secured by a mortgage on property owned by the corporation. Since the bonds usually extend over a number of years, the interest dates are specified. Bonds are generally issued in denomination of $1,000.00 and occasionally in smaller amounts such as $500.00 and $100.00.

There are two principal kinds of bonds:

(a) *Registered Bonds.* The names and addresses of the owners are recorded in the books of the corporation, and the interest is sent to the bondholders of record on the interest dates. When this type of bond is sold, the corporation must be notified.

(b) *Coupon Bonds.* The bonds have interest coupons attached. When they become due, the bondholder clips the coupon and cashes it like a check.

There is a fundamental difference between stocks and bonds. A share is evidence of ownership in a corporation. The shareholder invests his money in the business. When the directors declare dividends, he shares the corporation's profits. A bondholder lends his money to the corporation and is therefore a creditor. He receives a fixed interest rate on his loan on specified dates and when the bonds mature, the principal.

The *par value* of a bond is the face value. The price at which the bond may be bought or sold is the market value, which is expressed as a percentage of the par value. A bond, par value $1,000.00, quoted at $95\frac{1}{4}$ can be bought at $952.50 ($1,000 \times .95\frac{1}{4}$). When the market value is more than the face value, the bond sells at a *premium*. When the price is less than face value, it sells at a *discount*.

The designation of the bond shows who issued the bond, the rate of interest, and year of maturity. Thus, "So Pacific $4\frac{1}{2}$ '81" was issued by Southern Pacific R. R., pays $4\frac{1}{2}\%$ interest, and will be paid in 1981. "Treas. $2\frac{1}{2}$ s 72" is the name of a series of U. S. Treasury bonds paying $2\frac{1}{2}\%$ interest and maturing in 1972.

Bonds are bought and sold through brokers, like stocks. The brokerage fee in the New York Stock Exchange is based upon the price of the bond. The commission rates are $.75 for bonds selling under $10.00; for bonds priced at $10.00 but less than $100 the rate is $1.25; for bonds selling at $100 and above the rate is $2.50. A special rate of $1.25 is charged for bonds maturing in six months to five years.

Problem 6: Find the cost of 5 American T. & T. 4⅜s 85 @ 94.

$940.00 .... Price per bond
  2.50 .... Brokerage per bond
―――――
$942.50 .... Cost per bond
$942.50 × 5 = $4,712.50 ... Cost of 5 bonds

Proof: 5 × $940.00 = $4,700.00
     5 ×   2.50 =   12.50
―――――
             $4,712.50

EXERCISE 38

Find the cost including brokerage.

No.	Bond	Price	Brokerage	Total Cost
1. 10	Armour 5s 84	96	......	......
2. 25	Beth Steel 4½s 90	95	......	......
3. 5	Con Edison 4½s 86	91	......	......
4. 50	General Foods 3⅜s 76	88	......	......
5. 10	Phila. Electric 2¾s 70	90	......	......

BONDS WITH ACCRUED INTEREST

When bonds are purchased between interest dates, the interest accumulates from the last interest date to the day before the purchase is made. Accrued interest on bonds is normally computed on a 30-day month and a 360-day year basis. The buyer advances the accrued interest because he will collect it on the next interest date.

Problem 7: On July 1 Mr. Simpson bought 10 Minneapolis-St. Louis 6s 85 @ 101 (par value $1,000). The interest dates are April 1 and October 1. How much do the bonds cost?

Given: Par value, market price, bond rate of interest, interest date, date of purchase.

Find: Accrued interest, gross receipts, brokerage, net proceeds.

Solution:	*Explanation:*

1. $\left\{\begin{array}{l} \text{April 1-July 1 — 3 months} \\ \text{Interest on \$1,000.00 for 3} \\ \text{months @ 6\% ......\$ 15.00} \end{array}\right.$

Number of months from April 1 to June 30 is 3.

2. Price per bond 1,010.00
   Gross Receipts for 1 bond 1,025.00

Add accrued interest and price per bond to find the selling price per bond.

3. Brokerage for 1 bond 2.50
   Net Proceeds for 1 bond.. 1,022.50

The brokerage is deducted from the gross receipts.

4. $10 \times \$1,022.50 =$ 255.00

The net proceeds of 10 bonds is ten times the proceeds of 1 bond.

EXERCISE 39

Find the total cost, including accrued interest and brokerage.

	No. of Bonds	Par Value	Int. Rate	Quotation	Last Int. Date	Date of Purchase
1.	10	$1,000	5	$104\frac{1}{2}$	July 1	Sept. 14
2.	5	$1,000	$4\frac{1}{2}$	$95\frac{5}{8}$	Apr. 1	July 1
3.	20	$ 500	4	$86\frac{1}{2}$	Oct. 1	Jan. 14
4.	6	$1,000	$5\frac{1}{2}$	85	Apr. 15	July 23
5.	8	$ 500	$3\frac{3}{4}$	$107\frac{1}{2}$	July 15	Sept. 15

IV

USEFUL FACTS AND FIGURES

WEIGHTS AND MEASURES

LONG OR LINEAR MEASURE

12 inches (in.) = 1 foot (ft.).
3 feet = 1 yard (yd.).
$5\frac{1}{2}$ yds. or $16\frac{1}{2}$ ft. = 1 rod (rd.) or pole (p.).
40 rods = 1 furlong (fur.).
8 furlongs = 1 mile (mi.).
320 rods or 5,280 ft. = 1 mile.
3 miles = 1 league.

Note—A line equals $\frac{1}{12}$ in.

SQUARE MEASURE

144 square inches = 1 square foot (sq. ft.).
9 square feet = 1 square yard (sq. yd.).
$30\frac{1}{4}$ sq. yds. $\Big\}$ = 1 square rod (sq. rd.).
$272\frac{1}{4}$ sq. ft.
160 square rods = 1 acre (A.).
640 acres = 1 square mile (sq. mil.).

Note—A perch (P.) is a square rod.

CUBIC MEASURE

1,728 cubic inches (cu. in.) = 1 cubic foot (cu. ft.).
27 cubic feet = 1 cubic yard (cu. yd.).
$24\frac{3}{4}$ cubic feet = 1 perch (P.).

WOOD MEASURE

16 cubic feet = 1 cord foot.
8 cord feet or 128 cubic feet = 1 cord (cd.).

Note—A cord of wood, as generally piled, is 8 ft. long, 4 ft. wide, and 4 ft. high.

Liquid Measure

4 gills (gi.) = 1 pint (pt.).
2 pints = 1 quart (qt.).
4 quarts = 1 gallon (gal.).

Note—In the United States, a gallon contains 231 cu. in.; 31 gallons are considered a barrel (bbl.), and 63 gallons a hogshead (hhd.).

Apothecaries' Fluid Measure

60 minims = 1 fluid dram (fl. dr.).
8 fluid drams = 1 fluid ounce (fl. oz.).
16 fluid ounces = 1 pint (O.).
8 pints = 1 gallon (C.).

Dry Measure

2 pints (pt.) = 1 quart (qt.)
8 quarts = 1 peck (pk.).
4 pecks = 1 bushel (bu.).

Note—In the United States, a bushel contains 2,150.42 cu. in.; in Great Britain, 2,218.2.

Troy Weight

24 grains (gr.) = 1 pennyweight (pwt. or dwt.).
20 pennyweights = 1 ounce (oz.).
12 ounces = 1 pound (lb.).

Note—1 lb. troy equals 5,760 grains. In weighing diamonds 1 carat equals 3.168 troy grains, and is divided into quarters, which are called carat grains.

Apothecaries' Weight

20 grains (gr.) = 1 scruple (sc.).
3 scruples = 1 dram (dr.).
8 drams = 1 ounce (oz.).
12 ounces = 1 pound (lb.).

Note—The pound, ounce and grain have the same weight as those of troy weight.

Mariners' Measure
6 feet = 1 fathom.
120 fathoms = 1 cable length (or cable).
7$\frac{1}{2}$ cable lengths = 1 mile.
5,280 feet = 1 statute mile.
6,085 feet = 1 nautical mile.

Avoirdupois Weight
27$\frac{11}{32}$ grains = 1 dram (dr.).
16 drams = 1 ounce (oz.).
16 ounces = 1 pound (lb.).
25 pounds = 1 quarter.
4 quarters or 100 pounds (U.S.) = 1 hundredweight (cwt.).
112 pounds (Gt. Brit.) = 1 hundredweight.
20 hundredweight or 2,000 pounds (U.S.) = 1 ton (T.).

Note—1 lb. avoirdupois equals 7,000 grains. The "long ton" is also used in the United States.

Measures of Angles or Arcs
60 seconds (″) = 1 minute (′).
60 minutes = 1 degree (°).
90 degrees = 1 right angle or quadrant (L.).
360 degrees = 1 circle.

Common Units
12 units = 1 dozen (doz.).
12 dozen = 1 gross (gr.).
144 units = 1 gross.
12 gross = 1 great gross.
20 units = 1 score.

Paper Measure
24 sheets = 1 quire.
20 quires = 1 ream (480 sheets).
500 sheets = 1 ream (commercial).
2 reams = 1 bundle.
5 bundles = 1 bale.

Time Measure

60 seconds (sec.) = 1 minute (min.).
60 minutes = 1 hour (hr.).
24 hours = 1 day (da.).
7 days = 1 week (wk.).
365 days = 1 common year (yr.).
12 months = 1 common year.
366 days = 1 leap year.
100 years = 1 century.

Kitchen Weights and Measures

4 large tablespoonfuls = $\frac{1}{2}$ gill.
1 teacup = 1 gill.
1 glass (ordinary tumbler) = $\frac{1}{2}$ pint.
2 cups = 1 pint.
2 pints = 1 quart.
1 tablespoonful = $\frac{1}{2}$ ounce.
1 wine glass (large) = 2 ounces.
16 tablespoonfuls = 1 cup.
60 drops = 1 teaspoonful.
3 teaspoonfuls = 1 tablespoonful.
4 tablespoonfuls = $\frac{1}{4}$ cup.
1 tablespoonful = $\frac{1}{2}$ fluid ounce.
1 ordinary cup = 2 gills.

Common Equivalents (Approximate)

One Cup of	Weighs
butter	$\frac{1}{2}$ pound.
cornstarch	$\frac{1}{4}$ pound.
lard	$\frac{1}{2}$ pound.
granulated sugar	$\frac{1}{2}$ pound.
flour	$\frac{1}{4}$ pound.
rice	$\frac{1}{2}$ pound.
cornmeal	5 ounces.
stale bread crumbs	2 ounces.
chopped meat	$\frac{1}{2}$ pound.

The Metric System

The fundamental unit of the metric system is the meter—the unit of length. From this the units of capacity (liter) and of weight (gram) were derived. All other units are the decimal subdivisions or multiples of these. These three units are simply related; e.g., for all practical purposes one cubic decimeter equals one liter, and one liter of water weighs one kilogram. The metric tables are formed by combining the words "meter," "gram" and "liter" with the six numerical prefixes, as in the following tables:

Prefixes	Meaning	Notation
Milli-	one-thousandth	.001
Centi-	one-hundredth	.01
Deci-	one-tenth	.1
Unit	one	1
Deka-	ten	10
Hecto-	one hundred	100
Kilo-	one thousand	1,000

Measures of Length

Name	Metres	Equivalent
myr'i-a-me"ter	10,000 m.	6.214 miles
kil'o-me"ter	1,000 m.	0.62137 mile (3,280 ft., 10 in.)
hec'to-me"ter	100 m.	328 feet, 1 inch
dec'a-me"ter	10 m.	393.7 inches
me'ter	1 m.	39.37 inches
dec'i-me"ter	$\frac{1}{10}$ m.	3.937 inches
cen'ti-me"ter	$\frac{1}{100}$ m.	0.3937 inch
mil'li-me"ter	$\frac{1}{1000}$ m.	0.03937 inch

Factors for Conversion: One inch equals 0.0254 meter; one foot equals 0.3048 meter; one mile equals 1,609.35 meters.

Abbreviations: cm. equals centimeter, dm. equals decimeter, km. equals kilometer, m. equals meter, mm. equals millimeter.

Measures of Surface

Name	Sq. Meters	Equivalent
hec'tare	10,000 m2.	2.471 acres
are	100 m2.	119.6 square yards
cen'tare	1 m2.	1,550 square inches

Factors for Conversion: One square inch equals 0.06452 square meter; one square yard equals 0.836 square meter; one acre equals 4,047 square meters.

Abbreviations: a. equals are, ha. equals hectare, m2. equals square meter.

Measures of Capacity

Name	Liters	Cubic Measure	Dry Measure
kil'o-li''ter (stere)	1,000	1 cu. m.	1.308 cu. yds.
hec'to-li''ter	100	$\frac{1}{10}$ cu. m.	2 bu., 3.35 pks.
dec'a-li''ter	10	10 cu. dm.	9.08 qts.
li'ter	1	1 cu. dm.	0.908 qt.
dec'i-li''ter	$\frac{1}{10}$	$\frac{1}{10}$ cu. dm.	6.1022 cu. in.
cen'ti-li''ter	$\frac{1}{100}$	10 cu. cm.	0.6102 cu. in.
mil'li-li''ter	$\frac{1}{1000}$	1 cu. cm.	0.061 cu. in.

Name	Liters	Cubic Measure	Liquid Measure
kil'o-li''ter (stere)	1,000	1 cu. m.	264.17 gals.
hec'to-li''ter	100	$\frac{1}{10}$ cu. m.	26.42 gals.
dec'a-li''ter	10	10 cu. dm.	2.64 gals.
li'ter	1	1 cu. dm.	1.0567 qts.
dec'i-li''ter	$\frac{1}{10}$	$\frac{1}{10}$ cu. dm.	0.845 gill.
cen'ti-li''ter	$\frac{1}{100}$	10 cu. cm.	0.338 fl. oz.
mil'li-li''ter	$\frac{1}{1000}$	1 cu. cm.	0.27 fl. dr.

Factors for Conversion: One cubic inch equals 0.0164 liter; one bushel equals (U. S.) 35.25 or (British) 36.35 liters; one quart (dry measure) equals 1.1011 liters; one peck equals (U. S.) 8.81 or (British) 9.09 liters; one cubic yard equals 765 liters; one fluid dram equals 0.00369 liter; one fluid ounce equals 0.0296 liter; one gill equals 0.1183 liter; one quart (liquid measure) equals 0.9463 liter; one gallon standard (231 cubic inches) equals 3.785 liters; one gallon imperial (277 cubic inches) equals 4.543 liters.

Abbreviations: cl. equals centiliter, cm³. equals cubic centimeter, dal. equals decaliter, dl. equals deciliter, dm³. equals cubic decimeter, hl. equals hectoliter, 1. equals liter, m³. equals cubic meter, ml. equals milliliter, mm³. equals cubic millimeter.

WEIGHTS

Name	Grams	Water at Maximum Density	Avoirdupois Weight	
mil″lier′ (tonneau)	1,000,000	1 cu. m.	2,204.6	lbs.
quin′tal	100,000	1 hl.	220.46	lbs.
myr′i-a-gram	10,000	10 l.	22.046	lbs.
kil′o-gram	1,000	1 l.	2.204	lbs.
hec′to-gram	100	1 dl.	3.527	ozs.
dec′a-gram	10	10 cu. cm.	0.353	oz.
gram	1	1 cu. cm.	15.432	grs.
dec′-i-gram	$\frac{1}{10}$	$\frac{1}{10}$ cu. cm.	1.543	grs.
cen′ti-gram	$\frac{1}{100}$	10 cu. mm.	0.154	gr.
mil′li-gram	$\frac{1}{1000}$	1 cu. mm.	0.015	gr.

Factors for Conversion: One grain equals 0.0648 gram; one avoirdupois ounce equals 28.3495 grams; one troy ounce equals 31.103 grams; one pound equals 453.59 grams.

Abbreviations: cg. equals centigram, dg. equals decigram. g. equals gram, kg. equals kilogram, mg. equals milligram, q. equals quintal, t. equals tonneau (millier).

USEFUL VALUES

To find diameter of a circle, multiply circumference by .31831.
To find circumference of a circle multiply diameter by 3.1416.
To find area of a circle multiply square of diameter by .7854.
To find side of an equal square multiply diameter by .8862.
To find cubic inches in a ball multiply cube of diameter by .5236
Doubling the diameter of a pipe increases its capacity four times.
One cubic foot of anthracite coal weighs about 53 pounds.
One cubic foot of bituminous coal weighs 47 to 50 pounds.

One ton of coal is equivalent to two cords of wood for steam purposes.

A gallon of water (U. S. standard) weighs 8⅓ pounds and contains 231 cubic inches.

A cubic foot of water contains 7½ gallons, 1728 cubic inches, and weighs 62½ pounds.

A horsepower is equivalent to raising 33,000 pounds one foot per minute, or 550 pounds one foot per second.

To find the pressure in pounds per square foot of water, multiply the height of column in feet by .434.

Steam rising from water at its boiling point (212 degrees) has a pressure equal to the atmosphere (14.7 pounds to the square inch).

To evaporate one cubic foot of water requires the consumption of 7½ pounds of ordinary coal or about 1 pound of coal to 1 gallon of water.

REFERENCE TABLES

ROMAN NUMERALS

I 1	XI 11	XXX 30	CCC 300
II 2	XII 12	XL 40	CCCC 400
III 3	XIII 13	L 50	D 500
IV 4	XIV 14	LX 60	DC 600
V 5	XV 15	LXX 70	DCC 700
VI 6	XVI 16	LXXX or	DCCC 800
VII 7	XVII 17	XXC 80	CM 900
VIII 8	XVIII 18	XC 90	M or
IX 9	XIX 19	C 100	clc 1000
X 10	XX 20	CC 200	MM 2000

Note—A dash line over a numeral, multiplies the value by 1,000; thus, $\overline{X} = 10,000$; $\overline{L} = 50,000$; $\overline{C} = 100,000$; $\overline{D} = 500,000$; $\overline{M} = 1,000,000$; $\overline{CLIX} = 159,000$; $\overline{DLIX} = 559,000$.

Other general rules in Roman numerals are as follows: (1), repeating a letter repeats its value—XX = 20; CCC = 300; (2), a letter placed after one of greater value adds thereto—VI = 6; DC = 600; (3), a letter placed before one of greater value subtracts therefrom—IV = 4.

Arabic numerals are those now commonly in use—0, 1, 2, 3, 4, 5, 6. 7, 8, 9, etc.

Interest Tables

THREE PER CENT

TIME	$1	$2	$3	$4	$5	$6	$7	$8	$9	$10	$100	$1000
4 DAY	0	0	0	0	0	0	0	0	0	0	3	33
8 "	0	0	0	0	0	0	0	1	1	1	7	67
12 "	0	0	0	0	1	1	1	1	1	1	10	1.00
16 "	0	0	0	1	1	1	1	1	1	1	13	1.33
20 "	0	0	1	1	1	1	1	1	2	2	17	1.67
24 "	0	0	1	1	1	1	1	2	2	2	20	2.00
28 "	0	0	1	1	1	1	2	2	2	2	23	2.33
1 MO	0	1	1	1	1	2	2	2	2	3	25	2.50
2 "	1	1	2	2	3	3	4	4	5	5	50	5.00
3 "	1	2	2	3	4	5	5	6	7	8	75	7.50
6 "	2	3	5	6	8	9	11	12	14	15	1.50	15.00
1 YR	3	6	9	12	15	18	21	24	27	30	3.00	30.00

FOUR PER CENT

TIME	$1	$2	$3	$4	$5	$6	$7	$8	$9	$10	$100	$1000
4 DAY	0	0	0	0	0	0	0	0	0	0	4	44
8 "	0	0	0	0	0	1	1	1	1	1	9	89
12 "	0	0	0	1	1	1	1	1	1	1	13	1.33
16 "	0	0	1	1	1	1	1	1	2	2	18	1.78
20 "	0	0	1	1	1	1	2	2	2	2	22	2.22
24 "	0	1	1	1	1	2	2	2	2	3	27	2.67
28 "	0	1	1	1	2	2	2	2	3	3	31	3.11
1 MO	0	1	1	1	2	2	2	3	3	3	33	3.33
2 "	1	1	2	3	3	4	5	5	6	7	67	6.67
3 "	1	2	3	4	5	6	7	8	9	10	1.00	10.00
6 "	2	4	6	8	10	12	14	16	18	20	2.00	20.00
1 YR	4	8	12	16	20	24	28	32	36	40	4.00	40.00

FIVE PER CENT

TIME	$1	$2	$3	$4	$5	$6	$7	$8	$9	$10	$100	$1000
4 DAY	0	0	0	0	0	0	0	0	1	1	6	56
8 "	0	0	0	0	1	1	1	1	1	1	11	1.11
12 "	0	0	1	1	1	1	1	1	2	2	17	1.67
16 "	0	0	1	1	1	1	2	2	2	2	22	2.22
20 "	0	1	1	1	1	2	2	2	3	3	28	2.78
24 "	0	1	1	1	2	2	2	3	3	3	33	3.33
28 "	0	1	1	2	2	2	3	3	4	4	39	3.89
1 MO	0	1	1	2	2	3	3	3	4	4	42	4.17
2 "	1	2	3	3	4	5	6	7	8	8	83	8.33
3 "	1	3	4	5	6	8	9	10	11	13	1.25	12.50
4 "	2	3	5	7	8	10	12	13	15	17	1.67	16.67
5 "	2	4	6	8	10	13	15	17	19	21	2.08	20.83
6 "	3	5	8	10	13	15	18	20	23	25	2.50	25.00
1 YR	5	10	15	20	25	30	35	40	45	50	5.00	50.00

SIX PER CENT

TIME	$1	$2	$3	$4	$5	$6	$7	$8	$9	$10	$100	$1000
4 DAY	0	0	0	0	0	0	0	1	1	1	7	67
8 "	0	0	0	1	1	1	1	1	1	1	13	1.33
12 "	0	0	1	1	1	1	1	2	2	2	20	2.00
16 "	0	1	1	1	1	2	2	2	2	3	27	2.67
20 "	0	1	1	1	2	2	2	3	3	3	33	3.33
24 "	0	1	1	2	2	2	3	3	4	4	40	4.00
28 "	0	1	1	2	2	3	3	4	4	5	47	4.67
1 MO	1	1	2	2	3	3	4	4	5	5	50	5.00
2 "	1	2	3	4	5	6	7	8	9	10	1.00	10.00
3 "	2	3	5	6	8	9	11	12	14	15	1.50	15.00
4 "	2	4	6	8	10	12	14	16	18	20	2.00	20.00
5 "	3	5	8	10	13	15	18	20	23	25	2.50	25.00
6 "	3	6	9	12	15	18	21	24	27	30	3.00	30.00
1 YR	6	12	18	24	30	36	42	48	54	60	6.00	60.00

From "A Personal Book for Executives," copyright, 1935, through courtesy of Dartnell Corporation

How Money Grows at Compound Interest

Interest as Earned Added to the Principal Every 6 Months

Years	$500				Years	$1,000			
	3%	4%	5%	6%		3%	4%	5%	6%
1	$ 515.11	$ 520.20	$ 525.32	$ 530.45	1	$1,030.22	$1,040.40	$ 1,050.63	$ 1,060.90
2	530.68	541.22	551.91	562.76	2	1,061.35	1,082.43	1,103.81	1,125.51
3	546.72	563.08	579.85	597.03	3	1,093.43	1,126.16	1,159.69	1,194.05
4	563.24	585.83	609.20	633.39	4	1,126.48	1,171.66	1,218.40	1,266.77
5	580.27	609.50	640.04	671.96	5	1,160.53	1,218.99	1,280.08	1,343.92
6	597.80	634.12	672.45	712.88	6	1,195.60	1,268.24	1,344.89	1,425.76
7	615.87	659.74	706.49	756.30	7	1,231.73	1,319.48	1,412.97	1,512.59
8	634.48	686.40	742.26	802.36	8	1,268.95	1,372.79	1,484.51	1,604.71
9	653.65	714.13	779.83	851.22	9	1,307.30	1,428.25	1,559.66	1,702.43
10	673.41	742.98	819.31	903.06	10	1,346.81	1,485.95	1,638.62	1,806.11
11	693.76	772.99	860.79	958.05	11	1,387.51	1,545.98	1,721.57	1,916.10
12	714.72	804.22	904.37	1,016.40	12	1,429.44	1,608.44	1,808.73	2,032.79
13	736.32	836.71	950.15	1,078.30	13	1,472.64	1,673.42	1,900.29	2,156.59
14	758.58	870.51	998.25	1,143.97	14	1,517.15	1,741.02	1,996.50	2,287.93
15	781.51	905.68	1,048.79	1,213.63	15	1,563.01	1,811.36	2,097.57	2,427.26
16	805.13	942.27	1,101.88	1,287.54	16	1,610.25	1,884.54	2,203.76	2,575.08
17	829.46	980.34	1,157.66	1,365.96	17	1,658.91	1,960.68	2,315.32	2,731.91
18	854.52	1,019.95	1,216.27	1,449.14	18	1,709.04	2,039.89	2,432.54	2,898.28
19	880.35	1,061.15	1,277.84	1,537.39	19	1,760.69	2,122.30	2,555.68	3,074.78
20	906.96	1,104.02	1,342.53	1,631.02	20	1,813.91	2,208.04	2,685.06	3,262.04
21	934.37	1,148.62	1,410.50	1,730.35	21	1,868.73	2,297.24	2,821.00	3,460.70
22	962.61	1,195.03	1,481.91	1,835.73	22	1,925.21	2,390.05	2,963.81	3,671.45
23	991.70	1,243.31	1,556.93	1,947.52	23	1,983.39	2,486.61	3,113.85	3,895.04
24	1,021.67	1,293.54	1,635.75	2,066.13	24	2,043.33	2,587.07	3,271.49	4,132.25
25	1,052.54	1,345.80	1,718.56	2,191.96	25	2,105.08	2,691.59	3,437.11	4,383.91
26	1,084.35	1,400.17	1,805.56	2,325.45	26	2,168.70	2,800.33	3,611.11	4,650.89
27	1,117.12	1,456.73	1,896.96	2,467.06	27	2,234.24	2,913.46	3,793.92	4,934.12
28	1,150.88	1,515.59	1,993.00	2,617.31	28	2,301.76	3,031.17	3,985.99	5,234.61
29	1,185.66	1,576.81	2,093.89	2,776.70	29	2,371.32	3,153.62	4,187.78	5,553.40
30	1,221.50	1,640.52	2,199.90	2,945.80	30	2,442.99	3,281.03	4,399.79	5,891.60
31	1,258.41	1,706.79	2,311.27	3,125.20	31	2,516.82	3,413.58	4,622.53	6,250.40
32	1,296.44	1,775.75	2,428.27	3,315.53	32	2,592.88	3,551.49	4,856.54	6,631.05
33	1,335.62	1,847.49	2,551.22	3,517.44	33	2,671.24	3,694.97	5,102.41	7,034.88
34	1,375.99	1,922.13	2,680.36	3,731.66	34	2,751.97	3,844.25	5,360.72	7,463.31
35	1,417.57	1,999.78	2,816.05	3,958.91	35	2,835.14	3,999.56	5,632.10	7,917.82
36	1,460.41	2,080.57	2,958.62	4,200.01	36	2,920.82	4,161.14	5,917.23	8,400.02
37	1,504.55	2,164.63	3,108.40	4,455.79	37	3,009.09	4,329.25	6,216.79	8,911.58
38	1,550.02	2,252.08	3,265.76	4,727.15	38	3,100.03	4,504.15	6,531.51	9,454.30
39	1,596.86	2,343.06	3,431.09	5,015.05	39	3,193.72	4,686.12	6,862.17	10,030.10
40	1,645.12	2,437.72	3,604.79	5,320.45	40	3,290.24	4,875.44	7,209.57	10,640.90
41	1,694.84	2,536.21	3,787.28	5,644.45	41	3,389.68	5,072.41	7,574.55	11,288.90
42	1,746.06	2,638.67	3,979.01	5,988.20	42	3,492.12	5,277.33	7,958.01	11,976.40
43	1,798.83	2,745.27	4,180.45	6,352.90	43	3,597.66	5,490.54	8,360.89	12,705.80
44	1,853.20	2,856.18	4,392.08	6,739.80	44	3,706.39	5,712.35	8,784.16	13,479.60
45	1,909.21	2,971.57	4,614.40	7,150.25	45	3,818.41	5,943.13	9,228.80	14,300.50
46	1,966.91	3,091.62	4,848.04	7,585.70	46	3,933.81	6,183.24	9,696.07	15,171.40
47	2,026.35	3,216.52	5,093.47	8,047.65	47	4,052.70	6,433.04	10,186.93	16,095.30
48	2,087.60	3,346.47	5,351.32	8,537.75	48	4,175.19	6,692.93	10,702.64	17,075.50
49	2,150.69	3,481.67	5,622.24	9,057.70	49	4,301.37	6,963.33	11,244.47	18,115.40
50	2,215.69	3,622.33	5,906.86	9,609.30	50	4,431.37	7,244.65	11,813.72	19,218.60

From "A Personal Book for Executives," copyright, 1935, through courtesy of Dartnell Corporation

Rapid Table of Multiplication and Division

A figure in the top line (19) multiplied by a figure in the last column on the left (18) produces the figure where the top line and the side line meet (342), and so on.

A figure in the table (342) divided by the figure at the top of that column (19) results in the figure (18) at the extreme left; also, a figure in the table (342) divided by the figure (18) at the extreme left gives the figure (19) at the top of the column, and so on.

1	2	3	4	5	6	7	8	9	10	11	12	13	14	15	16	17	18	19	20	21	22	23	24	25	1
2	4	6	8	10	12	14	16	18	20	22	24	26	28	30	32	34	36	38	40	42	44	46	48	50	2
3	6	9	12	15	18	21	24	27	30	33	36	39	42	45	48	51	54	57	60	63	66	69	72	75	3
4	8	12	16	20	24	28	32	36	40	44	48	52	56	60	64	68	72	76	80	84	88	92	96	100	4
5	10	15	20	25	30	35	40	45	50	55	60	65	70	75	80	85	90	95	100	105	110	115	120	125	5
6	12	18	24	30	36	42	48	54	60	66	72	78	84	90	96	102	108	114	120	126	132	138	144	150	6
7	14	21	28	35	42	49	56	63	70	77	84	91	98	105	112	119	126	133	140	147	154	161	168	175	7
8	16	24	32	40	48	56	64	72	80	88	96	104	112	120	128	136	144	152	160	168	176	184	192	200	8
9	18	27	36	45	54	63	72	81	90	99	108	117	126	135	144	153	162	171	180	189	198	207	216	225	9
10	20	30	40	50	60	70	80	90	100	110	120	130	140	150	160	170	180	190	200	210	220	230	240	250	10
11	22	33	44	55	66	77	88	99	110	121	132	143	154	165	176	187	198	209	220	231	242	253	264	275	11
12	24	36	48	60	72	84	96	108	120	132	144	156	168	180	192	204	216	228	240	252	264	276	288	300	12
13	26	39	52	65	78	91	104	117	130	143	156	169	182	195	208	221	234	247	260	273	286	299	312	325	13
14	28	42	56	70	84	98	112	126	140	154	168	182	196	210	224	238	252	266	280	294	308	322	336	350	14
15	30	45	60	75	90	105	120	135	150	165	180	195	210	225	240	255	270	285	300	315	330	345	360	375	15
16	32	48	64	80	96	112	128	144	160	176	192	208	224	240	256	272	288	304	320	336	352	368	384	400	16
17	34	51	68	85	102	119	136	153	170	187	204	221	238	255	272	289	306	323	340	357	374	391	408	425	17
18	36	54	72	90	108	126	144	162	180	198	216	234	252	270	288	306	324	342	360	378	396	414	432	450	18
19	38	57	76	95	114	133	152	171	190	209	228	247	266	285	304	323	342	361	380	399	418	437	456	475	19
20	40	60	80	100	120	140	160	180	200	220	240	260	280	300	320	340	360	380	400	420	440	460	480	500	20
21	42	63	84	105	126	147	168	189	210	231	252	273	294	315	336	357	378	399	420	441	462	483	504	525	21
22	44	66	88	110	132	154	176	198	220	242	264	286	308	330	352	374	396	418	440	462	484	506	528	550	22
23	46	69	92	115	138	161	184	207	230	253	276	299	322	345	368	391	414	437	460	483	506	529	552	575	23
24	48	72	96	120	144	168	192	216	240	264	288	312	336	360	384	408	432	456	480	504	528	552	576	600	24
25	50	75	100	125	150	175	200	225	250	275	300	325	350	375	400	425	450	475	500	525	550	575	600	625	25

ANSWERS TO MATHEMATICS EXERCISES AND PROBLEMS

Exercise 3 (page 229)

1. 17%
2. 95%
3. 90%
4. $7\frac{3}{4}$%
5. 75%
6. $\frac{1}{2}$%
7. $\frac{1}{2}$%
8. $33\frac{1}{3}$%
9. $16\frac{2}{3}$%
10. $87\frac{1}{2}$%

Exercise 4 (page 230)

1. 35%
2. $12\frac{1}{2}$%
3. $6\frac{1}{2}$%
4. $15\frac{1}{4}$%
5. $83\frac{1}{3}$%
6. $87\frac{1}{2}$%
7. $6\frac{1}{4}$%
8. $\frac{1}{2}$%
9. $\frac{1}{4}$%
10. 110%
11. $333\frac{1}{3}$%
12. $162\frac{1}{2}$%

Exercise 5 (page 230)

13. .15
14. .125
15. .75
16. $.08\frac{1}{3}$
17. .8
18. .9375
19. .135
20. .005
21. .0425
22. $1.33\frac{1}{3}$
23. 2.5
24. .00005

Exercise 6 (page 230)

25. 75%
26. $62\frac{1}{2}$%
27. $83\frac{1}{3}$%
28. $41\frac{2}{3}$%
29. 25%
30. $35\frac{1}{2}$%
31. 40%
32. 70%
33. 19%
34. 40%
35. $33\frac{1}{3}$%
36. $26\frac{2}{3}$%

Exercise 8 (page 232)

1. 40%
2. $16\frac{2}{3}$%
3. $12\frac{1}{2}$%
4. 40%
5. $37\frac{1}{2}$%
6. 20%
7. 20%
8. 30%
9. 70%
10. 50%

Exercise 9 (page 232)

1. $600
2. $2320
3. $720
4. $840
5. $256
6. $1536
7. $40
8. $1800
9. $48
10. $15
11. $9000
12. $12,000

13. $88,800
14. $12,000
15. $30
16. $40
17. $400
18. $90
19. $50
20. $179.20

Exercise 10 (page 233)

1. 240
2. 220
3.   72
4. 7000
5.   18
6.   40
7. 480
8. 1000
9. 700
10. 300

Exercise 11 (page 233)

1.   12
2. 100
3. 180
4. 200
5.   90
6. 800
7. 112
8. 2000
9. 800
10.   .64

Problems (page 235)

1. $75
2. 5%
3. $1.75
4. $17,000.00
5. $364.00
6. $60.00
7. $6,320.00
8. $28,636.00
9. $37\frac{1}{2}$%
10. 60%
11. $451.13
12. $48,000.
13. 3%
14. B's gross profit is $150 more than A's
15. $223.43 gain.

Exercise 12 (page 244)

1. $ .70
2. $ 8.00
3. $ .13
4. $10.69
5. $ 3.00
6. $14.25
7. $15.00
8. $15.00
9. $ 2.50
10. $ 9.00

% Mark-up on Sales

11. $33\frac{1}{3}$%
12. 10%
13. $33\frac{1}{3}$%
14. 25%
15. 20%

% Mark-up on Cost

16. $33\frac{1}{3}$%
17. 25%
18. 20%
19. $14\frac{2}{7}$%
20. $11\frac{1}{9}$%

Exercise 13 (page 247)

	Equiv. Rate	Gr. Profit	S.P.
1.	25%	1.00	5.00
2.	$66\frac{2}{3}$%	.50	1.25
3.	50%	1.05	3.15
4.	60%	.39	1.04
5.	20%	.30	1.80
6.	$33\frac{1}{3}$%	6.00	24.00
7.	$66\frac{2}{3}$%	3.00	7.50
8.	50%	2.50	7.50
9.	100%	3.50	7.00
10.	20%	1.60	9.60

Exercise 14 (page 249)

1. 30.00
2. 3.00
3. 1.50
4. 1.90
5. 2.00

Exercise 15 (page 250)

1. 4.50
2. 1.32
3. 1.35
4. 2.70
5. 2.50

Problems (page 250)

1. $2.75
2. 40%
3. $2.00
4. $700.00
5. A's price is **$.45 less**
6. $5.25
7. $1.33⅓

8. 68%; 32%; 23%; 9%
9. 28⅞%
10. Hat   3.40
    Coat   23.00
    Gloves   .81
    Shoes   10.63
    Tie   1.49
    Neckwear 1.19

Exercise 16 (page 255)

1. 46¾ hrs.
2. 31¾ "

3.

	Am't. Due	$10	$5	$2	$1	.50	.25	.10	.05	.01
				Currency Sheet						
32	$32.67	3	..	1	..	1	..	1	1	2
33	24.75	2	..	2	..	1	1	..	..	..
34	33.26	3	..	1	1	..	1	..	..	1
35	26.73	2	1	..	1	1	..	2	..	3
36	32.67	3	..	1	..	1	..	1	1	2
37	24.75	2	..	2	..	1	1	..	..	..
38	25.24	2	1	..	..	..	..	2	..	4
39	22.57	2	..	..	..	1	..	..	1	2
40	20.67	2	..	1	..	1	..	1	1	2
Total	$243.31	21	2	8	2	7	3	7	4	16

Currency Memo

$10.00	21		$210.00	.25	3		.75
5.00	2		10.00	.10	7		.70
2.00	8		16.00	.05	4		.20
1.00	2		2.00	.01	16		.16
.50	7		3.50			Total	$243.31

4.

	Amt. Due	$10	$5	$2	$1	.50	.25	.10	.05	.01
				Currency Sheet						
S. Sanford	$42.77	4	..	1	..	1	1	..	..	2
T. Ober	41.58	4	..	..	1	1	..	..	1	3
F. Kulikowski	41.58	4	..	..	1	1	..	..	1	3
L. Stoller	23.76	2	..	1	1	1	1	..	..	1
V. Whipple	31.68	3	..	..	1	1	..	1	1	3
J. Stewart	26.73	2	1	..	1	1	..	2	..	3
N. Wheeler	24.95	2	..	2	..	1	1	2	..	..
S. Mound	40.99	4	..	..	..	1	1	2	..	4
Total	$274.04	25	1	4	5	8	4	7	3	19

Currency Memo

$10.00	25	$250.00
5.00	1	5.00
2.00	4	8.00
1.00	5	5.00
.50	8	4.00
.25	4	1.00
.10	7	.70
.05	3	.15
.01	19	.19
	Total	$274.04

Exercise 17 (page 258)

1. $ 9.46
2.   8.97
3.   32.71
4.   5.94
5.   5.54

Exercise 18 (page 259)

1. $ 5.40
2. $25.65
3. $ 8.40
4. $ 1.60
5. $ 8.50
6. $ 2.74
7. $13.10
8. $29.07
9. $ 4.74
10. $ 9.00

Exercise 19 (page 260)

1. 33½%
2. 43%
3. 47½%
4. 33⅓%
5. 56.7%
6. 37.65%
7. 56.35%
8. 35.795%
9. 21.03%
10. 50%

Problems (page 260)

1. $ 25.65
2. $134.66
3. $ 55.08
4. $ 80.00
5. $105.00
6. $ 30.00
7. $ .87 decrease

Exercise 20 (page 262)

1. $1144.22
2. $2,980.83
3. $ 459.05
4. $2302.51
5. $1657.25
6. $3275.20
7. $ 518.29
8. $ 990.48
9. $ 764.11
10. $1379.41

Problems (page 262)

1. $4565.45
2. $6404.81
3.   26.95%
4. $ 900.00
5. $2115.45 gain
6. $3877.57
7. $2655.62
8. $ 102.00

Exercise 21 (page 264)

	Per $1	Per $100	Per $1000
1.	.015	1.50	15.00
2.	.005	.50	5.00
3.	.0175	1.75	17.50
4.	.0125	1.25	12.50
5.	.03	3.00	30.00

Exercise 22 (page 265)

	Per $100	Per $1000
1.	3.50	35.00
2.	3.50	35.00
3.	2.00	20.00
4.	2.75	27.50
5.	2.75	27.50
6.	1.864	18.64
7.	8.225	82.25
8.	7.50	75.00
9.	7.50	75.00
10.	1.864	18.64

Exercise 23 (page 265)

1. $178.75
2. $210.96
3. $206.35
4. $365.00
5. $ 20.50
6. $377.43

7. $ 78.62
8. $105.59
9. $215.20
10. $ 85.56

Exercise 24 (page 266)
1. .0175
2. $32000.00
3. $2353.13
4. .00125
5. $850000.00

Exercise 25 (page 268)

	2%	3%	4%	6%
1.	10.00	15.00	20.00	30.00
2.	4.00	6.00	8.00	12.00
3.	2.00	3.00	4.00	6.00
4.	4.00	6.00	8.00	12.00
5.	1.00	1.50	2.00	3.00
6.	50.00	75.00	100.00	150.00
7.	4.00	6.00	8.00	12.00
8.	4.00	6.00	8.00	12.00
9.	.40	.60	.80	1.20
10.	.40	.60	.80	1.20

Exercise 27 (page 270)

	6%	5%	7%	4%	2%
1.	9.00	7.50	10.50	6.00	3.00
2.	18.00	15.00	21.00	12.00	6.00
3.	48.00	40.00	56.00	32.00	16.00
4.	1.80	1.50	2.10	1.20	.60
5.	8.80	7.33	10.27	5.87	2.93
6.	9.00	7.50	10.50	6.00	3.00
7.	12.00	10.00	14.00	8.00	4.00
8.	30.00	25.00	35.00	20.00	10.00
9.	60.00	50.00	70.00	40.00	20.00
10.	120.00	100.00	140.00	80.00	40.00

Exercise 28 (page 272)
1. 59 days
2. 89 days
3. 30 days
4. 60 days
5. 46 days
6. 92 days
7. 30 days
8. 90 days
9. 66 days
10. 60 days

Exercise 29 (page 273)
1. March 6
2. May 11
3. April 9
4. June 1
5. August 23
6. September 7
7. August 26
8. September 24
9. December 29
10. December 20

Exercise 30 (page 275)
1. $1,522.50
2. $4,567.50
3. $ 505.00
4. $5,050.00
5. $3,618.00
6. $4,422.00
7. $ 282.80
8. $ 447.62
9. $ 741.60
10. $ 816.00

Exercise 31 (page 275)
1. 50 days
2. 48 days
3. 20 days
4. 25 days
5. 80 days
6. 49 days
7. 33 days
8. 117 days
9. 41 days
10. 85 days

Exercise 32 (page 276)

	Disc.	Net. Proceeds
1.	$10.10	$ 999.90
2.	6.19	602.81
3.	14.98	1,233.47
4.	6.97	902.03
5.	4.17	449.33
6.	13.92	1,478.13
7.	3.83	761.98
8.	20.30	2,009.70

Exercise 33 (page 279)
1. $127.50
2. $393.75
3. $ 55.13

4. $292.50
5. $ 76.50

9. $ 24.64
10. $ 8,844.36

Exercise 34 (page 280)

1. $ 4,000.
2. 10,000.
3. 12,800.
4. 20,000.
5. 48,000.

Exercise 36 (page 289)

1. 10 %
2. 3%
3. 8%
4. 6%
5. 1¼%
6. 2¾%
7. 2¼%
8. 5%

Exercise 35 (page 280)

	Insurance Required	Part of Loss Collectible
1.	$ 4,000.	50%
2.	$10,000.	80%
3.	$12,800.	75%
4.	$20,000.	75%
5.	$48,000.	50%

Exercise 37 (page 289)

1. $1,500.00
2. $1,000.00
3. $ 112.50
4. $ 900.00
5. $5,000.00
6. $ 400.00
7. $1,400.00
8. $2,400.00

Problems (page 280)

1. $10,000.
2. $6,250.
3. $40,000.
4. $15,625.
5. A, $12,500. B, $8,333.33.
6. $20,000.
7. $15,000.
8. { A, B, $1000 each; C, $3000. D, $2000.
9. $8,333.33
10. $351.25

Exercise 38 (page 291)

	Brokerage	Cost
1.	$ 25.00	$ 9,625.00
2.	$ 62.50	$23,812.50
3.	$ 12.50	$ 4,562.50
4.	$125.00	$44,125.00
5.	$ 25.00	$ 9,025.00

Exercise 39 (page 292)

1. $10,576.40
2. 4,849.00
3. 8,814.40
4. 5,204.82
5. 4,345.00

Problems (page 287)

1. $18,296.20
2. $ 3,861.13
3. $ 1,449.62
4. $ 98.44
5. $10,062.64
6. $12,099.65
7. $ 6,814.14
8. $ 8.33 (loss)